Fashioning the Self

Identity and Style in British Culture

Edited by
Emily Priscott
Independent scholar

Curating and Interpreting Culture

Vernon Press

Copyright © 2024 by the authors.

All rights reserved. No part of this publication may be reproduced, stored in a retrieval system, or transmitted in any form or by any means, electronic, mechanical, photocopying, recording, or otherwise, without the prior permission of Vernon Art and Science Inc.

www.vernonpress.com

In the Americas:
Vernon Press
1000 N West Street, Suite 1200
Wilmington, Delaware, 19801
United States

In the rest of the world:
Vernon Press
C/Sancti Espiritu 17,
Malaga, 29006
Spain

Curating and Interpreting Culture

Library of Congress Control Number: 2023937355

ISBN: 978-1-64889-870-9

Also available: 978-1-64889-179-3 [Hardback]; 978-1-64889-707-8 [PDF, E-Book]

Product and company names mentioned in this work are the trademarks of their respective owners. While every care has been taken in preparing this work, neither the authors nor Vernon Art and Science Inc. may be held responsible for any loss or damage caused or alleged to be caused directly or indirectly by the information contained in it.

Every effort has been made to trace all copyright holders, but if any have been inadvertently overlooked the publisher will be pleased to include any necessary credits in any subsequent reprint or edition.

This book is an original multi-author monograph with five chapters, each of which has been written by its individual authors. Each author has contributed a chapter based on their original research, developed in the field of their own specialism specifically for this volume.

Table of contents

	Table of figures	vii
	Abstract	ix
	Introduction	xi
	Emily Priscott	
	Independent scholar	
	Margaret D. Stetz	
	University of Delaware	
Chapter 1	**Creole conversation pieces: portraits in eighteenth-century Jamaica**	1
	Chloe Northrop	
	Tarrant County College, Texas	
Chapter 2	**Fashion, colonialism and nationalism: changing notions of everyday dress codes in British-colonial Sri Lanka**	33
	Ramesha Jayaneththi	
	University of Peradeniya, Sri Lanka	
Chapter 3	***Tilda's New Hat*: a case study in Edwardian fashion and working-class identity**	63
	Petra Clark	
	Independent scholar	
Chapter 4	**Refashioning spinsterhood: Edith Sitwell's singular style in British interwar literary culture**	109
	Emily Priscott	
	Independent scholar	
Chapter 5	**British Jewish identity: Linda Grant as a flâneuse and 'thoughtful dresser'**	137
	Margaret D. Stetz	
	University of Delaware	
	List of contributors	163
	Index	165

Table of figures

Figure 1.1: "Portrait of the Taylor Family," photograph of Daniel Gardner, Sir John Taylor, His Wife Elizabeth, His Brother Simon Taylor, and Four of their Six Children, c. 1785.   6

Figure 1.2: Pompeo Batoni, *Portrait of John Blagrove*, 1774.   8

Figure 1.3: Richard Cosway, "Brodbelt Children," 1788, in Geraldine Nutt Mozley, Letters to Jane from Jamaica, 1788-1796.   10

Figure 1.4: After George Robertson, "A View in the Island of Jamaica of Part of the River Cobre Near Spanish Town" 1778, aquatint.   12

Figure 1.5: Philip Wickstead, *Portrait of Benjamin and Mary Pusey*, c.1775.   16

Figure 1.6: Philip Wickstead, *Richard and Jane Pusey* [William Pusey and His Wife], c. 1785.   19

Figure 1.7: Philip Wickstead, *Edward Pusey and His Family* [Edward East and His Family] c.1775.   21

Figure 1.8: Philip Wickstead, *James Henry and His Family*, before 1784.   24

Figure 2.1: From a fresco on Sigiriya rock   39

Figure 2.2: The Bodhisattva Tara. Gilded bronze, Sri Lanka, 8th century CE.   40

Figure 2.3: Portrait of Queen Consort Venkata Rangammal Devi of Kandy in South Indian attire, drawn by W. Daniell, R.A. Engraved by R. Woodman, early 1800s.   44

Figure 2.4: Traditional Kandyan women's attire, unknown author, Ceylon India, 1880.   44

Figure 2.5: Reception of the envoys of the King of Kandy by Governor Iman Falck, Carel Frederik Reimer, 1772.   45

Figure 2.6: An advert for the Singer Manufacturing Co., 1892.   50

Figure 2.7: Front center (seated): John Henry Meediniya Adigar with his family. Rear center (standing): his daughter, Alice, who married the low-country newspaper magnate D. R. Wijewardena in 1916. Self-taken photograph, 1905.   56

Figure 2.8: Women's Health magazine launch a new cover in 2012, showing off a skimpy mini-dress.   59

Figure 3.1: Portrait of a seated young woman in Edwardian dress.   63

Figure 3.2: Edwardian fashion plate, depicting two fashionably dress women in picture hats.   82

Figure 3.3: Edwardian fashion plate, depicting a fashionable Edwardian hat with feathers.   107

Figure 4.1:	Edith Sitwell, 1926.	110
Figure 4.2:	Edith Sitwell, Renishaw estate, 1930.	125
Figure 5.1:	Linda Grant, *The Thoughtful Dresser*.	140
Figure 5.2:	1954 Dior cocktail dress	154
Figure 5.3:	A *flâneuse's* paradise, Oxford Street, 2006.	158

Abstract

This book takes an interdisciplinary approach to examining the link between personal style and identity, moving across academic disciplines such as art history, English literature and cultural studies. Comprising five chapters by individual authors, this collection of essays explores the relationship between identity and style, both collective and individual. Each chapter is designed to address a specific interpretation of this broad subject, interrogating what people wear and why, and examining how style can relate to wider social systems to create a person's sense of themselves and their social position. Rather than focusing on one specific time-period or cultural moment, it moves through time and geographical boundaries to explore the relationship between different style practices and their social contexts, with each piece illustrating the tension between individual identity and external structures. It is a series of snapshots, a collage of different images which explores the radically diverse uses of style and its different meanings, highlighting its multiplicity within British society. The impact of colonialism and its legacy is a significant part of British culture and its heritage, which this collection reflects in its diverse choice of subjects, bringing into focus intersectional issues such as race, class and gender.

Introduction
Fashioning the self

Emily Priscott
Independent scholar

Margaret D. Stetz
University of Delaware

"On the subject of dress almost no-one…feels truly indifferent…it is dangerous…it has a flowery head, but deep roots in the passions."[1]

Personal adornment is itself an aesthetic act, and as Mary Ellen Roach and Joanne Bulbolz Eicher have written, "all aesthetic acts are acts of speaking."[2] As the sociologist and dress theorist Fred Davis has argued, individual style is a statement of self, but it is also a social practice, a form of visual communication with deeper meanings.[3] Style is a rich conceptual framework through which to view history and culture, a way of exploring identity and its relationship to both the self and society. While fashion is an external category related to capitalist commodity culture, style can be far more subjective. Yet its meaning is slippery; it can suggest an externally agreed upon set of characteristics that conform to received beauty norms, but it can also signify the opposite, a defiance of beauty standards in favor of self-expression. More often, it is a negotiation between the two. Style, like fashion can, as Vike Martina Plock has written, "facilitat[e] the analysis of modern subject identity…at once receptive and defensive towards external influences and pressures,"[4] with the relationship between originality and uniformity in personal style highlighting the tension between individual and group identity, internal versus external

---

[1] Elizabeth Bowen, "Dress," in *Collected Impressions* (New York: Knopf, 1950) p. 112.
[2] Mary Ellen Roach and Joanne Bubolz Eicher, "The Language of Personal Adornment," in *The Fabrics of Culture: The Anthropology of Clothing and Adornment*, ed. Justine M. Cordwell and Ronald M. Schwarz (New York: De Gruyter Mouton, 2011), p. 7.
[3] Fred Davis, *Fashion, Culture and Identity* (Chicago: University of Chicago Press, 1994), p. 3.
[4] Vike Martina Plock, *Modernism, Fashion and Interwar Women Writers* (Edinburgh: Edinburgh University Press, 2017), p. 2.

influences.⁵ This way of approaching the issue of style has inspired not only scholarly study but new work in the arts in Britain, including displays and installations at museums and galleries, which have generated enormous popular interest.

In 2018, the Victoria and Albert Museum staged its summer/autumn exhibition, *Frida Kahlo: Making Her Self Up*, drawing huge crowds that queued both inside and outside of the main doors to see it. By the time it closed in mid-November, after being extended an additional two weeks, several hundred thousand people had viewed glass cases filled with artworks, photographs, jewelry, medical devices (such as plaster casts painted with decorations), jars and bottles that had once held cosmetics, but most of all with clothes—especially with a series of spectacular Tehuana dresses, shawls and skirts of intricate design that were collected and worn by the artist during her too-brief and pain-filled lifetime. The focus throughout was on illuminating the persona that Kahlo had created by such material means, while asserting her linkage to indigenous communities in Mexico. When offering a rationale for what had been put on show, co-curators Claire Wilcox and Circe Henestrosa wrote in "Fashioning Frida," their Introduction to the exhibition catalog, "The symbiotic relationship in Kahlo's life and work between her art and dress cannot be overestimated."⁶

This link between style and identity has, in recent years, received a substantial amount of academic attention and enjoys far greater legitimacy in scholarly circles than it once did. It is no longer revolutionary simply to state that style expresses deeper aspects of the self: most people now know that clothing matters, be it fashionable or otherwise. As a field of study, dress is both fascinating and hugely significant. However, while we no longer have to defend the idea that style is a significant social phenomenon, it is how we use it that counts, and it provides researchers with a rich analytical tool through which to interrogate the past. As Davis notes, clothing and style signify far more than surfaces, and also more than the basic categories of class and social status, but can denote ideas about gender, sexuality, race and, in fact, "any aspect of self about which individuals can, through symbolic means, communicate with others in the instance of dress, through nondiscursive visual [...] symbols, however [...] elusive these may be."⁷ In other words, dress

---

⁵ Plock, *Modernism, Fashion and Interwar Women Writers*.
⁶ Claire Wilcox and Circe Henestrosa, "Introduction: Fashioning Frida," in *Frida Kahlo: Making Her Self Up*, edited by Claire Wilcox and Circe Henestrosa (London: V&A Publishing, 2018), p. 18.
⁷ Wilcox and Henestrosa, "Introduction: Fashioning Frida," *Frida Kahlo: Making Her Self Up*, p. 16.

can work symbolically at micro levels of consciousness to express subtle codes, varieties and manners, as well as broader categories. Age, marital status and sexuality are all significant aspects of identity which, in earlier eras as well as today, personal style has been used to elucidate. Hope Howell Hodkins's 2016 study, *Style and the Single Girl*, for instance, examines the relationship between singleness and dress in the novel from the 1920s to the 1970s, a period of intense upheaval in gender norms, of which fashion and style were important signifiers.[8] Likewise, dress is not only relevant to women's history and need not be ghettoized as a "women's issue." Academic interest in menswear, from nineteenth-century dandyism[9] to gay male subcultural styles,[10] has also grown over the past few decades, providing a rich background of literature on diverse sets of style practices, along with important interdisciplinary arts exhibitions, such as the Victoria and Albert Museum's *Fashioning Masculinities: The Art of Menswear* in 2022.

That the study of clothing can teach us about lives and cultures, the connections between how individuals both perceive and present themselves, and the historical contexts of their circumstances, has clearly been well established in the fields of dress and fashion research. While its value as a source was once denigrated, due to the traditionally subordinate position of fashion in both scholarship and the arts, the rise of design history, material culture and popular culture studies has, as Cheryl Buckley and Hilary Fawcett have written, "given a legitimacy to the study of fashion."[11]

However, the broad acceptance of fashion as a legitimate cultural source of knowledge in academic circles is only half the story and it seems that, elsewhere, the debate rages on. As Robyn Gibson, Australian arts educator and author of *The Memory of Clothes*, wrote in 2015, "Almost every fashion writer…insists anew on the importance of fashion. However[,] typical responses from outside the discipline boarder on cynicism, ambivalence or irony."[12] The source of this enduring squeamishness about dress, as Margaret D. Stetz has written, is apparently its "long associat[ion] with feminine preoccupations," often being

---

[8] Hope Howell Hodgkins, *Style and the Single Girl: How Modern Women Re-Dressed the Novel, 1922-1977* (Columbus: Ohio State University Press), 2016.
[9] Margaret D. Stetz, "Fabricating Girls: Clothes and Coming-of-Age Fiction by Women of Color," *Humanities Bulletin*, vol. 2, no. 1 (2019), pp. 122-134, p. 122.
[10] See, for instance, Shaun Cole, *Don We Now Our Gay Apparel* (Berg 3PL, illustrated edition, 2000).
[11] Cheryl Buckley and Hilary Fawcett, *Fashioning the Feminine: Representation and Women's Fashion from the Fin de Siècle to the Present* (London: I. B. Taurus Publishers, 2002), p. 1.
[12] Robyn Gibson, "Introduction," in *The Memory of Clothes*, ed. Robyn Gibson (Rotterdam: Sense Publishers, 2015), xiii–xvii, p. xiii.

"taken as a sign of vanity or insufficient intellectual or political seriousness,"[13] an enduring sentiment in some circles.

Though it was enthusiastically embraced by British museum-going audiences, even the V&A's Frieda Kahlo exhibition was not without controversy, demonstrating once again that some cultural critics remain to be convinced of the wider significance of fashion and dress. Reviewing the exhibition for the UK's *Guardian* newspaper, the art critic Jonathan Jones wrote disapprovingly of what he saw as a lack of attention to Frida Kahlo's "blazing, visionary paintings[,]" which took "a back seat at the V&A to Kahlo's clothes, makeup and iconic image." He went on to decry what seemed an inappropriate effort to define Kahlo through the display of such ephemera, dismissing it as merely "a dead woman's stuff[,]" and insisting, "I feel a far greater intimacy looking into Kahlo's eyes in her paintings than I do wandering among 80-year-old clothes."[14] According to Jones, moreover, the legitimate purpose of an art museum such as the V&A risked being compromised, when it was confused with a project of archaeology that involved digging up and placing on view Kahlo's sartorial remains, however visually striking the result.

In this recent disparagement of dress as the feature of an art exhibition, it is difficult to avoid hearing echoes of the long debate—a gendered debate, at that—between those (often, critics who were men) who have argued that attention to clothing could never be a serious or important matter and those (often, writers who were women) who have asserted the opposite. Readers can find it already in 1929, underpinning Virginia Woolf's lecture-into-essay, *A Room of One's Own*. There, the speaker told her audience, "But it is obvious that the values of women differ very often from the values which have been made by the other sex; naturally, this is so. Yet it is the masculine values that prevail. Speaking crudely, football and sport are 'important'; the worship of fashion, the buying of clothes 'trivial'."[15]

In a similar vein, Edith Sitwell's most recent biographer, Richard Greene, devotes little space to discussing her highly individualistic appearance in his 2011 biography of the poet. Although his decision to focus primarily on her literary output might be welcomed as an over-due corrective to her often subordinate position in discussions of modernist literature, the picture it

---

[13] Margaret D. Stetz, "Fabricating Girls: Clothes and Coming-of-Age Fiction by Women of Color," *Humanities Bulletin*, vol. 2, no. 1 (2019), pp. 122-134, p. 123.
[14] Jonathan Jones, "Frida Kahlo Making Her Self Up Review: Forget the Paintings, Here's Her False Leg," *Guardian* (UK), 12th June 2018. https://www.theguardian.com/artanddesign/2018/jun/12/frida-kahlo-making-her-self-up-review-v-and-a-london
[15] Virginia Woolf, *A Room of One's Own*, 1929, p. 60 https://gutenberg.net.au/ebooks02/0200791.txt

Introduction

paints is incomplete. This well-intentioned desire to situate Sitwell as a significant modernist poet as opposed to an eccentric clothes horse has resulted in an important reassessment of her literary reputation, but, as Chapter Four of this collection shows, Sitwell's flamboyant image was inseparable from her art, expressing the same decorative sensibility as her poetry.

Such self-conscious evocations of this disagreement over cultural values had also appeared in 2009, and could be seen throughout the British novelist and journalist Linda Grant's collection of essays, *The Thoughtful Dresser*. Grant deplored the fact that "Writing and thinking about clothes is generally relegated to the fashion pages of newspapers and magazines or to the scholarly works of the costume historians [. . .] Fashion is lightweight, trivial, and obsession with appearance the sign of a second-rate mind."[16] Eighty years after Woolf's observations, Grant still found it necessary to employ sarcasm to defend those (mainly women) who are "interested in fashion and might, quite wrongly, feel a little ashamed of this passion. Might fear that they are not going to be taken seriously [. . . unlike] our male counterparts who have mature and adult preoccupations, without which the human race could not survive, such as moving balls from one end of a grassy field to the other, with the aid of the human foot."[17]

Even today, this dispute remains far from resolved in mainstream, non-academic circles. For the *Times* (UK) newspaper on 18 July 2021, the Black British feminist author Otegha Uwagba, who has published on topics such as race and money, described a lifetime of having "feared being taken less seriously as a writer if I was perceived as being too fashion-conscious [. . . as] in some corners it is assumed that women who are overtly focused on fashion and how they dress must be intellectual lightweights"; whether consciously or unconsciously echoing Woolf, she wrote, "It also hasn't escaped my attention that it is fashion — an arena often categorised as a 'female' interest — that is frequently reduced to the level of mere triviality."[18] That she still felt it necessary to defend her interest in fashion and style speaks volumes about the ongoing precarity of the status of clothing as a "serious" matter among the British intelligentsia.

---

[16] Linda Grant, "In Which a Woman Buys a Pair of Shoes," in *The Thoughtful Dresser* (London: Virago, 2009), p. 7.
[17] Grant, "In Which a Woman Buys a Pair of Shoes," *The Thoughtful Dresser*, pp. 10–11.
[18] Otegha Uwagba, "Otegha Uwagba: 'I Love Fashion—So Should I Be Taken Less Seriously?'" *Times* (UK), 18th July 2021. https://www.thetimes.co.uk/article/otegha-uwagba-i-love-fashion-so-should-i-be-taken-less-seriously-5zmcvk89b

And yet the use of dress as way of defining aspects of British identity has never been more openly on display, given the opportunities that new forms of social media now offer. Indeed, the creation, curation and circulation of images of dressed bodies across multiple online platforms has provided one answer to a problem articulated nearly twenty years ago. As Chris Weedon noted in a 2004 essay on "Identity and Belonging in Contemporary Black British Writing," "Identity is an important issue in contemporary Britain where there are ongoing struggles to redefine both 'Britishness' and the nature of a desirable, culturally diverse society."[19] Its importance is now greater than ever, due to political factors such as the complexities of Brexit and public responses to fresh waves of immigration. Deciding for oneself what it means to be British, giving that claim visual expression through what one wears and posting the results publicly, can now be accomplished quickly and with relative ease via Instagram and its ilk. If, as Weedon has suggested, "identity [. . . is] a process, constituted at least in part in and through cultural production[,]" then dress is among the most accessible forms of cultural production through which to initiate the process of constructing identity externally, and social media has become one of the major ways to disseminate whatever has been created.[20]

Nonetheless, the Internet has by no means been the sole vehicle for this or even the chief one. In their 2017 study of two international cities, *Fashion and Everyday Life: London and New York*, Buckley and Clark have emphasized the significance of the urban scene and its streets, arriving at the conclusion that "fashion is an (increasingly) integral part of everyday life in the long twentieth century[,]" for "as visual spectacle and material object" it has "offered the potential for the extraordinary to occur [. . .] thus enabling transformation in appearance and identities."[21] Buckley and Clark remind readers, moreover, that in cities such as London, "substantial social and cultural shifts occurred which challenged the location of power and created new narratives of gender, race, identity, sexuality, national identity, age and generation," all of which produced "overlapping subjectivities," shaped "the lived experiences of individuals[,]" and, therefore, influenced how they chose "to dress, style and fashion themselves."[22] One need not travel to the V&A Museum to see a

---

[19] Chris Weedon, "Identity and Belonging in Contemporary Black British Writing," in *Black British Writing*, edited by R. Victoria Arana and Lauri Ramey (Houndmill, UK: Palgrave Macmillan, 2004), p. 74.
[20] Weedon, "Identity and Belonging in Contemporary Black British Writing," *Black British Writing*, p. 75.
[21] Cheryl Buckley and Hazel Clark, *Fashion and Everyday Life: London and New York* (London: Bloomsbury, 2017), p. 2.
[22] Buckley and Clark, *Fashion and Everyday Life: London and New York*, p. 5.

display of distinctive and often eccentric dress being used to forge a public persona. Due to the greater turnover of retail clothing in the age of "fast fashion" and the affordability of goods manufactured abroad by underpaid workers, London and its environs can sometimes seem like a veritable parade of *fashioned* British identities, fully realized yet simultaneously in flux.

Approaches and Sources

This collection of essays reflects the increasingly interdisciplinary nature of fashion studies: art history meets Edwardian drama, popular newspapers and modernist poetry, reflecting the far-reaching significance of dress as a method of historical inquiry. The sources used here are not material, but textual; they do not concern the material reality or substance of clothing itself, but the textual significance of dress as a social and cultural marker, making a contribution to a well-established method of using novels, plays, poetry and paintings as sources of fashion history. This approach is not without its criticisms; in her 2000 study, *The Fashioned Body: Fashion, Dress and Social Theory*, Joanne Entwistle addressed what she saw as the failure of fashion studies to consider the bodily experience of wearing clothes, or, as she expresses it, the "totality of the dressed body in everyday life."[23] By using only textual sources that ignore the body's role in the lived reality of dress, Entwistle argues, fashion theorists have sometimes shied away from the experience of dress as a "situated bodily practice"[24] in favor of a more abstract approach. This apparent dismissal of the body from dress and fashion studies is indeed ironic; however, the textual approach also has its merits, and simply provides the opposite (but, as the authors in this volume would assert, an equal) approach to the subject, a means of examining the social and cultural meanings of different styles through representation rather than lived reality.

As Lou Taylor has argued, the social significance of clothing is multi-faceted, providing what he calls "a powerful analytical tool" for diverse academic disciplines.[25] The eclecticism of this collection is proof of this: the wide scope of geographical locations and time periods, ranging from eighteenth-century colonial Jamaica to post-war London, demonstrates the deep significance of dress, style and fashion across barriers of time, place and culture. Likewise, the diversity of sources used indicates the extent to which style and fashion have saturated different levels of society. Using literary and artistic sources is

---

[23] Joanne Entwistle, *The Fashioned Body: Fashion, Dress and Social Theory* (Cambridge: Polity Press, 2015), p. xi.
[24] Entwistle, *The Fashioned Body: Fashion, Dress and Social Theory*, p. xi.
[25] Lou Taylor, *The Study of Dress History* (Manchester: Manchester University Press, 2002), p. 1.

a well-established approach to dress history and offers a fascinating insight into the "cultural meaning of clothes,"[26] highlighting prevailing discourses and attitudes as well as providing details of dress itself. As Taylor has suggested, literary and artistic sources provide dress historians with a deeper understanding of "the past through [their] coded signaling of gender, culture, politics and social stratum," exemplifying what Ann Buck has called "dress in action."[27]

Fine art, for instance, an obvious source for dress historians, may provide researchers with vital visual details of dress style that have otherwise been lost,[28] while novels, poetry and plays can help to "pinpoint period socio-economic issues"[29] as well as evoking detailed visual images. As Buck tells us, "[..]where dress is used to express character and illuminate social attitudes and relationships, the novel can give more. It then shows dress in action within the novelist's world."[30] The same goes for other, non-literary textual sources such as letters, diaries and autobiography, all of which are used here to further illuminate the significance of cultural depictions, offering personal insights into writers' subjective responses to dress.

Chapters

As Davis notes, while we are not simply "passive recipients" of our social markers, we are influenced and conditioned by "strong collective currents" which help to shape our sense of self within society, and which, in turn, fashion feeds off.[31] In a broad sense, then, the essays in this collection concern the tensions between the individual self and its social context, while considering the subtler ways that dress can denote identity and meaning. While these essays are intentionally eclectic, each uses clear case studies, situated within distinct contexts, to explore the theme of style and identity across time and place. Building on existing work in this field by researchers such as Buckley and Fawcett, Davies and Ribeiro, this collection interrogates what people have worn and why, examining how dress and style have worked within social systems to "fashion" a person's sense of themselves and their social identity.

---

[26] Taylor, *The Study of Dress History*, p. 2.
[27] Taylor, *The Study of Dress History*, p. 91.
[28] Taylor, *The Study of Dress History*, p. 15.
[29] Taylor, *The Study of Dress History*, p. 91.
[30] Ann Buck, "Clothes in Fact and Fiction, 1825-1865," *Costume*, 17 (1983), p. 83.
[31] Fred Davis, *Fashion, Culture and Identity* (Chicago: University of Chicago Press, 1994), pp. 16-17.

Introduction xix

Within an intersectional framework, each essay represents a link between style and its deeper ties to social identity categories. Rather than focusing on one specific time period or cultural moment, this volume moves through time and place to explore the relationship between different style practices and their social contexts, with each chapter examining specific tensions between individual identity and external structures. What results is a series of snapshots, in both close-up and panoramic visions—a collage of different images illuminating the radically diverse uses of style and its wider significance, highlighting its multiplicity within British culture. The impact of colonialism and its legacy is a significant part of British culture and its heritage, which this collection foregrounds in its diverse choice of subjects, bringing into focus issues such as race, class and gender identity. Given this legacy of British imperialism, it is essential to expand the definition of British identity beyond the borders of the British Isles; by taking this approach, this collection aims to challenge narrow, parochial definitions of British culture and to explore the role of colonialism in constructions of style and the self, a vital move as we continue to reckon with the legacies of Britain's imperial past and its role in the slave trade. As a colonial power with far-reaching global territories, Britannia's attempt to "rule the waves" has had consequences that must be explored and interrogated.

As Buckley and Fawcett remark, fashion and style can both "transgress" and "reinforce dominant modes of representation,"[32] a theme which this collection explores through case studies of both elite and popular style practices. By placing these chapters side by side, we not only see the far-reaching significance of dress as a cultural source, but a series of contrasts and intersections between elitist and dissident styles. Yet the relationship between the two is not as clear-cut as one might initially assume. While, in Chapter One, for instance, we find an elite class of Creole planters using fashion as a means of asserting their sense of racial and class superiority within a colonial context, Chapter Four explores a very different type of elite dress culture through a case study of the aristocratic modernist poet and eccentric Edith Sitwell. Although her class privilege and sense of aristocratic hauteur situated Sitwell firmly at the top of the social scale, her status as a spinster, combined with her lavishly eccentric dress, did little to reinforce the dominant dress codes of her class. Likewise, Chapters Two, Three and Five all, implicitly or explicitly, consider this distinction between elite and popular styles, featuring, respectively, case studies of everyday dress codes in colonial Sri Lanka, working-class female fashions in the Edwardian drama *Tilda's New Hat* and dress and Jewish identity in post-war Britain.

---

[32] Davis, *Fashion, Culture and Identity*, p. 7.

Chapter One of this collection focuses on the society of white Creole planters in eighteenth-century colonial Jamaica,[33] and the use of conversation pieces as signifiers of status, of which clothing was an important part. Concentrating on objects of material culture, such as portrait paintings and fashionable dress, Chloe Northrop analyzes the construction of a British identity on the part of an image-conscious Creole class, highlighting the relationship between taste, style, manners. In this essay, Northrop discusses the ways in which style can function as part of a system of oppression to promote the ideology of colonial supremacy. Through the eighteenth-century portraiture of Philip Wickstead, she examines the relationship between Creole planters and what they regarded as the metropolitan center of elite British culture. By dressing themselves in fashionable clothes, the Creole sitters in Wickstead's conversation pieces aligned themselves with British taste and material culture, using their garments to shape a conspicuously British identity in colonial Jamaica.

From here we travel to colonial Sri Lanka where, in Chapter Two, Ramesha Jayaneththi discusses the link between dress and Sri Lankan identity politics. Jayaneththi examines the significance of fashion as a cultural, historical, social and political phenomenon, tracing transformations in both elite and popular dress and fashions within a colonial context and looking at the role of style and aesthetics in different phases of colonial rule. As part of Sri Lanka's material culture, everyday dress could be utilized for different political purposes. As well as reinforcing the values of colonialism, national dress also became part of the symbolism of anti-colonial nationalism, playing a role in the processes of decolonization itself. In this chapter, Jayaneththi brings to the fore the relationship between dress and Sri Lankan national identity through distinct dress codes, both from the perspective of colonial rulers and nationalist rebels, while also considering the significance of both elite and populist styles. She also weighs the role of cultural artefacts, such as paintings and statuary, in the creation of these dress codes, and illustrates Buckley and Fawcett's argument that fashion and style can both "transgress" and "reinforce dominant modes of representation."[34]

These first two essays both utilize examples of elite cultural representations, such as Philip Wickstead's conversation pieces and images of Sri Lankan sculpture, to open up the question of the relationship between dress and

---

[33] See David Lambert, *White Creole Culture, Politics and Identity During the Age of Abolition* (Cambridge: Cambridge University Press, 2010).
[34] Cheryl Buckley and Hilary Fawcett, *Fashioning the Feminine: Representation and Women's Fashion from the Fin de Siècle to the Present* (London: I. B. Tauris Publishers, 2002), p. 7.

national identity, with the first chapter focusing on white, upper-class styles, and the second on the imposition of British colonial dress on the populace of Sri Lanka and subsequent nationalist resistance. While the women of Wickstead's portraits are represented as part of wider family groups, gender is an implicit theme of Chapter One, with women's status within the eighteen-century family denoted through formal poses and dress styles. Chapter Two also explores the ways in which some women used Western dress in post-colonial Sri Lanka to assert a new kind of female identity, independent of orthodox religious doctrine or colonial authority. Nevertheless, this fashion for mini-skirts and trouser suits, though free from overt colonial power structures, also represented a continuation of Western influence.

Gender and class move to center stage in Chapter Three, which takes us to Edwardian England in the form of a critical Introduction to the 1908 one-act play *Tilda's New Hat* by George Paston (Emily Morse Symonds). In her critical essay, Petra Clark explores the play's intersecting themes of fashion, gender and class, presenting it as a fascinating case study of female identity in Edwardian society, while also looking at its reception. Included as part of the chapter is the transcript of the play which, with its dominant themes of fashion and class, is itself a creative and critical essay on Edwardian attitudes to identity and style, despite being little known by scholars and theatre audiences today.

Tilda's New Hat offers a feminist perspective on working-class Edwardian women's style, and it provides Clark with a distinctive case study through which to elucidate two very different approaches to fashionable dress in the central female characters of Tilda and Daisy. A neglected, if not all-but-forgotten, work of Edwardian drama, this play foregrounds discussions of dress as a significant mode of self-expression for working-class women of the period, with Tilda herself representing a flamboyant type of Edwardian femininity.

Building on the theme of individual aesthetics and identity, Chapter Four explores the link between style and singleness in interwar Britain, using the poet Edith Sitwell as its central case study. As Hope Howell Hodgkins has written, the received image of single women changed significantly after the First World War, becoming closely allied to fashionable dress and modernity.[35] Yet in this age of "surplus women," Sitwell built a reputation as a "formidable spinster," making a theatrical display of her own singleness which seemed as much a part of her sensibility as her poetry. While female poets, novelists and painters were encouraged to cultivate stylish, photogenic publicity profiles,

---

[35] Hope Howell Hodgkins, *Style and the Single Girl: How Modern Women Re-Dressed the Novel, 1922-1977* (The Ohio State University Press, 2016), p. 52.

Sitwell adorned herself in flamboyant costumes, fashioning an image that reinforced her uncategorizable uniqueness and subverted the standards of normative femininity. Using the personal diaries and correspondence of her wide circle of literary friends, this chapter examines the ways in which Sitwell's outlandish sense of style reinforced the perception of her as an eccentric spinster.

Chapter Five foregrounds the notion of the British Jewish *flâneuse* in the aftermath of the Second World War. Challenging the notion of the *flâneur* as essentially masculine, Margaret Stetz builds upon Lauren Elkin's 2016 study *Flâneuse* and, from a feminist perspective, turns to Linda Grant's collection of essays, *The Thoughtful Dresser* (2009), to reveal how British Jewish identity has been expressed through the relationship between women's shopping and urban culture. While shopping has traditionally been coded as a superficial female pursuit that links women to materiality and consumer culture, Stetz affirms Grant's claim that its aesthetic aspects, and the ability of clothes to transform one's identity, serve as a means of observing and participating in the urban scene. As Grant suggests, moreover, shopping and fashionable dress have been necessary social instruments, especially in the twentieth century, for Jewish women in Britain whose right to feel themselves part of the nation has often been contested and challenged.

Chapters Three, Four and Five all feature women's testimony about clothes, either theirs or other women's, in real or fictional settings. While Tilda's flamboyant feather hats and flashy jewelry align her with the gleefully gaudy end of Edwardian womenswear, Edith Sitwell's style is far more of an anti-fashion statement. Linda Grant, on the other hand, discusses her own style, and that of the novelist Anita Brookner and clothing retailer Catherine Hill, in the context of their Jewish identity. Recalling a single red high-heeled shoe among the discarded footwear on display at the museum at Auschwitz, Grant experiences an overpowering desire to purchase a pair of flamboyant, impractical pumps in order to assert her own identity through what she wears, and to fashion her body as a visual statement in the British urban landscape, in a way that cannot be ignored.

Each of these protagonists views clothing primarily as a means of pleasing herself; yet, given their radically different backgrounds, this means different things to each of them. All, however, rebel against their mothers' ideas of how girls should dress, from Tilda's gentle, teasing conflict with her mother (a clear case of generational difference) to Sitwell's dramatic defiance of early-twentieth-century dress codes and Grant's rejection of her mother's ladylike, New Look glamour in favor of the bohemian, eccentric chic of the 1970s. Recalling the increasingly Western-influenced styles of Sri Lankan women in Chapter Two, and standing in stark contrast to the elitist conformity to colonial ideals discussed in Chapter One, these latter chapters give a central place to women's experiences of dress. The horrors of the Holocaust, so central to Grant's discussion of dress and her sense of identity as a British Jewish woman, are juxtaposed here with the depictions of enslaved men and boys in Wickstead's conversation pieces; though presented as marginal figures at the edges of these polished society portraits, they demand our attention and hold our collective gaze.

In this collection of essays, we see how style has functioned through time as an expression of self, both through individualist self-expression and as a wider representation of identity in response to social and political developments in British history. Embracing topics as various, yet significant, as eighteenth-century portraiture, Sri Lankan dress culture, Edwardian working-class glamour, early-twentieth-century modernism and post-Holocaust Jewish *flânerie*, *Fashioning the Self* offers an eclectic approach to contemporary fashion studies. We hope that, by foregrounding issues of gender, class, ethnicity and race in these diverse contexts, this collection will contribute to the wider understanding of fashion and style as significant markers of identity, rich with both personal and political meaning.

Bibliography

Primary Sources

Bowen, Elizabeth. "Dress." In *Collected Impressions*. New York: Knopf, 1950.

Grant, Linda. "In Which a Woman Buys a Pair of Shoes." *The Thoughtful Dresser*. London: Virago, 2009.

Jones, Jonathan. "Frida Kahlo Making Her Self Up Review: Forget the Paintings, Here's Her False Leg." *Guardian* (UK), 12th June 2018. https://www.theguardian.com/artanddesign/2018/jun/12/frida-kahlo-making-her-self-up-review-v-and-a-london

Uwagba, Otegha. "Otegha Uwagba: 'I Love Fashion—So Should I Be Taken Less Seriously?'" *Times* (UK), 18th July 2021. https://www.thetimes.co.uk/article/otegha-uwagba-i-love-fashion-so-should-i-be-taken-less-seriously-5zmcvk89b

Wilcox, Claire and Circe Henestrosa. "Introduction: Fashioning Frida." In *Frida Kahlo: Making Her Self Up*, edited by Claire Wilcox and Circe Henestrosa. London: V&A Publishing, 2018.

Woolf, Virginia. *A Room of One's Own*. 1929, p. 60: https://gutenberg.net.au/ebooks02/0200791.txt

Secondary Sources

Buck, Ann. "Clothes in Fact and Fiction, 1825-1865." *Costume*, no. 17 (1983).

Buckley, Cheryl and Hazel Clark. *Fashion and Everyday Life: London and New York*. London: Bloomsbury, 2017.

Buckley, Cheryl and Hilary Fawcett. *Fashioning the Feminine: Representation and Women's Fashion from the Fin de Siècle to the Present.* London: I. B. Taurus Publishers, 2002.

Cole, Shaun. *Don We Now Our Gay Apparel.* Berg 3PL, illustrated edition, 2000.

Davis, Fred. *Fashion, Culture and Identity.* Chicago: University of Chicago Press, 1994.

Entwistle, Joanne. *The Fashioned Body: Fashion, Dress and Social Theory.* Cambridge: Polity Press, 2015.

Gibson, Robyn. "Introduction." In *The Memory of Clothes*, edited by Robyn Gibson. Rotterdam: Sense Publishers, 2015. xiii–xvii.

Hodgkins, Hope Howell. *Style and the Single Girl: How Modern Women Re-Dressed the Novel, 1922-1977.* Columbus: Ohio State University Press, 2016.

Lambert, David. *White Creole Culture, Politics and Identity During the Age of Abolition.* (Cambridge: Cambridge University Press, 2010).

Plock, Vike Martina. *Modernism, Fashion and Interwar Women Writers.* Edinburgh: Edinburgh University Press, 2017.

Roach, Mary Ellen and Joanne Bubolz Eicher. "The Language of Personal Adornment." In *The Fabrics of Culture: The Anthropology of Clothing and Adornment*, edited by Justine M. Cordwell, and Ronald M. Schwarz. New York: De Gruyter Mouton, 2011.

Stetz, Margaret D. "Fabricating Girls: Clothes and Coming-of-Age Fiction by Women of Color." *Humanities Bulletin*, vol. 2, no. 1 (2019), pp. 122-134.

Taylor, Lou. *The Study of Dress History.* Manchester: Manchester University Press, 2002.

Weedon, Chris. "Identity and Belonging in Contemporary Black British Writing." In *Black British Writing*, edited by R. Victoria Arana and Lauri Ramey. Houndmill UK: Palgrave Macmillan, 2004.

Chapter 1

Creole conversation pieces: portraits in eighteenth-century Jamaica

Chloe Northrop
Tarrant County College, Texas

Abstract: While scholars like Temi Odumosu, David Bindman, Tim Barringer, and Kay Dian Kriz have examined art from eighteenth-century Jamaica, a study of the portraits focusing on the colonial gentry remains unexamined. While one, or a few of the paintings produced by artist Philip Wickstead appear in recent works, there has not been a comprehensive project focusing on Wickstead's career. Particularly in light of the latest publication concerning conversation pieces by Kate Retford, contextualizing Wickstead's paintings from Jamaica will show an attempt by a British artist to travel to a colonial landscape and imitate and "creolize" those produced in the metropole.

Philip Wickstead departed for Jamaica in 1773 to create portraits for the plantation gentry in Jamaica, accompanying a wealthy plantation owner, William Beckford of Somerly, who acted as a connection between the Creole families and Wickstead. He painted several portraits for the Pusey family, as well as the East and Henry families who owned plantations in this important outpost of empire, and his paintings assist in the Creole fashioning of a British identity through material objects. Additionally, the garments depicted display a consciousness of the tastes and modes of the metropolitan center. His renditions appear around the same time as the conversation pieces rose in popularity in England. Although in a different climate, and in a different environment than that in the British Isles, the extant pieces have a connection to those produced in the metropolitan imperial center, while portraying differences as well. These works are unique in that they represent some of the only visual sources created in the West Indies of the plantocracy. The remaining paintings are important for demonstrating a counterpart to the executions rendered in the British Isles.

Keywords: Eighteenth-century Jamaica, Philip Wickstead, colonialism, slavery, conversation pieces, portraiture, Creole, material culture, fashion.

***

During the eighteenth century, portraiture became more accessible to patrons in middling ranks, and as the prestige of having one's likeness rendered in a permanent form grew, many artists began to experiment with the genre. Despite the enduring popularity of the stately, full-length portraits that mirrored those seen in the halls and galleries of manors and estates around England, other, less formal, renditions began to emerge above the mantelpieces of urban and country homes alike. These appeared more like the *genre pieces* that had been fashionable in the seventeenth and early eighteenth centuries. Labeled "conversation pieces," these specialized portraits typically depicted groups engaged in an activity that replicated everyday behavior,[1] and tea tables, outdoor scenes and large parties populated these prospects. Dominated by artists like William Hogarth and Arthur Devies, they waned in popularity in the mid-eighteenth century until the arrival of Johann Zoffany in metropolitan England.

His homecoming marked a renaissance of sorts for these pieces. While Zoffany created prodigious works for the nobility, wealthy gentry families and even the royal family, other artists struggled to perfect this genre. Recent scholarship on the conversation piece by Kate Retford has shown its diversity and enduring status, while noting its ability to encompass many different scenes and groupings.[2] Retford and other scholars of eighteenth-century art have studied pieces from England, Scotland and Ireland, while even examining some pieces created in India. This range, however, leaves out a piece of this genre that appeared for a short time in colonial Jamaica. Philip Wickstead, a student of Zoffany's, departed for Jamaica in 1773 to create portraits for the plantation gentry, and these renditions appeared around the same time as conversation pieces rose in popularity in England. Philip Wickstead's portraits, while not considered masterpieces, still contribute to the discussion of conversation pieces outside of the metropole.

Conversation pieces crafted by Wickstead in Jamaica demonstrate a desire among the colonial gentry to participate in this fashionable depiction of landed gentility, displayed in their homes as both a decorative object and a

---

[1] For a contemporary artistic depiction of eighteenth-century conversation pieces in the Caribbean see, Hyacinth, M. Simpson, "Re-framing the Colonial Caribbean: Joscelyn Gardner's "White Skin, Black Kin: A Creole Conversation Piece," *Postcolonial Studies*, 15 (2012), pp. 87-104.
[2] Kate Retford, *The Conversation Piece: Making Modern Art in 18th Century Britain*, published for the Paul Mellon Centre for Studies in British Art (New Haven: Yale University Press, 2017).

visual display of their family and cultural acumen. Additionally, white Creole inhabitants in the Caribbean used this material culture to establish and display their connections to the British metropole and demonstrate their "Britishness," through luxury goods including fashionable items such as dresses, accessories and other material items.[3] The role dress played in expressing status in the eighteenth century has been proven by many scholars, including Aileen Ribeiro, Beverly Lemire, and Hannah Grieg.[4] Like their metropolitan counterparts, colonial subjects fashioned their identity through both dress and the consumption of goods, like conversation pieces.[5] The clothing chosen for these pictorial displays was carefully selected, with portraits a particularly significant part of this style of colonial consumption. As Beth Fowkes Tobin reminds us, these portraits became a "hybrid" in these spaces "out of the convergence of English painting's visual codes and the colonial subjects that British artists sought to portray."[6] Conversation pieces in the West Indies, therefore, underwent a "subtle generic and ideological" change "when these quintessential English genres incorporated alien subject matter."[7] By combining the familiar with the "exotic," conversation pieces in this tropical landscape underwent a creolization process, which increased their significance for the plantocracy. Further, these items held more value than merely merchandise for colonial inhabitants: through fashion and the consumption of popular British material culture, such as Wickstead's conversation pieces, these colonial inhabitants could signify their own taste and distinguish themselves in the British Atlantic, attempting to legitimize

---

[3] Creole refers to an inhabitant who was either born in the Caribbean or had spent enough time there to "creolize." In these eighteenth-century British Caribbean examples, "Creole" does not refer to racial heritage. For more on Creole culture in the West Indies see David Lambert, *White Creole Culture, Politics and Identity During the Age of Abolition* (Cambridge: Cambridge University Press, 2010); Kamau Braithwaite, *The Development of Creole Society in Jamaica, 1770-1820* (Jamaica: Ian Randle, Kingston, 2006).

[4] See Aileen Ribeiro, *The Art of Dress: Fashion in England and France 1750 to 1820* (New Haven: Yale University Press, 1995); Beverly Lemire and Giorgio Riello, *Dressing Global Bodies: The Political Power of Dress in World History* (Abingdon Oxon: Routledge Taylor & Francis Group, 2020); Hannah Greig, *The Beau Monde: Fashionable Society in Georgian London* (Oxford: Oxford University Press, 2013).

[5] See Jennifer M. Jones, *Sexing La Mode: Gender, Fashion, and Commercial Culture in Old Regime France* (Oxford and New York: Berg, 2004).

[6] Beth Fowkes Tobin, *Picturing Imperial Power: Colonial Subjects in Eighteenth-Century British Painting* (Durham: Duke University Press, 1999), p. 20.

[7] Tobin, Picturing Imperial Power, p. 21.

their wealth and position through these objects.⁸ For, as Maya Jasanoff argues, "By accumulating material wealth, objects and property," these colonial inhabitants "had the ability to transform themselves."⁹ While Jasanoff examines British individuals in India, those in the sugar plantations of the Caribbean could also fit this lens. Although tainted in their own eyes by the association of enslavement, contact with African bodies, infidelity and the sultry climate, these objects assisted in crafting the persona of legitimacy that many colonial inhabitants desired.¹⁰ By employing a British artist in this colonial outpost, the plantocracy could display their connections to the metropole, and craft an image of themselves as British subjects whilst inhabiting what they regarded as this torrid zone of empire. While not quite reaching the masterly quality as those by Hogarth and Zoffany, Wickstead's portraits do show an attempt to both emulate and create permanent renditions of family life in this sugar island residence. Although in a different climate, and in a different environment than that of the British Isles, the extant pieces have a connection to those produced in the metropolitan imperial center.

While the celebrated career of Zoffany is well known, the lives and oeuvres of his students remain obscure. Zoffany, artist and future founding member of the Royal Academy, had arrived in England in 1760, his brief tenure in Rome resulting in his possible meeting with his future pupil, Philip Wickstead. They might have also associated with William Beckford of Somerly, an absentee Jamaican planter from the famed Beckford family who also resided in Rome at the same time as the two artists. Both Zoffany and Wickstead were back in England in the 1760s, and this is most likely when Wickstead began his work in Zoffany's studio. Art Historian David Wilson reports that Wickstead won a prize in 1765 for a drawing of a classical tale of *Tarquin and Lucretia*.¹¹ This prize was for artists under the age of twenty, and the records of the

---

⁸ For an examination of an individual's consumption habits, including the procurement of portraits in eighteenth-century England, see Christa M. Beranek, "Beyond Consumption: Social Relationships, Material Culture, and Identity," in The Materiality of Individuality: Archaeological Studies of Individual Lives, edited by Carolyn L. White (New York: Springer, 2009), p. 163-183.
⁹ Maya Jasanoff, "Collectors of Empire: Objects, Conquests and Imperial Self-Fashioning," *Past & Present*, 184, August 2004, p. 110.
¹⁰ For an excellent work on female slaveholders in Jamaica, see Christine Walker, *Jamaica Ladies: Female Slaveholders and the Creation of Britain's Atlantic Empire*, Omohundro Institute of Early American History and Culture, Williamsburg, Virginia (Chapel Hill: University of North Carolina Press, 2020).
¹¹ David Wilson, "Roubiliac's Missing Model of *Tarquin and Lucretia*: its possible purchase by Johan Zoffany in 1762 or later," *Sculpture Journal*, 18 (2009), pp. 122-123.

Committee on Polite Arts reported that Wickstead created his submission in Zoffany's studio in London. Zoffany biographer Mary Webster notes his lack of students, with Wickstead making up one of the four known pupils.[12] While Zoffany's career ascended, with his election to the Royal Academy in 1768, not much is known of Wickstead during this period.

Connections between Zoffany and the conversation pieces with individuals with holdings in the West Indies include the Young family's 1770 monumental rendition. Commemorating Sir William Young's appointment as Governor of Dominica and his elevation to a baronetcy, this painting by Zoffany depicts the family seated outside their estate in England, donning van Dyckian costumes.[13] The lustrous fabrics glow in contrasting colors as the figures sit theatrically in the outdoor scene, elegantly combining the van Dyckian style of the seventeenth century with a more contemporary eighteenth-century composition.[14] The only connection between this piece and their West Indian position is the inclusion of an enslaved young Black child assisting one of the smaller Youngs off a horse. While no direct connection between Beckford and the Youngs appear, Zoffany's composition and conversation pieces undoubtedly affected Wickstead's own style and paintings.[15]

---

[12] Mary Webster, *Johan Zoffany: 1733-1810*, National Portrait Gallery, London, 1976, p. 612. The other three were James Rubey, Henry Walton, and Geroge Huddesford.

[13] See Tobin, *Picturing Imperial Power*, pp. 39-43. See also Felicity A. Nussbaum, *The Global Eighteenth Century* (Baltimore, M. D.: Johns Hopkins University Press, 2003), p. 176; Mia L. Bagneris, *Colouring the Caribbean: Race and the Art of Agostino Brunias* (Manchester: Manchester University Press, 2018); Kay Dian Kriz, *Slavery Sugar and the Culture of Refinement: Picturing the British West Indies 1700-1840* (New Haven: Yale University Press, 2008). For Van Dyckian (or vandyke) costume, see Jennifer Van Horn, *The Power of Objects in Eighteenth-Century British America*, Omohundro Institute of Early American History and Culture, Williamsburg, Virginia (Chapel Hill: University of North Carolina Press, 2017), pp. 222-229.

[14] See https://www.liverpoolmuseums.org.uk/artifact/family-of-sir-william-young.

[15] Sir William Young notably solicited Agostino Brunias to produce works from the islanded ceded from the Seven Year's War. Brunias produced, as Robert S. DuPlessis notes, "in a tropical version of the 'conversation piece,' an informal group portrait in a realistic setting that was a popular eighteenth-century genre," in *The Material Atlantic: Clothing, Commerce, and Colonization in the Atlantic World, 1650-1800* (Cambridge: Cambridge University Press, 2015), p. 297; For more on Brunias see Kay Dian Kriz, *Slavery, Sugar, and the Culture of Refinement Picturing the British West Indies, 1700-1840* (New Haven: Yale University Press, 2008); Sarah Thomas, "Envisaging a Future for Slavery: Agostino Brunias and the Imperial Politics of Labor and Reproduction," *Eighteenth-Century Studies* vol. 52 (2008), pp. 115-33; David Bindman, "Representing Race in the Eighteenth-Century Caribbean: Brunias in Dominica and St Vincent," *Eighteenth-

Figure 1.1: "Portrait of the Taylor Family," photograph of Daniel Gardner, Sir John Taylor, His Wife Elizabeth, His Brother Simon Taylor, and Four of their Six Children, c. 1785.

Courtesy of National Gallery of Jamaica.

Absentee planters and those with means and connections to travel to England typically had their likenesses done by metropolitan artists. Since colonial inhabitants often lacked access to talented British artists, they had to seize opportunities while in metropolitan centers, and when colonists left the tropics for places like London, they were quick to take advantage of the available talent and possibilities for portraits. These pieces often pictorially separated these individuals from slavery, the source of their wealth.[16] Beckford's cousin, also William Beckford, heir to a large fortune and the author of *Vathek*, sat for Sir Joshua Reynolds for his portrait, now housed in the National Portrait Gallery in London. Portraits like these, as Geoff Quilley reminds us, assist in "dissociating their display of cultural refinement from the source of their prosperity."[17] Likewise, Simon Taylor, possibly the largest

---

Century Studies vol. 1 (2017), pp. 1-17; Mia Bagneris, *Colouring the Caribbean Race and The Art of Agostino Brunias* (Manchester: Manchester University Press, 2018).

[16] For pictorial renditions of the Black population in the West Indies, see Temi Odumosu, *Africans in English Caricature 1769-1819: Black Jokes, White Humour* (London: Harvey Miller Publishers, 2017); Tim Barringer, Gillian Forrester, and Barbaro Martinez-Ruiz, *Art and Emancipation in Jamaica: Isaac Mendes Belisario and His Worlds* (New Haven: Yale Center for British Art in association with Yale University Press, 2007).

[17] Geoff Quilley, and Kay Dian Kriz, *An Economy of Colour: Visual Culture and the Atlantic World, 1660-1830* (Manchester: Manchester University Press, 2003), p. 107.

landowner and the richest man in the British Empire, is purported to appear in a pastel by Daniel Gardner from 1785. In his recent biography of Taylor, Christer Petely stated that Taylor was not in England at the time of the rendition,[18] which suggests that the inclusion could be of someone else, but is most likely that of the absent, yet powerful relative.

The artist depicted Taylor, whether present or in absentia, on the left side of the group portrait with his brother, Sir John Taylor and his wife Elizabeth and their four children. Simon's nephew, namesake and heir, is included with the children. On the far right of the image, John Taylor wears a suit with jeweled buckles on the breeches, while to his left, Elizabeth dons an ensemble that was most likely a posing gown.[19] Such ensembles could be adapted, as seen by the accessorizing of her yellow gown with a black belt and jeweled adornments, and with her powdered hair and rogued cheeks, she epitomizes high fashion in the mid-1780s. She glances down at one of their four children, who appear in an angelic arrangement with white gowns and flowered accouterments. On the far-left Simon Taylor appears in a black suit with a lacey, frilled white shirt, gazing off to the right while holding one of the children. Fashionably dressed, this group represents the height that sugar plantation wealth could achieve in metropolitan England.[20] Intended for a private display of this extended family, the Taylors pose in a familiar, yet stylish pastel.[21]

---

[18] Christer Petely, *White Fury: A Jamaican Slaveholder and the Age of Revolution* (Oxford: Oxford University Press, 2018), p. 85.

[19] Ribeiro notes that although these ensembles are often imaginary, they also include "specific contemporary styles" as well. Aileen Ribeiro, in *John Singleton Copley in America*, Metropolitan Museum of Art, New York. Distributed by H.N. Abrams, p. 107. See also Claudia Kidwell, "Are Those Clothes Real? Transforming the Way Eighteenth-Century Portraits Are Studied," *Dress*, vol. 24 (1998), pp. 3-15 for more on the authenticity of dress in eighteenth-century portraits.

[20] Although physically removed from the plantation and enslaved labor that provided the wealth on display in the Taylor family portrait, elements of their unsavory dealings remain, with goods whose supply depended on triangular trade routes surrounding them. For more on fabrics and colonial trade see Amelia Rauser, *The Age of Undress* (London: Yale University Press, 2020); Jane Ashelford, "'Colonial livery' and the Chemise à la Reine, 1779–1784,'" *Costume*, vol. 52, no. 2 (2018) pp. 217-239.

[21] Daniel Gardner excelled in pastel and gouache. Katherine Marjorie Shelley Baetjer believes that Gardner studied with Benjamin West and Johann Zoffany and served as an assistant to Joshua Reynolds. See Katharine Marjorie Shelley Baetjer, *Pastel Portraits: Images of 18th-Century Europe*, Metropolitan Museum of Art, (New York and New Haven: Yale University Press, 2011), p. 50. In his account book this grouping is entitled, "The Watson-Taylor Family Group. The family of Sir John Taylor, Bart. (1) Mr. Simon Taylor, of Jamaica (the stout old gentleman, brother of Sir John.) (2) Sir John Taylor, F.R.S., Bart., *ob.* 1788. (3) Lady Taylor, daughter and heir of Philip Houghton of Jamaica.

Figure 1.2: Pompeo Batoni, *Portrait of John Blagrove*, 1774.

Courtesy of the National Gallery of Jamaica.

Other methods of obtaining a portrait were available during the "Grand Tour." Going on the Grand Tour to continental Europe, particularly to Rome, represented an important milestone for young gentlemen of fortune,[22] and

---

The four children were afterwards: – (4) Sir Simon Taylor (*ob.* 1815). (5) Mrs. Watson-Taylor (*ob.* 1853). (6) Mrs. Mayne. (7) Mrs. Graeme. This group formerly belongs to Mrs. Keatinge, of Teffont Manor, near Salisbury, and was sold at the Watson-Taylor sale, at Colston Park, in 1832," George Charles Williamson, *Daniel Gardner, Painter in Pastel and Gouache: A Brief Account of His Life and Works*, John Lane, The Bodley Head, London, and the John Lane Company, Vigo St. W. New York, 1921, p.128.

[22] See Jeremy Black, *The British Abroad: The Grand Tour in the Eighteenth Century* (Stroud: History Press, 2011).

when Wickstead himself spent time in Rome, he possibly completed a conversation piece involving seven British gentlemen.[23] These grand tours also provided opportunities for Creole planters who journeyed to the ancient city to sit for a portrait. John Blagrove, for instance, of Cardiff Hall, Jamaica sojourned to Europe in the late 1770s and had his likeness produced by Pompeo Batoni in 1779.[24]

Standing erect in this half-length portrait, he gazes at the viewer, and with a powdered coif and a smart suit, appears as a young British gentleman of fashion and fortune.[25] His light waistcoat contrasts with the dark coat trimmed in gold, his lace collar and sleeves completing the outfit. Nothing in this portrait indicates his origin or the imperial source of his wealth from sugar plantations. This conventional Grand Tour portrait removes those unsavory elements to craft a persona rooted in the popular motifs of the time for metropolitan British young men, one that was far removed from the taint of bondage and the by-products of sugar.

Children who crossed the Atlantic for their education in the British Isles often had their portraits produced while matriculating, including both single and group portraits. Possibly the most famous young Creole from Jamaica to appear in a portrait, Sara Barrett Moulton, appeared in a 1794 painting by Thomas Lawrence. Now housed at the Huntington Library and entitled *Pinkie,* this portrait depicts a young girl in an outdoor setting, wearing a white flowing dress accessorized with a pink ribbon and hat.[26] The looseness of her

---

[23] This portrait is now in a private collection. Recent scholarship attributes it to artist John Brown. It includes Mr. John Corbet, Tollemache, Earl Talbot, James Byres, Sir John Rous, John Staples, and William McDouwall (http://www.nationaltrustcollections.org.uk/object/1139726). Kate Retford notes that portraits on the Grand Tour containing multiple sitters often had to be copied for each person, and was both time-consuming, unprofitable, and a nuisance for many artists. See "The conversation of a well chosen friend," in *The Conversation Piece*. It is likely the Wickstead also produced a painting Baicco, the Roman Dwarf while in Rome. More information about this piece can be found in the Frick Collection Library.

[24] Pompeo Batoni was a leading portrait painter in Rome for those on the Grand Tour. The portrait of John Balgrove follows his conventional poses for those visiting his studio in Rome. See Hugh Belsey, *History Today* vol. 32, no. 8 (August 1982), pp. 46-48.

[25] For more on Cardiff Hall and John Blagrove see James Hakewill, *A Picturesque Tour in the Island of Jamaica, from Drawings Made in the Years 1820 and 1821,* Hurst and Robinson, London, Pall-Mall: E. Lloyd, Harley Street, 1825, Section 1; Rosalie Smith McCrea, "John Blagrove of Cardiff Hall, St. Ann Jamaica, 1753-1824," *Journal of Caribbean History* vol. 47 (2013), pp. 123-152. See also https://www.ucl.ac.uk/lbs/person/view/1305465018.

[26] See https://www.huntington.org/pinkie. For more on children in eighteenth century art, see Marcia Pointon, "The State of A Child," in *Hanging the Head: Portraiture and Social*

posture renders her in a dance-like pose, which must have delighted her family, particularly after her untimely death, possibly from a cough a year after this sitting. One of her contemporaries, who left their island home of Jamaica and attended school with Moulton in England, was Jane Brodbelt. Like the Barrett-Moultons, the Brodbelts sought a metropolitan artist to record a permanent recollection of their children while in Great Britain. In a miniature by the popular London artist Richard Cosway, the children of Dr. Francis Rigby Brodbelt of Spanish Town, Jamaica, who were all attending schools in the British Isles, came together for their portrait.[27] The eldest, a son named Rigby, was depicted in van Dyckian costume, and is accompanied by his two sisters Nancy and Jane, who don more contemporary fashions.

Figure 1.3: Richard Cosway, "Brodbelt Children," 1788, in Geraldine Nutt Mozley, Letters to Jane from Jamaica, 1788-1796.

(London: Published for the Institute of Jamaica by the West India Committee, 1938), Frontispiece.

Formation in Eighteenth Century England (New Haven: Yale University Press, 1997), pp. 177-226.
[27] See Stephen Lloyd, *Richard Cosway* (London: Unicorn Press, 2005).

Costume historian Aileen Ribeiro notes that masquerade fashion, including van Dyck dress was particularly popular for boys at this time.[28] Their mother wrote of receiving the image and placing it in the home for her neighbors and friends to come and view, demonstrating the public nature of such private family images.[29] Such behavior also indicates the importance of these objects in displaying connections to British fashions and the visualization of familial connections. The desire to craft visual renditions of British identity through pictorial scenes indicates the aspiration of Creole families in the Caribbean. Transatlantic families in Jamaica desired not only to appear in fashionable ensembles in metropolitan locations like Kingston and Spanish Town, but also to have these moments commemorated. Family scenes of planters, though, remain quite rare, as many families experienced separation across the Atlantic. Therefore, those with the means to travel to metropolitan centers eagerly sat for portraits, demonstrating the desirability to participate in this fashionable and practical form of artistic patronage.

While the prospect of sitting for a portrait in London appealed to planters in the West Indies, many remained on the island without the possibility of venturing across the Atlantic. When William Beckford of Somerley relocated to Jamaica in 1773 he invited Wickstead and landscape artist George Robertson to accompany him.[30] It appears that Wickstead traveled directly with Beckford, and the pair were later joined by Robertson. Beckford's family owned extensive properties in Jamaica, and as the illegitimate son of Richard Beckford, brother of William Beckford, the infamous art patron and lord-

---

[28] Aileen Ribeiro, "The dress worn at masquerades in England, 1730 to 1790, and its relation to fancy dress in portraiture," Thesis, Courtauld Institute of Art, 1975, p. 205.
[29] Chloe Northrop, "Education, Material Culture, and the Coming of Age in Eighteenth-Century British Jamaica, *Transversea*, 2 (2012), pp. 67-68.
[30] George Robertson accompanied William Beckford in order to create landscapes of estates in Jamaica. According to Geoff Quilley and Kay Dian Kriz, Robertson was a "protégé" of Beckford's and his *Descriptive Account* contained descriptions of Roberton's career. Further, John Boydell engraved six of the paintings which were taken in Jamaica. These "picturesque" scenes serve as a visual counterpart to Wickstead's portraits, as they are also devoid of the cruelties of the sugar plantations and enslavement. See Geoff Quilley, and Kay Dian Kriz, *An Economy of Colour: Visual Culture and the Atlantic World, 1660-1830*, Manchester University Press, Manchester, 2003, pp. 106-113. Frank Cundall notes that Robertson "painted views in the island, and, returning to England, exhibited pictures of Jamaica scenes, twenty-six in all, with the Incorporated Society of Artists (of which body he was for some time vice-president) from 1775 to 1778. Most of them appeared as "A View in Jamaica. The names given are Roaring River, Fort William and Wiliamsfield. These views were admired, and when engraved created some interest..." (Cundall, Frank. *Historic Jamaica*, Pub. for the Institute of Jamaica by the West India Committee, London, 1915, p. 364).

mayor of London, he still stood to inherit land in Jamaica.[31] The Beckford family possessed vast estates in Westmoreland, and he relocated in order to efficiently run them from Jamaica rather than as an absentee planter, like many of his relatives and other landowners residing in England. Westmoreland, a parish on the southwest corner of the island, contained many plantations owned by the Beckfords, including Fort William, Hertford, Roaring River, Smithfield and Williamsfield (Figure 1.4).[32]

Figure 1.4: After George Robertson, "A View in the Island of Jamaica of Part of the River Cobre Near Spanish Town" 1778, aquatint.

Aaron and Marjorie Matalon Collection, Courtesy of the National Gallery of Jamaica.

By soliciting two artists to accompany him to Jamaica, he acted as a patron of the arts, bringing a form of imperialist culture and an opportunity for accessible artistic renditions for his fellow planters.

---

[31] Jill H. Casid, *Sowing Empire: Landscape and Colonization* (Minneapolis: University of Minnesota Press, 2005), p. 60.
[32] https://www.ucl.ac.uk/lbs/person/view/2146634868. George Robertson depicted a landscape from Roaring River, a copy of which is housed at the John Carter Brown Library. The tropical paradise background includes enslaved persons near the water.

Contemporary to the execution of these conversation pieces, metropolitan observers bemoaned the Creole people of the West Indies for their apparent lack of restraint with regards to food and alcohol, sexual immorality and contact with the tropical climate and enslaved people from Africa.[33] While derived from English culture, the equatorial location rendered it, as scholar Roger Buckley has termed it, as lacking in "refinement, like civilized societies, and that it was dominated by the climate and the soil. A civilized life, it was argued by some, was better calculated to make man virtuous than the life of nature. Jamaican society, like other primitive societies, was too much the product of the whims of climate."[34] Other scholars, like Trevor Burnard, have pointed out the lack of success in crafting a settler society. Burnard posits: "West Indian planters failed all tests. They did not create self-sustaining and morally upstanding 'neo-Britains' in the tropics. Their proclivity for sexual relationships outside marriage with allegedly promiscuous black women was deeply problematic when they could not develop a settled white community."[35]

Wickstead's contemporaries at the time of his tenure in Jamaica put much of the blame on the white women themselves for the failure of the white population to reproduce. Noting the white men's proclivity for engaging in illicit sexual activities with enslaved Black women, historian and Jamaican inhabitant Edward Long suggested in his 1774 *History of Jamaica*: "To allure men from these illicit connexions, we ought to remove the principal obstacles which deter them from marriage. This will be chiefly affected by rendering women of their own complexion more agreeable companions, more frugal, trusty and faithful friends, than can be met with among the African ladies."[36]

By examining the Wickstead portraits, we see the rendering of stable families, possibly generations of white families who were reproducing white children, as well as retaining respectability in this tropical landscape. Whether or not this was a conscious attempt on Wickstead's or the sitters' part to counter such rhetoric as Long's, we can still see the delineation of stable British families, emulating proper gentry settings in these conversation

---

[33] See Sarah E. Yeh, "'Sink of All Filthiness': Gender, Family and Identity in British Atlantic, 1688-1763," *The Historian* 68 (March 2006), pp. 66-88.
[34] Roger N. Buckley, "The Frontier in the Jamaican Caricatures of Abraham James," *The Yale University Library Gazette* 58, 1984, p. 153.
[35] Trevor Burnard, and Richard Follett, "Caribbean Slavery, British Anti-Slavery, and the Cultural Politics of Venereal Disease," *The Historical Journal* 55 (2012), p. 447; See also Trevor Burnard, "A Failed Settler Society: Marriage and Demographic Failure in Early Jamaica," *Journal of Social History* vol. 28 (1994), pp. 63-82.
[36] Edward Long, *The History of Jamaica: Or, General Survey of the Antient and Modern State of the Island: With Reflections on its Situation Settlements, Inhabitants, Climate, Products, Commerce, Laws, and Government* (London: T. Lowndes, 1774), p. 330.

pieces. These portraits, then, can be seen to have a dual purpose. Not only are they marking generational likenesses on a permanent canvas, but they can also be seen as a means of self-fashioning a British identity in this colonial sphere, their fashionable dress assisting in solidifying their "Britishness" in these depictions.

Patronage still played a large role in introducing artists to potential clients, and, particularly for portrait painting, such forms of introduction were necessary. Jennifer Van Horn notes that after the British artist Joseph Blackburn worked in Bermuda, he carried letters of introduction to colonial North America. Bostonians received him and commissioned portraits based on these letters, which acted as a sort of credit in this colonial scene.[37] Since Wickstead accompanied a plantation owner, such letters were not necessary, as Beckford could personally introduce him to the individuals who would patronize his services. Therefore, Wickstead was poised to "creolize" these conversation pieces in this imperial landscape.

Portraitists working in transatlantic locations such as Jamaica had to operate within a tenuous cultural position. While rooted in the fashions of metropolitan England, they also had to adapt to reflect local customs and traditions. These conversation pieces could be tailored to the client's tastes, preferences and the climate itself, and while retaining some of the recognizable elements of those produced in metropolitan centers, they also possess some distinctive qualities. This balance, as T. H. Breen reminds us, was necessary, for to be "successful in this provincial market, they had to craft images that resonated with broadly shared cultural meanings."[38] Conversation pieces meshed well with both the local market and personal tastes in this colonial context.

Wickstead began his career in Jamaica memorializing families and individuals in the latest style. Eschewing the approach of Joshua Reynolds, who preferred his sitters to appear in more "timeless" ensembles, Wickstead employed settings that resembled some of Zoffany's compositions.[39] While many of these paintings are difficult to date, and the individuals are not always precisely noted, these scenes provide a glimpse into the white plantation owner's familial life in the 1770s. This period marks one in which

---

[37] Van Horn, *Power of Objects,* pp. 1-9.

[38] T. H. Breen, "'The Meaning of Likeness,' Portrait-Painting in an Eighteenth-Century Consumer Society," in *The Portrait in Eighteenth-Century America,* ed. Ellen G. Miles (Newark and London: University of Delaware Press and Associated University Presses, 1993), p. 39.

[39] Ian McIntyre, *Joshua Reynolds: The Life and Times of the First President of the Royal Academy* (London: Allen Lane, 2003), p. 112, p. 242.

the white settlers were still attempting to form a settler colony against the backdrop of a massive slave population conducting extreme labor in the heat of the Caribbean.[40] The sugar plantations in the 1770s were experiencing some insecurity as tensions rose with the mainland North American colonies and the mother country.[41] In contrast to reports of high mortality rates, debauched bachelors and the debilitating influence of a climate and contact with enslaved persons on these transplanted Britons, the portraits by Wickstead show stable, polite gentry families.[42] Many of the families are portrayed in the popular "conversation piece" tradition, and, as Kate Retford notes, "it is this sense of exchange between figures that sets the conversation piece apart from other painted groups."[43] These familial exchanges can be seen in all of the extant portraits by Wickstead that contain more than one person, rooting these figures in the style that was then popular in England and transplanting it to this colonial outpost.

Wickstead's portraits, many of which are now housed at the National Gallery of Jamaica and in private collections, portray families in scenes similar to those in conversation pieces from England from the second half of the eighteenth century. According to historian Frank Cundall, restoration attempts to many of the Wickstead pieces rendered their sitters' identities indefinite at best.[44] However, Wickstead did send some pieces back to England for exhibition at the Society of Artists for the 1777, 1778 and 1780 exhibitions. The now lost painting, *A Mulatto Woman Teaching Needlework to Negro Girls*, made it back to London, as well as *Portrait of a well-known beggar at Rome* and *A Conversation*.[45] This demonstrates that his conversation pieces crossed the Atlantic and might have been viewed by a London audience, though the exact nature of the exhibited pieces remains a mystery. Considered "natural and expressive" by contemporaries, these portraits, according to art historian David Bindman, "give strong hints that Wickstead

---

[40] According to Trevor Burnard, the population of Jamaica in 1774 was 209,617, with the white population 12,737. See, Trevor Burnard, "European Migration to Jamaica, 1655-1780," *The William and Mary Quarterly*, vol. 53 (1996), p. 772.

[41] See Andrew Jackson O'Shaughnessy, *An Empire Divided: The American Revolution and the British Caribbean* (Philadelphia: University of Pennsylvania Press, 2000).

[42] See Sarah E. Yeh, "'A sink of all filthiness': gender, family, and identity in the British Atlantic, 1688-1763," *The Historian*, vol. 68 (2006), pp. 66-89.

[43] Retford, *The Conversation Piece*, p. 1.

[44] Frank Cundall, "Philip Wickstead of Jamaica," *Conosseuir*, vol. 94 (1934), pp. 174-175.

[45] Algernon Graves, *The Society of Artists of Great Britain, 1760-1791; the Free Society of Artists, 1761-1783: A Complete Dictionary of Contributors and Their Work from the Foundation of the Societies to 1791* (London: George Bell and Sons, 1907), p. 277.

was capable of reflecting interestingly on the complexities of a slave-owning society."[46] Out of Wickstead's paintings, only portraits remain extant.

While exhibiting paintings in England might provide some prestige in that metropolitan center, portraits were the principal means to financial success, however tenuous, in this colonial scene. Around 1775 Wickstead executed several paintings for the Pusey family, the first, likely portraying Benjamin and Mary Pusey, unfolding a companion portrait of a mature couple.

Figure 1.5: Philip Wickstead, *Portrait of Benjamin and Mary Pusey*, c.1775.

Courtesy of the National Gallery of Jamaica.

The Puseys owned land in Clarendon, the parish directly next to St. Catherine, which contained the capital Spanish Town. Pusey Hall Estate was part of Vere Parish but is now part of Clarendon.[47] This portrait of Benjamin

---

[46] David Bindman and Henry Louis Gates Jr., *Image of the Black in Western Art: From the "Age of Discovery" to the Age of Abolition* (Cambridge, Mass.: Harvard University Press, 2010), p. 270.
[47] See https://thelastgreatgreathouseblog.wordpress.com/tag/pusey-hall-great-house/

Creole conversation pieces

and Mary depicts the couple sitting together in an open room festooned with dark red curtains. In a scene that is indoors but with an opening to the prospect beyond, the lighting illuminates the couple.[48] With a bright carpet on the floor, and books and a globe indicating learning and sophisticated knowledge, Benjamin appears as a country sage. He gestures towards the enslaved young man in livery, who appears to be unveiling an oval painting balanced on a chair upholstered in a dark blue fabric. The red in the young man's vest and pantaloons both compliments the jacket strewn next to Benjamin, while contrasting to the fabric of his stockings and jacket. He is positioned at the edge of the indoor space and the outside, indicating his marginalized position within the family, and his inclusion aligns with Tobin's analysis of the Black page in Zoffany's portrait of the Young family: "He is included in the family portrait, like the animals, as an accoutrement or prop to help communicate this family's qualities."[49] This sanitized portrayal of slavery removes the individual from the backbreaking labor of the sugar plantations. His enslavers sit comfortably by, enjoying the fruits of labor not done by their own efforts, depicted in a position pictorially satisfying to the patron's wishes, without even hinting at the sweat and blood that paid for this image.

The interior of the home sets the background for the painting. Retford argues that the exact locations in conversation pieces cannot always be readily determined, for: "Exterior spaces in conversation pieces range from evocative pastoral settings to precise locations in front of country houses."[50] This could, therefore, be the space in which the Pusey family lived, but it could also be some creation that Wickstead crafted for his sitters. Regardless of location, however, the scene is removed and disconnected from the exterior labor. The back wall, bare except for a single framed landscape, contains a tropical scene, the only indication that this piece takes place in the tropics.

Benjamin, in an all-black suit, leans towards his wife, who is bent towards him in contemplation. A single necklace and earrings accessorize her loose, pale gown, unadorned except for lace frills and a white fichu.[51] A contrasting

---

[48] This scene is reminiscent of a 1775 conversation piece by Johan Zoffany of the Gore Family. In Zoffany's family portrait, four of the family members gather around a harpsichord, while two women sit in the opening of the room. A red cloth also hangs atop this painting. While Wickstead likely did not see this piece before his departure from England, the similarity of the backdrops indicates that Zoffany influenced Wickstead's style.
[49] Tobin, *Picturing Imperial Power*, p. 42.
[50] Retford, *Conversation Piece*, p. 129.
[51] See Kidwell, "Are Those Clothes Real?"

shawl on her lap and a modest cap complete her ensemble. Such small visual details could help to distinguish Mary from her colonial compatriots, since, as fashion historian Kimberly Chrisman-Campbell argues, it was "trimmings and accessories that determined whether or not a person was in style."[52] She gently lifts the folds of her skirt, which guides the viewer's gaze to the dog on the bottom right. Signaling fidelity, the couple appears content and reputable.

This painting placed them pictorially with the fashionable portrayals of gentry in England. Further, the attention to dress is reminiscent of paintings by Agostino Brunias, who painted West Indian scenes in the 1770s. According to Tobin, his "careful rendering of the dress and adornment of his Caribbean subjects reflect not only natural history's concern with surfaces but the Caribbean societies obsession with clothing. Brunias's attention to clothing is matched by descriptions of dress in the journals of Caribbean planters and in the narratives of British visitors to the West Indies."[53]

British observers noted the "obsession" that Creoles had for their dress. Edward Long, in his influential 1774 *History of Jamaica,* mentioned both the richness of white Creole women's attire, and also their tendency towards being "too much addicted to expensive living, costly entertainments, dress, and equipage.[54] Further, Long described: "Our English belles in Jamaica…do not scruple to wear the thickest winder silks and satins; and are sometimes ready to sink under the weight of rich gold or silver brocades. Their head-dress varies with the *ton* at home; the winter fashions of *London* arrive here at the setting in of hot weather; and thick or thin caps, large as an umbrella, or as diminutive as a half crown piece, are indiscriminately put on, without the smallest regard to the difference of climate."[55] These contemporary writers noted the fashion choices of these sugar plantation inhabitants, ensuring that the details in these conversation pieces place their sitters in a larger conversation regarding fashion. They demonstrate a fashionable grouping posing in companionable comfort and would not have gone unnoticed by the patrons of these portraits.

A similar companion portrait purports to be of Richard and Jane Pusey, but is likely Benjamin and Mary's son, William Pusey.

---

[52] Kimberly Chrisman-Campbell, "Fashioning (and Refashioning) European Fashion," in *Fashioning Fashion: European Dress in Detail, 1700-1915* (Munich: Delmonico Books, 2010), p. 17.
[53] Tobin, *Picturing Imperial Power*, p. 151.
[54] Long, *The History of Jamaica*, p. 265.
[55] Long, *The History of Jamaica*, p. 522.

Figure 1.6: Philip Wickstead, *Richard and Jane Pusey* [William Pusey and His Wife], c. 1785.

Courtesy of the National Gallery of Jamaica.

Later to become Speaker of the Jamaican House of Assembly in 1782, this depiction places the Pusey's home with possessions of respectability and refinement. As a colonel in the Middlesex Regiment of Horse Militia, William dons a red coat with detailed lacing framing his wrists, and breeches that contain an ample man who gestures out to the prospect beyond. Leaning against a small table containing a decorated black urn, he gazes towards his wife, attired in a blue silk gown trimmed with detailed black lace, her hair coiffed in a high style popular in the 1770s. Possibly to stand the discomfort of the heat, William's hair is cut short; he does not wear a wig and neither wears powder in their hair. A young, enslaved attendant stands with a hat and walking stick ready to receive instructions from William. While similar curtains frame the background as the first piece, the floor is bare and the books and globe which populated the previous portrait are missing.[56]

---

[56] See https://thelastgreatgreathouseblog.wordpress.com/category/clarendon/

The landscape beyond the house has more discernable details, with a house on the left and what appear to be tents lining the grounds.[57] Both are compositions of couples, with a horizontal orientation with complementary curtains in the background. They do not seem to portray the same room, and the resemblances are enough to make the differences charming and discernable to the viewers. These images craft a view of the stable subjects that these Creole inhabitants desired to display.

Wickstead executed two other conversation pieces in which the scene takes place outdoors.[58] One is of a Mr. Butler in Venetian style, who appears in a boat with his daughter, Mary.[59] The painting on wood contains a label stating that Mary later married a clergyman named William Pusey. This could perhaps be a couple present and mislabeled in one of the previous paintings, or another Pusey relative. Mary, wearing a pink gown with white trimmings, styles her hair up for their jaunt on the water. She sits in the wooden boat with a parasol shading her from the sun, while her father stands next to her with a fishing spear. The small boat is decorated with a red trim and a finely decorated hull. Guided by a Black man who wears a jacket with red cuffs that match the lining of the boat, they both look at the target, the lush green and blue background portraying a sense of outdoor indolence and ease.

Another outdoor scene crafted by Wickstead in Jamaica is unique, in that he paints a self-portrait of himself leaning against a large tree. This conversation piece presents Wickstead wearing a striped jacket and possibly sketching an unknown companion, who stands to his right. With her arm around him, the female acquaintance looks down at his drawing, her green riding habit suggesting she is ready for outdoor recreation. The bright hues of these two pieces, and their outdoor settings, mark them as some of the more coloristic of Wickstead's oeuvre.

While these domestic scenes illustrate the lives of paired Creole inhabitants, conversation pieces often represented entire families. For example, the

---

[57] A monument at Saint Peter's Anglican Church in Clarendon has a monument to William and Elizabeth Pusey on the interior walls of the church. https://thelastgreatgreathouseblog.wordpress.com/category/clarendon/

[58] A portrait of a single woman, *Portrait of an Unknown Lady,* also takes place outside. This fashionably dressed woman, stands in a gown of printed silk with lace trimmings. A large hat and parasol accessorize this outfit. She gestures towards the vista below, which displays boats in a river or inlet. A church and other buildings lines the bank. This could perhaps be Spanish Town, as the church appears to resemble the St. Catherine's Cathedral in Spanish Town. See Kriz, *Slavery, Sugar, and the Culture of Refinement*, Vol. 55; Mia Bagneris, *Colouring the Caribbean*, p. 160.

[59] For more on the use of Venetian style in the eighteenth century, see Michael Levey, *Painting in Eighteenth-Century Venice* (New Haven: Yale University Press, 1994), p. 7.

painting reported to be of Edward East and his family, now housed in the National Gallery of Jamaica, contains a family of four. This couple, accompanied by two children, is rendered in a similar composition to that of the Puseys, with one of the main differences being a horizontal orientation of the canvas. Unlike the other two conversation pieces, the wife and mother also stand in this arrangement. Labeled as both *Edward Pusey and His Family* as well as *Edward East and Family*, this painting likely depicts Edward East, a planter from Whitehall, Jamaica.

Figure 1.7: Philip Wickstead, *Edward Pusey and His Family* [Edward East and His Family] c.1775.

Courtesy of the National Gallery of Jamaica.

The East family had deep roots in Jamaica, as Edward's grandfather had been part of the conquest of Jamaica in 1655.[60] His first wife, Amy, of Hyde Hall, Jamaica, died in 1773, and he remarried in 1774 to Mary Wilkins. With his first wife he had a son, Edward-Hyde, who would later become a baronet, and a daughter, Amy-Anne. Edward-Hyde would have been twelve at the time of the painting, and was possibly in England for his education, rendering him unavailable for the sitting.[61] Mary had three children with Edward and her eldest, Hinton, is possibly the infant in this portrait. The four Easts, possibly the eldest Amy-Anne, his second wife Mary, infant Hinton and Edward himself, populate the image.

The family is arranged in a group, standing in front of imposing columns in an impressive estate. Edward dons an embroidered vest with a blue jacket, trimmed with lace around the wrists. The cravat with lace matches the trimming from the wrists and wraps high on the neck of a gentleman who appears with red cheeks, perhaps from the heat in such a warm outfit. Partially balding, he gazes towards his wife, who is also attired in a fashionable outfit of a pink silk, close-bodice gown, styled like a *robe a l'anglaise*, which is accessorized with lace trimmings. The tip of a shoe can be seen peaking from the bottom of her gown. British observers noted the attention to fashion that the Creoles demonstrated. Janet Schaw, a Scottish traveler in the 1770s remarked: "The people of Fashion dress as light as possible; worked and plain muslins, painted gauzes or light Lutstrings and Tiffities are the universal wear. They have the fashions every six weeks from London, and London itself cannot boast of more elegant shops than you meet with at St John."[62]

This ensemble marks the sitter as a woman of fashion. Further, she holds an infant, naked except for a cloth wrapping, showing that she was also a mother. Near the feet of the father is a small child. Wearing a loose gown, with a light blue ribbon, the eldest child stares directly at the viewer and holds an odd-looking brown and white dog. Curiously, the child is situated near her father and separated from her stepmother, and this blended family could account for the rather stiff formality of the poses. With high infant mortality, and the vagueness of the figures in the image, the identity of each person is

---

[60] See https://archive.org/stream/genealogicalhera00inburk#page/388/mode/2up
[61] For more on Edward-Hyde East, see https://www.ucl.ac.uk/lbs/person/view/16601.
[62] Janet Schaw, Evangeline Walker Andrews, and Charles McLean Andrews, *Journal of a Lady of Quality; Being the Narrative of a Journey from Scotland to the West Indies, North Carolina, and Portugal, in the Years 1774 to 1776* (New Haven: Yale University Press, 1921), p. 115.

questionable. Nevertheless, this conversation piece creates a striking image of a colonial family modeled on stability, respectability, fashion and taste.

Portraits often depicted families as a means of establishing genealogy and commemorating events like marriages and children. This image is particularly important as, at the time of its painting, Jamaica and the West Indian sugar plantation islands were experiencing a demographic crisis for the white population. Unable to maintain their own numbers through births, this portrait shows a white family actively participating in the establishment of an entrenched Creole settler society. The extreme paleness of the sitters likely demonstrates an absence of any racial "impurity" to potentially stain their family fortunes,[63] and if there were any mixed-race children fathered by the male sitter, they certainly are not depicted in this portrait. For, as Brooke Newman reveals in her recent work on the "genealogical concept of whiteness," eighteenth-century Jamaica saw several attempts on the part of mixed-race individuals to claim legal rights and inheritances.[64]

According to Newman, "White women's most crucial task in Jamaica therefore was to reproduce legitimate white children who could preserve white British hegemony and cultural identity despite the brutalities and demographic realities of colonial slavery."[65] This took on an even more significant role when, in 1761, the Jamaican Assembly passed a Devises Act, which prohibited mixed-race individuals from inheriting large properties and holdings. In the context of this, the "integrity of the white female body took on heightened significance, as only the progeny of white women's wombs could inherit substantial wealth and property."[66] This portrait, done over a decade after the passing of this law, depicts a family displaying their success at reproducing white, stable British families in this outpost of empire, who could carry on the colonial experiment for another generation.

While conversation pieces could depict a couple alone or with their children, often they included larger kinship networks. This correlates with the conversation pieces in England, which presented many different compositions of familial and kinship networks. For instance, in the painting

---

[63] For more on the extreme whiteness of white Creoles in the West Indies see, Deirdre Coleman, "Janet Schaw and the Complexions of Empire," *Eighteenth-Century Studies* vol. 36 (2003), p. 171.

[64] Brooke Newman, *A Dark Inheritance: Blood, race, and sex in colonial Jamaica*, Yale University Press, New Haven, 2019, p. 6. See Daniel Livesay, *Children of Uncertain Fortune: Mixed-Race Jamaicans in Britain and the Atlantic Family, 1733-1833* (Chapel Hill: University of North Carolina Press, 2018).

[65] Newman, *A Dark Inheritance*, p. 100.

[66] Newman, *A Dark Inheritance*, p. 126.

of James Henry of Jamaica and his family, ten individuals populate the canvas (Figure 1.8).

Figure 1.8: Philip Wickstead, *James Henry and His Family*, before 1784.

Courtesy of Woolley and Wallis Salisbury Salerooms Ltd.

These feature, according to an auction catalog, James Henry, originally a physician from Scotland, who relocated to Jamaica following the failed Jacobite Rebellion in 1745.[67] He married a Creole heiress and began working as a merchant and planter. This scene takes place on his plantation, Southfield, in St. Anne's on the north coast of the island. Depicted in this familial scene are James Henry and his wife, Elizabeth Jones Henry, their six children, the maternal grandmother Catherine and an unnamed tutor. Sadly, only one of the boys attained maturity and lived long enough to marry and produce heirs. This fate was quite common in this colonial context, where

---

[67] https://www.woolleyandwallis.co.uk/departments/paintings/pw170609/view-lot/300/. According to the catalog entry, this image was passed down in the Henry family until 1988. It was auctioned in 2009 and is now in a private collection.

disease and instability rendered the settlers prone to early deaths, and mortality loomed large.

Wickstead crafted this scene in a familiar arrangement, with the family inhabiting both outdoor and indoor spaces. On the right of the canvas, Elizabeth stands with flowers in her left hand and her right hand on her chest, wearing a light silk gown that gathers in the side, resembling a *robe à la polonaise*. The gown is similar in cut and style to the blue silk dress worn by Mrs. William Pusey in the conversation piece that placed her sitting next to her husband. Even the black-laced apron appears identical. The black lace trimming on the top of the gown matches the apron in the front, her elaborate lace cap rising high above her head in a style not seen in the other Wickstead pieces. Next to Elizabeth stands her husband, who wears a fashionable suit that resembles the one worn by William Pusey, with the alteration of the jacket to a lighter blue. He gestures towards his large family, which includes their only daughter, Elizabeth, who wears her hair down and is attired in a pink gown. Oriented towards her grandmother, she holds flowers and smiles slightly at the viewer. The grandmother gazes seriously, straight at the viewer, in a more somber ensemble of grey and white. Moving left across the canvas, the five sons lounge lazily in different positions around the table. One stands astride the family dog, while the other four seem to be successfully ignoring a geography lesson given by the tutor, who is smartly dressed in a black suit and points at a globe. Oddly proportioned, the sons don different shades of suits, from greenish to brown and grey.

Like other Wickstead pieces previously examined, the background has both an indoor and outdoor element, and an impressive library decorates the wall behind the sons and tutors. While many children went to England for their education, it appears that the Henry family employed a tutor, and demonstrated care for the upbringing and instruction of their large family. Two books lie open on the table and the globe indicates that their offspring are learning about the world beyond the sugar plantation island in which they reside. A charming vista meets the viewer outside. The vivid colors of the sunset, coupled with the gated lawn and open landscape, do not immediately place this group in a sugar plantation; rather, it could be any country home of a respectable British gentleman. James Henry died shortly after Wickstead executed this piece, and this charming family scene certainly took on a more sentimental significance following his untimely death.

Intended as private images for these Jamaican planter families, these portraits never had the critical gaze of a London audience, perhaps luckily for Wickstead, as the grace and ease which characterizes other conversation pieces are rather lacking in these renditions of the East and Henry families. The ambitious Henry family portrait depicts the youngest son with legs that are hardly proportional to a child. As Retford notes, the conversation piece was not an effortless art form: "For some other painters, these goals were arguably beyond their abilities, resulting in images that are often described as featuring overly regimented lines of sitters, mannered exchanges and a sense of puppetry."[68] This charge could certainly be leveled at Wickstead, whose portraits contain figures that do not match the talents of Zoffany, or even others working in colonial settings, such as John Singleton Copley.

London artists themselves produced work that did not receive general acclaim, and even those conversation pieces in England faced ridicule for unsuccessful renderings. When the *Drake Family of Shardeloes*, executed in 1778 by John Hamilton Mortimer, reached a London audience, the response was less than glowing. While generating a great deal of "attention" at the Royal Academy, where the artist was making his debut as an Associate, it showed that not all attention is necessarily beneficial to one's career. According to Retford, much of London "seem to have agreed that this was a 'very ugly' family, notably lacking in 'grace': 'a group of figures, whose countenance do not seem capable of depicting any other sensation besides the chagrin that generally accompanies the consciousness of deformity....'"[69] Even more damning, "the *Morning Chronicle* complained, 'the pictures which hang against the wainscot, are as strongly coloured as the main subjects of the piece', while the *General Advertiser* opined, 'the pictures in the background are too much in effect'."[70] The criticism aimed at the background was easily remedied by painting them out, but the family remained awkward and disagreeable. Perhaps luckily for Wickstead, few of his paintings had the lens of an Academic exhibition, where London audiences, curious to learn more about their West Indian contemporaries through such images, would have certainly found much to criticize.

Tragedy struck Wickstead's paintings when a hurricane battered Jamaica in 1780, a natural disaster which apparently destroyed many of his works.[71] Before this misfortune, Jamaican resident and diarist Thomas Thistlewood visited Wickstead's studio residence and reported: "Rode over to Mr. Wickstead's the painter, at the house of Mr. Fot's place near Smithfield. He showed me his portraits, very curious especially Mr. and Mrs Beckford and Capt.n Caning, Mr. and Mrs Beckford in another, George Pointz Ricketts and his Lady, Mr. George Inglish, Parson Poole, Jimmy Tomhnson [*sic*], etc., and a

---

[68] Retford, *The Conversation Piece*, p. 48.
[69] Retford, *The Conversation Piece*, p. 238.
[70] Retford, *The Conversation Piece*.
[71] Bindman, *Image of the Black in Western Art*, p. 269.

holegange of Negroes."[72] Unfortunately, many of these are now vanished to history, including pieces described by Beckford: "I had the picture of a holeing gang that was very naturally, and, with the negroes, their expression of features, and variety of action, at the same time very elegantly, described: but this performance, as well as many drawings of value, were unfortunately swept away by that tremendous hurricane of which I have ventured, however feebly, to convey a particular and a just account."[73]

Wickstead, like many others who had ventured to Jamaica, determined next to find success as a planter. Likewise, he apparently turned to alcohol and dissipation, and by 1790 he had passed away. Beckford eulogized him, stating that his "powers of painting were considerably weakened by his natural indolence, and more than all, by a wonderful eccentricity of character. His coloring was almost equal to any artist of his time."[74] His lack of ambition rendered him subject to indolence, which left him unable to succeed as a planter. Beckford finalized his homage: "Had he cultivated his profession with as much zeal as he displayed in friendship, and had he been as industrious as he was honest, he might have finished many works in Jamaica which would not only have added to the weight of his purse, but to the durability of his fame."[75]

Following Wickstead's short tenure in Jamaica, it does not seem that any other portrait painter ventured to the sugar plantation island. Tales of disease, unrest and the Napoleonic Wars of the 1790s likely deterred any future sojourns from talented artists, and subsequent renditions had to be

---

[72] Thomas Thistlewood as quoted in *Image of the Black in Western Art*, p. 269.

[73] William Beckford, *A Descriptive Account of the Island of Jamaica* (London: T. and J. Egerton, 1790), p. 315.

[74] Ibid., Beckford noted that Wickstead's drawings "were particularly apparent in his representation of negroes of every character, expression, and age. The negro-driver, a very strong and happy likeness! Was standing in front and leaning (p. 316) upon his stick; the other negroes were digging cane-holes in a circular line, and round the base of a hill, immediately before him: they were all portraits, and the marks of their country were preserved in their resemblance. Some were particularly clothed; and some, as far as decency would allow, displayed in their limbs the exertions of the body. Some had on hats, some handkerchiefs, and some had none. On one side was the water-carrier, a very picturesque and striking object; and behind her, a clump of plantain-trees, some of which were without fruit, upon some the fruit was shooting, and some green, and upon others ripe. And, in short, the picture, either taken all together, or divided into parts, would have been highly interesting to the planter, and not have proved unacceptable to the admirer of nature, and to the man of taste. The name of this incomparable, but unfortunate painter, was Wickstead; a name respectable in the arts, and which has (p. 317) often afforded amusement to the public!"

[75] Beckford, p. 317.

commissioned in the metropole. Wickstead created conversation pieces that resembled those executed in London; however, his renditions did not rival those created by Zoffany during his tenure in India.[76] While Wickstead's patrons might have been satisfied with his portraits, his lack of exposure in the metropole likely benefited his practice in this colonial outpost. Jasanoff reminds us that "possessions are critical indicators not only of personal taste, but also of social milieu, wealth, education and status. By acquiring them one can craft and advertise a particular persona."[77] Furthermore, objects brought back to Britain assisted in the formation of an "idea" of empire. For, as Jasanoff shows, it was "through objects that millions of Britain women and men literally 'saw their empire'."[78]

These conversation pieces, then, show an attempt to emulate popular British styles by the Creole plantocracy in Jamaica, and can be viewed, as Breen argues, through the "social process known as self-fashioning."[79] The clothing and accessory choices in these portraits certainly aided their quest to self-fashion their identity as respectable British colonists. Although Breen focused on Colonial America, his argument can apply aptly to those in eighteenth-century Jamaica. These individuals "wanted to present themselves on canvas, and by attending closely to those elements of self-fashioning that were distinctive products of an eighteenth-century commercial society, we are able to recapture the cultural meanings that the colonists, as opposed to the modern historian, brought to the creative exchange."[80] The fashionable attire worn by these inhabitants grounds them in the Creole aesthetic of emulating metropolitan fashions, as observed by eighteenth-century writers like Edward Long. This includes the stylish ensembles seen in these pieces, as well as the inclusion of women in attire such as posing gowns, which were fashionable in eighteenth-century conversation pieces.

When these Creole inhabitants commissioned such works, they "were at once objects in a consumer society and cultural commentary on that society."[81] This lens demonstrates the importance of the choices that the

---

[76] See Tobin, "Accommodating India: Domestic Arrangements in Anglo-Indian Family Portraiture," in *Picturing Imperial Power*, pp. 110-138.
[77] Jasanoff, "Collectors of Empire," p. 111.
[78] Jasanoff, "Collectors of Empire," p. 112.
[79] Breen, "'The Meaning of Likeness,' Portrait-Painting in an Eighteenth-Century Consumer Society," p. 39.
[80] Breen, "'The Meaning of Likeness,' Portrait-Painting in an Eighteenth-Century Consumer Society," p. 39.
[81] Breen, "'The Meaning of Likeness,' Portrait-Painting in an Eighteenth-Century Consumer Society," p. 39. For subsequent art in Jamaica, see Timothy John Barringer and Wayne Modest, *Victorian Jamaica* (London: Duke University Press, 2018).

sitters made in their dress, appearance, background and style. Carefully crafted, the ensembles allowed these individuals to participate in the fashionable styles present in the metropole in this colonial outpost. The clothing choices in these conversation pieces placed these sitters firmly in a mode popular in England and assisted in their presentation as fashionable and respectable British families. The remaining paintings are important for demonstrating a counterpart to the executions rendered in the British Isles. They express a conscious effort by Creoles in Jamaica to commission stylish pieces that outlasted their brutal regime.

Bibliography

Primary Sources

Images

"Portrait of the Taylor Family." Photograph of Daniel Gardner, *Sir John Taylor, His Wife Elizabeth, His Brother Simon Taylor, and Four of their Six Children.* c. 1785. Courtesy of National Gallery of Jamaica.

After George Robertson. "A View in the Island of Jamaica of Part of the River Cobre Near Spanish Town." 1778. aquatint, Aaron and Marjorie Matalon Collection. Courtesy of the National Gallery of Jamaica.

Batoni, Pompeo. *Portrait of John Blagrove.* 1774. Courtesy of the National Gallery of Jamaica.

Cosway, Richard. "Brodbelt Children." 1788. In Geraldine Nutt Mozley, *Letters to Jane from Jamaica, 1788-1796.* London: Published for the Institute of Jamaica by the West India Committee, 1938. Frontispiece.

Wickstead, Philip. *Edward Pusey and His Family* [Edward East and His Family]. c.1775. Courtesy of the National Gallery of Jamaica.

Wickstead, Philip. *James Henry and His Family.* before 1784. Courtesy of Woolley and Wallis Salisbury Salerooms Ltd.

Wickstead, Philip. *Portrait of Benjamin and Mary Pusey.* c.1775. Courtesy of the National Gallery of Jamaica

Wickstead, Philip. *Richard and Jane Pusey* [William Pusey and His Wife]. c.1785. Courtesy of the National Gallery of Jamaica.

Manuscripts

Beckford, William. *A Descriptive Account of the Island of Jamaica.* London: T. and J. Egerton, 1790.

Long, Edward. *The History of Jamaica: Or, General Survey of the Antient and Modern State of the Island: With Reflections on its Situation Settlements, Inhabitants, Climate, Products, Commerce, Laws, and Government.* London: T. Lowndes, 1774.

Schaw, Janet. *Journal of a Lady of Quality: Being the Narrative of a Journey from Scotland to the West Indies, North Carolina, and Portugal, in the Years*

1774 to 1776, edited by Evangeline Walker Andrews, Charles McLean Andrews, and Fund Frederick John Kingsbury Memorial. New Haven: Yale University Press, 1921.

Secondary Sources

Bagneris, Mia L. *Colouring the Caribbean: Race and the Art of Agostino Brunias*. Manchester: Manchester University Press, 2018.

Barringer, Tim, Gillian Forrester, and Barbaro Martinez-Ruiz. *Art and Emancipation in Jamaica: Isaac Mendes Belisario and His Worlds*. New Haven: Yale Center for British Art in association with Yale University Press, 2007.

Beranek, Christa M. "Beyond Consumption: Social Relationships, Material Culture, and Identity." In *The Materiality of Individuality: Archaeological Studies of Individual Lives*, edited by Carolyn L. White. New York: Springer, 2009.

Bindman, David. "Representing Race in the Eighteenth-Century Caribbean: Brunias in Dominica and St Vincent." *Eighteenth-Century Studies*, Vol. 1 (2017), pp. 1-17.

Bindman, David and Henry Louis Gates Jr. *Image of the Black in Western Art: From the "Age of Discovery" to the Age of Abolition*. Cambridge, Mass.: Harvard University Press, 2010.

Breen, T. H. "The Meaning of Likeness: Portrait-Painting in an Eighteenth-Century Consumer Society." In *The Portrait in Eighteenth-Century America*, edited by Ellen G. Miles. Newark: University of Deleware Press, 1993.

Buckley, Roger Norman. "The Frontier in the Jamaican Caricatures of Abraham James." *Yale University Library Gazette*, Vol. 58 (1984), pp. 152-162.

Burnard, Trevor and Richard Follett. "Caribbean Slavery, British Anti-Slavery, and the Cultural Politics of Venereal Disease." *The Historical Journal* Vol. 55 (2012), pp. 427-451.

Casid, Jill H. *Sowing Empire: Landscape and Colonization*. Minneapolis: University of Minnesota Press, 2005.

Chrisman-Campbell, Kimberly. "Fashioning (and Refashioning) European Fashion." In *Fashioning Fashion: European Dress in Detail, 1700-1915*. Munich: Delmonico Books, 2010.

Cundall, Frank. "Philip Wickstead of Jamaica." *Conosseuir*, Vol. 94 (1934), pp. 174-175.

Cundall, Frank. *Historic Jamaica*. London: Pub. for the Institute of Jamaica by the West India Committee, 1915.

DuPlessis, Robert S. *The Material Atlantic: Clothing, Commerce, and Colonization in the Atlantic World, 1650-1800*. Cambridge: Cambridge University Press, 2015.

Graves, Algernon. *The Society of Artists of Great Britain, 1760-1791; the Free Society of Artists, 1761-1783: A Complete Dictionary of Contributors and Their Work from the Foundation of the Societies to 1791*. London: George Bell and Sons, 1907.

Jasanoff, Maya. "Collectors of Empire: Objects, Conquests and Imperial Self-Fashioning." *Past and Present* Vol. 184 (2004), pp. 109-35.

Jones, Jennifer Michelle. *Sexing La Mode: Gender, Fashion and Commercial Culture in Old Regime France*. Oxford, New York: Berg, 2004.

Kidwell, Claudia. "Are Those Clothes Real? Transforming the Way Eighteenth-Century Portraits Are Studied." *Dress*, vol. 24 (1998), pp. 3-15.

Kriz, Kay Dian. *Slavery, Sugar, and the Culture of Refinement: Picturing the British West Indies, 1700-1840*. New Haven: Paul Mellon Centre for Studies in British, Art, Yale University Press, 2008.

Lloyd, Stephen. *Richard Cosway*. London: Unicorn Press, 2005.

McIntyre, Ian. *Joshua Reynolds: The Life and Times of the First President of the Royal Academy*. London: Allen Lane, 2003.

Newman, Brooke. *A Dark Inheritance: Blood, Race, and Sex in Colonial Jamaica*. New Haven: Yale University Press, 2019.

Northrop, Chloe. "Education, Material Culture, and Coming of Age in Eighteenth-Century British Jamaica." *Traversea* 2 (2013), pp. 60-79.

Nussbaum, Felicity. *The Global Eighteenth Century*. Baltimore, Md.: Johns Hopkins University Press, 2003.

Odumosu, Temi. *Africans in English Caricature 1769-1819: Black Jokes, White Humour*. London: Harvey Miller Publishers, 2017.

Petely, Christer. *White Fury: A Jamaican Slaveholder and the Age of Revolution*. Oxford: Oxford University Press, 2018.

Quilley, Geoff and Kay Dian Kriz. *An Economy of Colour: Visual Culture and the Atlantic World, 1660-1830*. Manchester: Manchester University Press, 2003.

Retford, Kate. *The Conversation Piece: Making Modern Art in 18th Century Britain*. New Haven: Paul Mellon Centre for Studies in British Art by Yale University Press, 2017.

Thomas, Sarah. "Envisaging a Future for Slavery: Agostino Brunias and the Imperial Politics of Labor and Reproduction." *Eighteenth-Century Studies*, vol. 5, no. 2 (2008), pp. 115-33.

Tobin, Beth Fowkes. *Picturing Imperial Power: Colonial Subjects in Eighteenth-Century British Painting*. Durham, N.C.: Duke University Press, 1999.

Van Horn, Jennifer. *The Power of Objects in Eighteenth-Century British America*. Chapel Hill: Omohundro Institute of Early American History and Culture, Williamsburg, Virginia by the University of North Carolina Press, 2017.

Walker, Christine. *Jamaica Ladies: Female Slaveholders and the Creation of Britain's Atlantic Empire*. Chapel Hill: Williamsburg, Virginia, Omohundro Institute of Early American History and Culture, Omohundro Institute of Early American History and Culture and the University of North Carolina Press, 2020.

Webster, Mary. *Johan Zoffany: 1733-1810*. London: National Portrait Gallery, 1976.

Wilson, David. "Roubiliac's Missing Model of Tarquin and Lucretia: its possible purchase by Johan Zoffany in 1762 or later." *Sculpture Journal* 18 (2009), pp. 122-123.

Yeh, Sarah E. "'A Sink of All Filthiness': Gender, Family and Identity in British Atlantic, 1688-1763." *The Historian* 68 (March 2006), pp. 66-88.

Chapter 2

Fashion, colonialism and nationalism: changing notions of everyday dress codes in British-colonial Sri Lanka

Ramesha Jayaneththi
University of Peradeniya, Sri Lanka

Abstract: The impact of colonialism and its legacy is a significant part of British culture and its heritage, which this chapter addresses through a case study of colonial Sri Lanka. Using archeological, art history and textual sources, such as travel journals and religious tracts, this chapter considers the cultural extent of British imperial influences and their impact on the everyday dress codes of the Sri Lankan populace, from the seventeenth century to the present. This sweeping perspective enables us to examine the impact of colonialism at its various stages, while also keeping in mind its continuing influence through the "soft power" form of Western consumerism, particularly evident in the cultural sphere of fashion and Westernized dress codes.

As part of Sri Lanka's material culture, everyday dress could be utilized for distinct political purposes. As well as reinforcing the values of colonialism, national dress also became part of the symbolism of anti-colonial nationalism, playing a role in the processes of decolonization itself. Contemporary attempts to ground so-called "modest" styles are also interrogated, and traced back, not to an ancient Sri Lankan cultural heritage, where topless dressing was the most elite, aspirational style of clothing, but to a complex combination of nineteenth-century British Victorian styles of dress and nationalist religious discourse. The role of cultural artefacts, such as paintings and statuary, in the creation of these dress codes, reveals a rich cultural heritage and challenges contemporary assumptions about pre-colonial Sri Lankan dress.

Keywords: Everyday dress codes, nationalism, Sri Lanka, British colonialism, social decorum, body politics.

***

Clothes are like windows into particular points in time.[1] As a social phenomenon, fashion develops in response to contemporary social and political circumstances, with changes to popular styles reflecting deeper transformations in society. As a mirror of society's values, fashion can reflect the progress of fundamental principles and belief systems, with the fashion industry itself often falling into line with dominant discourses and reproducing them in the form of fashionable dress.[2] As dress theorists such as Lehmann, Blumer and Laver have written, fashion not only reflects social, economic, political and cultural developments, but also conveys a sense of modernity, embodying the spirit of the times, or "zeitgeist."[3] This zeitgeist, defined by Blumer as a process of "collective selection," combines features such as change, novelty, self-expression and socio-economic forces to establish tastes and trends, to which people respond both collectively and as individuals.[4] In his 1969 research, Blumer discussed the relevance of fashion history, acknowledging the fact that, to the modern eye, historical styles can often appear as little more than elaborate displays of fancy and caprice, their social relevance obscured by both time and radically changing tastes. However, Blumer argued that far from being irrelevant, historical fashions can shed vital light upon the social customs of previous eras, the elaborate and often ostentatious styles of upper-class fashions acting as socially significant markers of power. Though over fifty years old, Blumer's work retains its value as a source through which to analyze and evaluate style from a sociological perspective. "Fashion," he wrote:

> seems to represent a kind of anxious effort of elite groups to set themselves apart by introducing trivial and ephemeral demarcating insignia, with a corresponding strained effort by non-elite classes to make a spurious identification of themselves with the upper classes by adopting these insignia. Finally, since fashion, despite its seeming frivolous content,

---

[1] Julia Vilaca, "Fashion Reflects social changes," 2021: https://fashinnovation.nyc/fashion-reflects-social-changes/

[2] Marilyn Revell DeLong, "Theories of Fashion," https://fashion-history.lovetoknow.com/fashion-history-eras/theories-fashion

[3] Herbert Blumer, "Fashion: From Class Differentiation to Collective Selection," *The Sociological Quarterly* 10, no. 3 (1969), pp. 275-291. See also, Ulrich Lehmann, *Tigersprung: Fashion in Modernity* (Cambridge, Mass.: MIT Press, 2000) and James Laver, *The Concise History of Costume and Fashion* (New York: Harry N. Abrams, 1969).

[4] Herbert Blumer, "Fashion: From Class Differentiation to Collective Selection," *The Sociological Quarterly* 10, no. 3 (1969), pp. 275-291.

sweeps multitudes of people into its fold, it is regarded as a form of collective craziness.[5]

While frequently applied to systems of Western style, Blumer's perspective is also applicable to a case study of Sri Lankan dress codes, in which power relations of both caste and colonial influence are clearly visible, particularly in the period of British rule. Indeed, the notion of British dress style is of interest here due to the profound and lasting influence of British colonialism in Sri Lankan culture as a whole. Over the centuries, and in many diverse and often conflicting ways, Sri Lankans themselves have created personalized fashion narratives and metaphoric, metonymic references by adopting their own fashion languages, relating them to broader issues of national identity. These narratives and references have, at various times, indicated both compliance with and resistance to prevailing dress conventions within wider consumer culture.

Beyond Blumer's sociological approach to fashion as a whole, however, more recent scholars have started to interrogate the relationship between fashion and nationalism, with Alexander Maxwell (2019), for instance, exploring the role of patriotic dressing within a national community context, considering the question of which groups and individuals are permitted, obliged and forbidden from adopting national dress codes and identity symbols.[6]

This discussion has expanded to include the Asian fashion industry, specifically highlighting issues of colonialism, identity politics and fashion's place within national discourse, with indigenous fashions now gaining attention from both Western and non-Western scholars. Among them, Rosemary Crill has examined many aspects of traditional Indian fashion and considered its role in shaping and expressing Indian cultural identity. Most notably, Crill has conducted extensive comparative research on the styles and techniques of traditional textiles in India through museum objects and paintings,[7] and in a 2022 talk on Indian textiles argued that "The abstract and geometric patterns of Indian textiles are as varied as the innumerable techniques used to produce them, encompassing woven, surface and embellished cloths of all kinds. Geometric structures form the basis of all

---

[5] Blumer, "Fashion: From Class Differentiation to Collective Selection," p. 276.
[6] Alexander Maxwell, "Analyzing nationalized clothing: nationalism theory meets fashion studies," *National Identities*, vol. 23, no. 1 (2019).
[7] *Rosemary* Crill, *The Fabric of India* (London: Victoria and Albert Museum, 2015), pp. 25-34.

cloth with intersecting warps and wefts, and as such stripes and checks are found in the oldest textiles known from South Asia."[8]

Asian fashions, which are stylistically distinct from European ones, often reflect the legacy of colonialism, and over the centuries have been subject to various innovations and industry forces that Asia absorbed from colonial practices.[9] The cotton and silk industries in India were particularly influential in constructing a conventional notion of fashion and style in the South Asian region. These cotton and silk productions had the potential to travel far beyond the Indian borders, often reaching as far as China. Many Indians and Sri Lankans now assume that decorum and modesty are indigenous to their cultures, yet as this chapter argues, they are actually British concepts that have been inherited from colonial ideas and practices.

From the sixteenth century, when Sri Lanka was first colonized by the Portuguese, up to the present, Sri Lankan dress culture has reflected a melting pot of different influences. Before this period, dress codes were far less concerned with modesty, with upper caste women frequently baring their breasts in displays which used elaborate jewelry in place of heavy top clothing. During ancient times, and until the colonial and Kandyan eras, elite dress codes reflected a greater acceptance of the naked body, something which, as time passed, became more closely associated with lower caste peasant women. However, while the first Portuguese and Dutch colonizers had a profound effect on society as a whole, it was the twin influence of the Tamil dynasty and British invaders in the nineteenth century that had the most significant influence on national dress, particularly in the southern coastal areas of Sri Lanka.

The earliest depictions of South Asian women show them wearing much lighter, less concealing clothes than the heavy, modesty-conscious attire of the Victorian colonial era, yet the styles depicted also clearly demarcated specific ethnic and religious identities. At the same time, the everyday dress styles in this region had a clear multicultural lineage. In 2017, Dev Nath Pathak and Sasanka Perera argued that the roots of Indian fashion have traveled a long way, weaving a story that documented the richness of a culture soaked in luxury, folklore, crafts and artisanal skills.[10] Fashion, culture and

---

[8] *Rosemary Crill, "Indian Textiles: 1,000 Years of Art and Design,"* 2022: https://oxfordasiantextilegroup.wordpress.com/tag/rosemary-crill
[9] Vinay Bahl, "Shifting Boundaries of 'Nativity' and 'Modernity' in South Asian Women's Clothes." In *Dialectical Anthropology*, vol. 29, no. 1 (2005), pp. 85-86.
[10] Dev Nath Pathak and Sasanka Perera, *Culture and Politics in South Asia: Performative Communication* (London: Taylor & Francis, 2017), p. 20.

dress politics themselves have a complex lineage and history in South Asia, which have combined with the Islamic influences of West Asian fashions.

Draped and wrapped fabrics were the most common kinds of traditional apparel in South Asia for both sexes, with the saree being a staple in women's wardrobes, which comes in a variety of sizes with various wrapping techniques, and is worn with or without a blouse. This style began as a simple drape worn by women thousands of years ago. The drape, a garment similar to the saree, may date back to the Indus Valley Civilization, which flourished in northwestern India between 2800 and 1800 BC, and the ancient carvings and sculptures dating from this period certainly depict both men and women wearing this distinctive style. These archaeological artifacts, taking the form of carvings, sculptures and paintings, are a crucial resource for both art and social historians, providing rich, detailed depictions of ancient dress styles and the social divisions that underpinned them.

As with fashions in other countries, South Asian dress styles developed in accordance with the cultural values of society, with different social classes being recognizable through their dress and jewelry. Typically, those from poorer or lower caste backgrounds wore minimalist and less elaborate clothes, while the upper castes wore garments of elaborate design, rich with colorful embroidery, beautiful muslins and heavy jewelry. These designs indicated specific class and caste hierarchies, acting as illustrative displays of social divisions, while also prominently denoting ethnic and religious identities; as a result of this, South Asian countries such as Sri Lanka have a socially complex concept of dress, which was further complicated by colonial influences. The different dress styles of the pre-colonial, colonial and post-colonial eras also reveal changing social customs, with dress becoming one of the visible symbols of both colonial social control and anti-colonial resistance.[11]

The influences of different dress narratives and their symbolism have particularly affected South Asian women, due to the historically close relationship between dress, gender, wealth and social status in South Asian communities. As a result of this, women's social class could easily be determined through their attire, and dress was frequently used in class and caste warfare to denote power and influence, since it was considered powerfully expressive of social difference. South Asian dress was also a significant instrument for negotiating and structuring social ties as well as enforcing class inequalities, since it could symbolize a person's culture,

---

[11] V. Bahl, "Shifting Boundaries of 'Nativity' and 'Modernity' in South Asian Women's Clothes," *Dialectical Anthropology*, vol. 29, no. 1 (2005), p. 85.

inheritance, moral code, economic standing and social status. In every era of South Asian society, dress has symbolized this social standing, becoming a conduit for many different social forces in the process, while the fashion and clothing industries also experienced significant changes due to the socio-economic dynamics of colonial and post-colonial Sri Lanka.

In recent decades many Sinhalese and Tamils in Sri Lanka have become increasingly keen to adopt what they regard as traditional clothing styles, finding a connection between their appearance and their sense of national heritage. National dress itself has been newly devised as a concept to boost nationalist consciousness and Sri Lankan national leaders have been eager to establish a specific dress style, the *Osariya*, as a national symbol, arguing that it is a traditional form of dress which represents authentic Sri Lankan culture. The *Osariya* has a similar draping method to that of the saree, the fabric being wrapped around the waist with one end slung over the shoulder, but unlike the Indian drape it has distinctive pleats at the waist which form a frill. Likewise, while puffed sleeves are common on Indian saree blouses, the *Osariya* is worn with a jacket, an underskirt and pieces of decorative jewelry.

To trace the threads of these different influences, it is worth looking at the development of dress and fashion in Sri Lanka during the pre-colonial era. According to archaeological and art history sources, such as pre-modern sculpture, the topless tradition in women's dress was idealized as far back as the 1st century B.C. Unlike today's trend for modest attire, in the 3rd century AD clothing, including the topless tradition, was utilized as a sign of royal social rank, seeking to show off the beauty of a woman's body rather than concealing it. The natural shape of the body was prized, with light-weight clothing, distinctive jewelry and a greater emphasis on ornamentation used to represent higher social status. Many poets in ancient Sri Lanka celebrated women's exquisite and oval-shaped breasts and honored them as a symbol of lust, an impression also evoked in the image below of topless, upper caste women from one of the frescoes on Sigiriya rock, believed to depict royal women engaging in Buddhist rituals.[12] As Nira Wickremasinghe explains:

> The royal ladies in the frescoes wear pleated robes from the waist upwards, save for necklace, armlets, wristlets, ear and hair ornaments and display their breasts. The ladies in waiting wear waist clothes, few ornaments and a firm 'breast bandage' or *thanapatiya*. The Sigiriya style of clothing — Sigiriya frescoes depict women wearing the cloth gracefully draped like a dhoti tied in a knot at the front and pulled

---

[12] Sigiriya Frescoes Art, Culture & Heritage https://www.artra.lk/visual-art/sigiriya-frescoes, 2022

down to expose the navel — must have survived a few centuries in Ceylon.[13]

Figure 2.1: From a fresco on Sigiriya rock

Commons.wikimedia.org, public domain.

According to some of the ancient literature from the 3rd century A. D., such as poems, chronicles and stone epigraphy, women in ancient Sri Lanka wore the bare minimum of clothing, their minimalist dress styles often the focus of sculptures and statues. This mode of attire is captured below in a bronze statue of the goddess Tara dating from the 7th to 8th century A. D., once again suggesting that, in the pre-modern Sri Lanka, bare breasted women represented an idealized kind of beauty. The extensive ornamentation and elaborate headdresses, often featuring huge gemstones, were also marks of distinction.

Sri Lankan temple sculptures often feature both the nude body and celebratory depictions of sex itself, with the Nalanda Gedige temple in Sri Lanka, for instance, being just one example of many that portray eroticized, naked bodies through beautiful carvings and religious symbols. As Nandasena Mudiyanse has noted, unless the religious practices performed at *Nalanda-*

---

[13] Nira Wickramasinghe, "Some Comments on Dress in Sri Lanka," International Centre for Ethnic Studies, *The Thatched Patio*, vol. 5, no. 1 (1992), p. 1.

gedige were of a Tantric nature, the presence of these erotic sculptures cannot otherwise be explained.[14]

Figure 2.2: The Bodhisattva Tara. Gilded bronze, Sri Lanka, 8th century CE.

Commons.wikimedia.org, public domain.

While we cannot assume that such depictions of elite dress represented mainstream trends, they do illustrate some of the aspirational ideals of the period and show that these styles were absorbed into the everyday wardrobes of the lower castes through a form of "trickle down" process. In lay societies as well as in religious life, bare-breasted women embracing their sexuality became a fairly common sight. During the colonial era, however, notions of fashionable dress changed dramatically. In this era, three separate European nations captured Sri Lankan territories and brought with them their own traditions, lifestyles and socio-economic practices, kicking off a wave of social transformation.

---

[14] Nandasena Mudiyanse, *Mahayana Monuments in Ceylon* (Maradana: M.D., Gunasena, 1967), p. 71.

This process began when the Portuguese colonized Sri Lanka in 1505, importing the first wave of Western culture and morals, after which it was captured by the Dutch (1658-1796) and then the British (1796-1948). While only the coastal regions had been colonized by previous invaders however, in 1815 the whole island was taken under British colonial rule. The inner territories of the Kandy had previously been under the rule of the Sinhala king and as a result, residents near the coast of Sri Lanka were more Westernized than those in the central highlands. During the last centuries of the Kandyan kingdom, the area was ruled by a Tamil dynasty called Nayakkar, which belonged to the Hindu royal house of South India, and which also practiced elements of Tamil culture within this Sinhalese kingdom. The subsequent influence of the Nayakkar dynasty led to changes in local styles of dress in the Kandyan provinces. This cultural fusion linked notions of everyday fashions with displays of virtue for Sinhalese women, and the *Osariya* (saree) style was extensively embraced by Kandyan upper-class women.[15] However, after 1815, Sri Lankan culture was exposed to an overwhelming British influence that precipitated waves of modernization, including novel ideas about dress and fashion, which affected the whole island.

Sri Lanka has been subjected to significant social and cultural changes since the Portuguese era, including the introduction of a mercantile economy and labor practices, the influence of Catholicism and its ethical framework, different marital traditions and changes to family structures, evolving class hierarchies and changes to the caste system. During the Dutch and British eras, adherence to Christianity and its moral tenets became a significant means of maintaining a collective social order. The colonial law makers imposed strict ideas about female chastity and purity, as well as their own indigenous ethical framework, through marital structures and inheritance laws. During the Dutch colonial era, Christian conversion and the Dutch education system became well-organized social initiatives. Dutch schools and churches also regulated marriage through a sophisticated legal framework, with a broader Roman-Dutch legal system being established to regulate social conduct. As Bulten writes:

> This period was characterised by a process of growing bureaucratisation, which led to the rise of colonial institutions like cadastral and census registration practices and an elaborate judicial system with several

---

[15] Nira Wickramasinghe, *Sri Lanka in the Modern Age: A History* (London: Oxford University Press, 2015), p. 93.

different colonial courts [...] With their growth, these institutions began to impact the daily lives of Sri Lanka's native population.[16]

Local reaction to the demands of colonial powers became a form of negotiation. The once-dominant top-down perspective of colonial authority was progressively replaced by a conceptual framework in which norms and values had to be transposed and negotiated on a regular basis. As society evolved under the influence of colonialism, bare-breasted styles of dress were devalued and marginalized and became increasingly associated with rural and lower-caste women, for whom the custom came to represent their social position. From the sixteenth century onwards, upper-caste women from wealthy families began covering their upper bodies with pieces of cloth, which eventually evolved into blouses.

With the introduction of Islamic, Hindu and Christian practices, Sri Lankans began to cover up for the sake of modesty, yet incorporating a hint of eroticism into these new, modest styles also became common through exposing specific areas of the body. Even so, this new style of dress stirred up a certain amount of discontent among women, seemingly indicative of a wider culture of shame surrounding women's bodies. The *Osariya* itself became an outward symbol of modesty; composed of a long length of cloth that was heavily draped around the body, it covered women's bodies from head to toe in order to outwardly express a sense of virtue. In the privacy of their own homes, however, Kandyan women preferred to go bare-breasted or to drape a cloth around themselves without a blouse. At home, they could reclaim erotic fashions for themselves, and the privacy of life afforded to them in the domestic sphere was a source of individual power and agency.

This new trend in the Kandyan era was diametrically opposed to how women had styled themselves in the ancient and medieval kingdoms, which had favored bare-breasted attire, demonstrating a marked change in response to rising feelings of bodily shame and embarrassment. In this region, the native kingdom of the central highlands that had remained untouched by colonialism until 1815, the South Indian influence on social values and dress codes had dominated. The political values which underpinned women's dress in this region prior to the British invasion were nicely illustrated by Robert Knox, an English sea captain with the British East India Company who became famous for his travel accounts of the Kingdom of Kandy, where he was captured by the Kandy king, Rajasinghe II in 1659. The memoirs of British travelers such as Robert Knox significantly influenced the narrative surrounding Sri Lankan

---

[16] Luc Bulten et al. "Contested conjugality? Sinhalese marriage practices in eighteenth-century Dutch colonial Sri Lanka," *Annales de démographie historique*, 2018, p. 1.

culture, creating a contemporary sociological account of colonial society. Knox was extremely critical of native women and their dress, which he frequently depicted in his travel accounts, and which he associated with loose morals. As he illustrated in his writings of 1681, styles of female dress were at this time dictated by the Kandyan caste hierarchy and closely bound by social norms:

> Men wear [their clothing] down half their legs and the women to their heels: one end which cloth the women fling over their shoulders and with the very end carelessly cover their Breasts; whereas the other sort of Women must go naked from waste upwards, and their clothes not hang down much below their knees: except before cold; for them either women or men may throw their clothes over their backs. But then they do excuse it to the *Handrews* [upper caste people] when they meet them saying, 'Excuse me, it is for warmth'.[17]

There is evidence that Kandyan noblewomen now fully covered themselves with modest attire and jewelry, while rural women remained bare-breasted in their own homes, and that showing less skin became a sign of social respectability as Kandyan dress customs developed. British colonialism had a significant impact on Sinhalese society during this period, but many South Indian traditions now also emphasized the need of concealing a woman's body: it seemed that, with the influences of both new religious and upper caste customs and foreign colonizers the female body was being politicized, with strict cultural norms developing to emphasize female virtue through women's dress. In the Kandyan kingdom during the nineteenth century, long, full dresses, mirroring the heavy frocks that were fashionable in Victorian Britain, became a powerful symbol of women's socialization and adaptation to the values of British colonialism.

The Kandyan kingdom in the highlands and the other lowlands of the coastal region were regarded as two separate regions from the sixteenth to the eighteenth century. Despite the fact that Sinhalese people from both areas were considered one ethnic group, their cultural practices and clothing norms diverged. In this diverse context, Kandyan women valued traditional clothing and fashions that covered the entire body and included traditional necklaces, such as the one seen in Figure 4 below. Figures 3 and 4 show two Kandyan ladies in distinct clothing styles; the first depicts the last queen of the Kandyan kingdom, who was of Tamil descent, while the second image depicts a humble Kandyan woman dressed in the traditional garb of the nineteenth century.

---

[17] Robert Knox, *An Historical Relation of the Island Ceylon* (London: Royal Society, 1681), pp. 66-67.

Figure 2.3: Portrait of Queen Consort Venkata Rangammal Devi of Kandy in South Indian attire, drawn by W. Daniell, R.A. Engraved by R. Woodman, early 1800s.

Commons.wikimedia.org, public domain.

Figure 2.4: Traditional Kandyan women's attire, unknown author, Ceylon India, 1880.

Commons.wikimedia.org, public domain.

The latter was included in the British Ceylon census of 1901 as a photographic depiction of colonial society and its different ethnic groups. Newly introduced European cameras were used to take snapshots of the colorful natives, with British photographers eager to document ethnic and cultural differences between local communities. These images reveal dress as a potent identity marker, with each woman's status being well-defined through their very different outfits and styles, despite the similarity of their hairstyles. The woman in traditional Kandyan attire illustrates the potentially problematic nature of such depictions of "native" women. Composed ostensibly for the purpose of documenting "authentic" views of foreign cultures, such pictures frequently exoticize sitters through the artist's white, European gaze. This perspective dominates in many of the pictures and travel documents of colonialists during this period, yet as cultural artifacts, they are valuable for the light they shed on this dynamic. During the Dutch and British eras many colonizers, as we have seen with Knox, provided painted and written observations of Sri Lankan society, with details such as dress a source of specific interest and disapproval.

Figure 2.5: Reception of the envoys of the King of Kandy by Governor Iman Falck, Carel Frederik Reimer, 1772.

Commons.wikimedia.org, public domain.

This fusion of different religious and cultural practices inevitably had a significant impact on Sri Lankan dress culture, and it was not only women who were affected. In Sinhalese culture men's social status was also clearly represented through their clothing and, like noblewomen during this period, noblemen were expected to dress lavishly and to cover their bodies. The upper caste *Radala* group, in particular, displayed their refined social manners and prestige through their stylish attire.

The British colonial era introduced many changes to the everyday dress of both men and women in Sri Lanka. Major Forbes, a soldier of the British colonial army when it conquered the Kandyan kingdom in 1815, observed in his travel diary that their court-dress consisted of:

> [..] a square cap of scarlet cloth resembling a huge pincushion. The jacket is of tissue, with short plaited sleeves, very full upon the shoulders. On the lower part of the body, over white trousers, which are tight at the ankle, a number of white cloths are bound in cumbrous folds round the waist by a broad gold belt.[18]

In comparison, apart from the addition of collars, frills and cuffs, the Dutch had had little influence on indigenous male attire in the coastal area. When the British arrived near the end of the colonial era, however, they triggered a complete shift in male dress culture, and donning Western dress became vital for securing a respectable position within the colonial system. Under British colonial rule, a man's social status was determined by his dress and many men followed the new styles and adhered to changing social customs. Within government institutions, for example, employees in the clerical classes and above were required to wear a Western suit that included a coat, waistcoat, pants, tie and hat. There was little need for coercion, particularly among the upper echelons of society, where Western attire was eagerly adopted by many. Aside from the men sweating in their three-piece suits, the ladies wore layered Victorian dresses with crinolines (stiffened petticoats) and accessories such as hats, gloves and umbrellas, which were equally unsuited to the weather.[19]

In light of prevailing dress standards and their political underpinnings, Nira Wickaramasinghe has emphasized the fact that, in South Asia, Western dress was not "consciously imposed upon the people by the colonisers, whether Portuguese, Dutch or British." Rather, she argues:

---

[18] Jonathan Forbes, *Eleven Years in Ceylon* (London: Richard Bently, 1840), p. 296.
[19] Richard Boyle, "Island Dress," 2016, http://serendib.btoptions.lk/article.php?id=1817 %EF%BB%BF

> At first the European conquerors did not in many instances dream of propagating, much less imposing, European forms of life on foreign peoples in tropical countries; rather they often tended to adopt the styles of life and particularly dress of the latter, which they realized were better suited to local conditions.[20]

Notably, lower caste communities in Sri Lanka had little choice in their clothing, which was designed to illustrate their low economic and social status. They were bound by both social convention and economic necessity to keep their status visible, often through their attire, and could not, in any case, afford to buy new clothes. Some lower caste groups, such as the *Rodiya* and *Kinnara*, had only the bare minimum of cultural capital and lacked access to fashionable clothing, and even in the British colonial era, both men and women in these groups continued to practice topless dressing in line with their perceived social inferiority. The caste system was just as rigid before the advent of colonial modernity. These isolated communities were inevitably poor, oppressed by discrimination, and remained excluded from the kinds of extravagant, ornamental fashions of higher castes. As Hussein has written of the hierarchical values that underpinned such caste distinctions:

> During Kandyan times both *Rodi* men and women were compelled to go bare-bodied and forced to reside in separate hamlets known as *kuppayam*. Their *rajakariya* (duties to the state) included the supply of rope made of animal hide for trapping wild beasts. During Knox's time the primary occupation of the *Rodi* was mendicancy and hardly anyone refused them. In more recent times the folk were given to professional entertainment. The women would sing hymns in praise of their legendary ancestress Ratnavalli and spin brass plates while the men played a one-sided drum known as Bum-mendiya.[21]

The bare-breasted *Rodi* women became an artistic target for British photographers and again show the troubling power relationship between colonial artists or photographers and colonized subjects. Many photographs of these lower caste women were published in British periodicals, their subjects' naked vulnerability exploited for public consumption and sensation.

---

[20] Wickramasinghe, Sri Lanka in the Modern Age, p. 99.
[21] Asiff Hussein, "The story of the Rodi: Sri Lanka's 'untouchables,'" http://www.lanka library.com/cul/rodi.htm#:~:text=During%20Kandyan%20times%20both%20Rodi,hide %20for%20trapping%20wild%20beasts.

A contemporary tale tells us that the Mount Lavinia Hotel in Colombo was established in 1810 as a private house for the British Governor. A *Rodiya* caste girl who worked for the Governor is said to have fallen in love with him, and the Governor, who was about to retire, asked the girl what he could do for her when he left the service. Much to his surprise she did not ask for his house at the old hotel, which he would have been happy to offer her. Instead, she requested formal permission to wear a cloth about her waist, a show of rank that *Rodiyas* had generally been denied by society, and to which he consented. Whether true or not, this folkloric tale reflects the changes to dress customs during the period of British rule, when the British government granted permission to *Rodiyas* to wear clothing to cover their bodies, subsequently abolishing the social convention of topless dressing.[22] Stories such as these reveal the extent to which the British government changed prevailing attitudes to dress in Sri Lanka. It is obvious that there was a noticeable movement among the general public to modify and change their everyday dress, and as in previous incidences, the British used such rules, and their own legal power, to modify the clothing of social outcast groups like the *Rodiyas*.

Of course, Western governmental hegemony exerted its influence considerably further than indigenous dress traditions, also reforming various social moral standards and regulations in Sri Lanka. For example, after establishing a colonial administrative framework on the island, the British declined to support Kandyan marriage rituals as a separate law. The whole country was affected by Ordinance No. 3 of 1870, which created a standard system for registering marriages and establishing the legal status of the family unit,[23] while Ordinances No. 13 of 1859, No. 3 of 1870, No. 23 of 1917 and No. 39 of 1938 were all adopted to unify the British and Kandyan legal systems.

The government had to push indigenous people to alter their traditions and to observe these new rules via both formal legal channels (by supporting marriage registration through different government organizations), and secondary influences such as missionaries and other vernacular authors. The latter were also affected by the modernization process, with many committing themselves to legitimizing colonial power, often promoting ideals about what they saw as civilized marriage. These third-party agents made use of a variety of unofficial media, and Christian institutions carried out the task

---

[22] N. Sarawanan, "Lovina Alphonso: A Rodi Waif who 'converted' a British Governor," https://thuppahis.com/2020/04/26/lovina-alphonso-a-rodi-waif-who-converted-a-british-governor/

[23] T. B. Dissanayake, and A. B. Colin de Soysa, *Kandyan Law, and Buddhist Ecclesiastical Law* (Colombo: Dharmasamya Press, 1963), pp. 8-20.

of altering traditional Sri Lankan customs as a result of their increasing social capital. According to missionary teachings, a decent Christian always avoided polygamy and polyandry by registering their marriage, and as a recent study suggests, American and British missionaries also dedicated themselves to finding beautiful Christian wives among the locals. It was not only about legalizing marriage, but about teaching women in particular to be more disciplined. These were the white man's moral traditions, and missionaries like Mrs. Harriet Winslow, who were assigned to Eastern Sri Lanka, were involved in these reformation efforts. As Alagiyawanna has written:

> The missionaries brought with them not only their religion. They also brought a whole culture - the entire gamut of attitudes and feelings; the discipline of developing modern societies, and a set of social, economic, and political ideas which were new to the East. These missionaries also became a force for the disorganization of the ancient cultures within which they chose to work, but they also opened the eyes of the peoples of such societies, like that of Sri Lanka, India and other Asiatic and African societies, to new vistas of progress and possibility.[24]

The British government sought to build a system of Victorian moral hegemony in Sri Lanka through both the regulation of marriage and property, for which new legislation was also introduced, and the colony's social norms and relationship patterns were quickly altered by this system. Virginity, chastity and female virtue became standard expectations in nineteenth-century Sri Lankan culture, and one of the vernacular poetesses wrote admiringly of the virginity of young brides, advising girls not to fear the wedding ceremony as long as they had safeguarded their chastity.[25] These freshly socialized young ladies were expected to dress modestly and to protect their virginity, and a woman's femininity and virtue were all-important in gaining societal acceptance. Her virginity and chastity were emphasized by her colonial-style attire, a form of clothing that was inspired by British Victorian dress. Because of this, and with legal marriage now highly regarded by colonial Sri Lankan society, bridal gowns, in a variety of styles, became popular among upper-caste women. In this era, the Victorian "angel of the

---

[24] K. L. V. Alagiyawanna, "The Social Impact of Missionary Activities in Sri Lanka in The Early 19th Century," *Journal of the Royal Asiatic Society of Sri Lanka New Series*, vol. 36 (1991/1992), pp. 1-12.
[25] Ramesha Jayaneththi, "Women's attitudes and their social status as discovered from the poems in colonial Sri Lanka," in *Sarathi* (Sri Lanka: Ministry of Cultural affairs, 2013).

house" also became the Sri Lankan ideal, promoted through the school system. An idealized image of chaste motherhood was celebrated, while girls and young women were taught virtuous, wifely activities such as embroidery, dressmaking, knitting, painting and cookery,[26] a process of socialization reflected in the new modest dress codes. An 1892 advertisement for Singer sewing machines (shown below) depicts an idealized domestic scene: the woman, seated at her sewing machine in what resembles a typical British Victorian ensemble of long skirt and neat white blouse while her husband stands beside her with his hand resting on a piece of blue cloth. Such advertisements, while designed to sell products through their depictions of an idealized lifestyle, promoted and reinforced the desirability of such everyday attire, which had become increasingly common among Sinhalese women in British Ceylon.

Figure 2.6: An advert for the Singer Manufacturing Co., 1892.

Commons.wikimedia.org, public domain.

In the nineteenth century, local attitudes were profoundly affected by this new emphasis on female decorum. Most newly-educated upper-class Sri Lankans, including several Kandyan chiefs, backed the government's moral efforts. Jeronis Pieris and James Alwis, two prominent upper-class and

---

[26] Indrani Meegama, *With a Fistful of Rice Buddhist Women and the Making of Mahamaya Girls' College* (Colombo: Mahamaya Old Girls Association, 2003), p. 185.

educated Sinhalese, challenged the existing marital patterns among Kandyan Sinhalese, with Pieris being particularly harsh in his criticisms of polyandry and polygamy in Sinhalese marriage. He maintained that polygamous arrangements were a "brutal practice," and that their customs as a whole were "barbarous" and "nasty," writing (with sincere conviction): "Look how barbarous the Kandyans are still! I wish all of them would soon turn Christians and leave off their old nasty customs."[27]

James Alwis, another member of the emerging national elite, claimed that "Marriage is regarded by the natives (especially by the Kandyans) as a matter of inconsiderable importance; they have no notion of the sacredness of its institution. Even that portion of the Singhalese who in fact are Christians, think it a matter of little or no consideration in the interior parts of Ceylon, 'where white man's foot never trod'; the people live in the rudest and most barbarous manner possible."[28] This sort of rhetoric aided British efforts to reform Sri Lankan customs in its own image, as they introduced a new moral framework for Sri Lankans citizens. These reformers brought up a number of moral and practical concerns about outdated marriage customs, such as issues around inheritance, further stressing their belief that what they saw as true marriage and proper sexual behavior had never been a part of traditional Sri Lankan culture. Clothing played an important role in establishing this new ideological framework, as upper-class Christian Sri Lankan women, models of Victorian propriety in their expansive crinolines and long, mutton-sleeved frocks, exhibited this new morality through their dress, the only apparent distinction between them and their British colonial counterparts being their brown skin.

In stark contrast to the rhetoric of Kandyan chiefs such as Pieris and Alwis, the impact of colonial modernity was met with a counter-response among Sinhala Buddhist national leaders, who followed a form of Buddhist nationalism with a different set of social norms and values to that of the general public. Sinhala Buddhist nationalism can be understood as a Sri Lankan political philosophy that blends Sinhalese culture and ethnicity with an emphasis on Theravada Buddhism. From the mid-nineteenth century, there was a revival in national culture among these groups, which extended to ideas about clothing and dress culture. Angarika Dharmapala and other Buddhist revivalists frequently criticized indigenous morality while advocating a new way of life for Sinhala Buddhists. Dharmapala was a classic example of a Buddhist modernizer and was possibly the most famous

---

[27] Michael Roberts, *Facets of Modern Ceylon History: Through the Letters of Jeronis Pieris* (Colombo: Hunsa Publishers Ltd., 1975), p. 28.
[28] Roberts, *Facets of Modern Ceylon History*, p. 28.

Protestant Buddhist in Sri Lanka at this time. His particular interest was what he saw as the compatibility between Buddhism and contemporary, Western-influenced social values. Dharmapala asserted that British rule was the finest type of foreign dominance, and the British themselves "the most enlightened, the most philanthropic, the most cultured of European races."[29] Dharmapala believed in the existence of distinct biological "races," and the assumption that the Sinhalese were Aryans gave him a sense of racial supremacy. To preserve their Aryan superiority over other ethnicities in Sri Lanka, Dharmapala believed that the Sinhalese should maintain themselves as a pure race and follow a strict social and moral code. He was particularly hostile to Sri Lanka's Muslims, whom he saw as predatory, referring to them as "Hambayas" — a pejorative term for Muslims which derived from the Malay "Sampan," meaning flat-bottomed boat.[30] He admired Sinhalese civilization as a disciplined and virtuous society and encouraged contemporary Sinhalese to adopt these values:

> Under the influence of the Tathagatha's (Buddha's) religion of righteousness, the people flourished. Kings spent all their wealth in building temples, public baths, dagobas, libraries, monasteries, rest houses, hospitals for man and beast, schools, tanks, seven-storied mansions, waterworks and beautified the city of Anuradhapura, whose fame reached Egypt, Greece, Rome, China, India and other countries.[31]

Furthermore, at a time when capitalism was redefining social ties, Buddhism's key institutions were connected to the feudal social order. If the Buddhist social fabric was to be preserved, it needed to adapt and discover new pathways. It was Dharmapala who enforced his view of the inseparable link between Buddhism and Sinhala society and supported the formation of a new relationship between religion and lay society in Sri Lanka:

> The Sinhalese people lived a joyously cheerful life in those bygone times…the streets were crowded day and night by throngs of pilgrims…The atmosphere was saturated with the fragrance of sweet-smelling flowers and delicate perfumes. There were no slaughter houses,

---

[29] Steven Kemper, *Rescued From The Nation: Anagarika Dharmapala and the Buddhist World* (Chicago: University of Chicago, 2015), p. 320.
[30] Shamara Wettimuny, "The Colonial History of Islamophobic Slurs in Sri Lanka," *The History Workshop*, September 20th, 2020. https://www.historyworkshop.org.uk/colonial-history-islamophobia/
[31] Ananda Guruge, Anagarika Dharmapala: Return to Righteousness (Colombo: Department of Cultural Affairs, 1991), p. 481.

no pawnshops, no brothels, no prisons and law Courts and no arrack (liquor) taverns and opium dens.³²

It became important for Sinhala Buddhists to define a code of lay ethics if they were to be organized into a functioning socio-political group. A traditional disregard for lay ethics was fully consistent with the Buddha's redemption objectives and techniques, but in the political climate of Dharmapala's day, such a unifying code was critical. As a result, Dharmapala prepared and published a lay code entitled "A Daily Code for the Laity," in which he outlined 200 rules for ordinary Buddhists, which had a considerable impact on local communities, particularly in relation to sexual morality and social values.

The early twentieth-century revival of ancient Sri Lankan Buddhist culture as part of anti-colonial nationalism meant that Buddist ideology as a whole became more conservative, and frequently criticized the contemporary moral climate. Old and modern Buddhist practices were often discussed through vernacular media, which reinterpreted the Buddhist moral code and reassessed the idea of sin. Many critiques focused upon men's and women's personal relationships, and extramarital relationships were reviled. In Sri Lanka, virginity and chastity were presented as vital components of women's lives, and Sri Lankan customs, social manners and styles of dress were often criticized.

At the same time, as a famous religious revivalist and social reformer, Anagarika Dharmapala attempted to reform Sinhalese dress. Dharmapala discouraged girls from wearing short dresses, claiming that it was only after the more modest, two-thousand-year-old Aryan traditions had died out four centuries ago that women had begun to expose their bodies.³³

The dress code which Dharmapala imposed on women effectively acknowledged the realities of what contemporary women really wore, which went against his strictures. As Seneviratne has written:

> This puritanical attitude toward the body, derived from missionaries but imagined by Dharmapala to be "Aryans" is expressed in the instructions Dharmapala gave "Aryan Sinhala" women as to how they should be clothed: without exposing the navel, breasts and legs. 'Aryans never exposed their limbs' Dharmapala wrote, and 'black Sinhala (female) legs should not be exposed'. Dharmapala objected to the two piece attire, consisting of a cloth (redda) wrapped casually around the waist and a top (hatte), a sensible tropical ensemble universally favored by Sinhala and

---

³² Kemper, *Rescued From The Nation*, p. 325.
³³ Guruge, *Anagarika Dharmapala: Return to Righteousness*, p. 85.

Kerala women. 'It is not appropriate', he wrote, 'for noble women to wear a half a cloth (kamba kalla) and a short blouse that exposes the midriff (udaraya)'.[34]

At the same time, covering up once again became a political and gendered statement as it served as a means of concealing the "evil, temptress woman." By associating sin with the female form, society quickly constructed a mechanism of restraint and a power structure which worked against women. Men did not need to be ashamed of their bodies, but women certainly did, and several contemporary poets expressed their opinions on the "proper" way for women to dress. These didactic poems were written about the common people's national character and encouraged them to follow a moralistic way of life.[35] While eventually the *Osariya* saree, which was so favored by these religious conservatives, would fall out of favor, its popularity during the early twentieth century forms a stark contrast to the British-inspired, Victorian-style frocks that had dominated a decade before. It is striking that, when looking through some contemporary family photo albums, I have seen pictures of weddings only a decade apart, in which women are dressed in Western attire, followed by another in which sarees dominate. As Nira Wickramasinghe explains:

> The evolution of patterns of dress consumption and production can only be understood within the broader picture of a small state being gradually integrated into the network of world capitalism. The sewing machine was the epitome of modernity and with its large-scale adoption the nature of people's relation to clothes and dress-making change dramatically.[36]

The traditional *Osariya* saree, was, then, designated their national dress. Revival leaders criticized the Tamil-style Indian saree, showing the significance of dress as a symbol of ethnic divisions. Tamil women in Jaffna and Muslim women in both Eastern Sri Lanka and other regions wore their sarees in distinct ways, principally that resembling the Indian style. The Indian style saree draping followed by these minority communities and Muslim women was designed to cover the head and was part of a different

---

[34] H. L. Seneviratne, *The New Buddhism in Sri Lanka* (Chicago: The University of Chicago, 1999), p. 117.
[35] Garrett Field, *Modernizing Composition: Sinhala Song, Poetry, and Politics in Twentieth century* (California: University of California, 2017), pp. 25-27.
[36] Nira Wickramasinghe, *Dressing the Colonised Body: Politics, Clothing, and Identity in Sri Lanka* (Hyderabad: Orient Longman, 2003), pp. 123-124.

tradition of saree draping to the Sinhalese *Osariya*. Young Tamil girls wore the *Pavadai thavani*, which took the form of draping the saree onto a long skirt, while Sinhalese girls, too young to wear a saree or *Osariya*, wore a *Lama sariya*, or "half-saree."

The ideological underpinnings and diversity of different styles of attire between different cultures came to the fore throughout the colonial era. Dress, it seemed, was a key element used in the separation of these parallel societies. It is notable that, in the nineteenth century, European social scientists and linguists had proposed Aryan theory as a linguistic and racial discourse, which India and Sri Lanka adopted as part of wider initiatives to demonstrate the social and racial purity of "Aryan races" in their countries, further legitimizing British colonial rule in their own eyes. The Sinhalese claimed to be an Aryan race and separated themselves from the Tamil "other." With this theoretical debate, the concept of a national dress code was created, and local business circles and print media made it popular among Sinhalese women.

Local populations were subjected to extensive propaganda aimed at promoting Sinhalese national attire, which cut across all socioeconomic strata. Propagandist stories circulated in the press regarding the development of the saree dress code, expressed in various leaflets and magazines. The *Osariya* leaflet, for instance, was circulated by a patriotic magazine named *Lanka Matha* in 1912 to elicit public enthusiasm among local Sinhalese women on the subject of national dress, expressing the popular Aryan ideology of the time and using women's attire to denigrate non-Aryans and other ethnic minorities. This outfit, which used the *Osariya* as its central garment, was presented as suitable attire for respectable "Aryan" women in Sinhalese society, forming part of an attempt to formally demarcate a strict social barrier between Sinhalese and non-Sinhalese women. Women's dress codes took on the weight of their own apparent purity, chastity and social respectability, while also shouldering the burden of representing the Aryan ideal of the developing nation.

Dress, then, became a potent cultural symbol that it was possible for many distinct groups to manipulate for their own ends. As the age of anti-colonial nationalism set in, national dress codes were imbued with a new significance, with ideas about tradition and heritage being constructed to give authority to the struggle for independence. As a reaction to colonial modernity, dress took on new meanings and interpretations, being presented to the general public as something to connect them to pre-colonialist ideas. This specific style of dress, however, did not accurately correspond to the dress code followed by early Sri Lankans during the pre-colonial era. The new national dress code was more concerned with encouraging a sense of virtue and a narrative of traditional femininity than truthfully representing the past, during which, as we have seen, topless dressing was common. Even men's dress went through a variety of politically-motivated changes that were intimately tied to pre-colonial or colonial socio-political organizations. Men were obliged to adopt a new style of dress, as both clothing and style choices became more clearly gendered and linked to national politics.

Figure 2.7: Front center (seated): John Henry Meediniya Adigar with his family. Rear center (standing): his daughter, Alice, who married the low-country newspaper magnate D. R. Wijewardena in 1916. Self-taken photograph, 1905.

Commons.wikimedia.org, public domain.

Addressing the issue of Sinhala men's new dress code, one national writer asserted that the Sinhalese man should abide by the following rules, and that he should:

> Not show the entire body like the Veddas (Aboriginals) who wear only a loin cloth.

Not wear a trouser like the fair Portuguese...

Not wear a hat wrapped in cloth, comb, collar tie, banian, shirt, vest coat, coat trousers,

cloth socks, shoes all at the same time. It is a ludicrous dress.[37]

The national dress of the Sinhalese man was now represented by a white sarong and long-sleeved shirt and established the notion of a standardized male dress code. It was popular among Sinhalese men for many different occasions, from wedding ceremonies and social gatherings to political meetings and rallies and provided them with a sense of national identity. It also demarcated the ethnic boundaries between Sinhalese men and male "others," such as Muslims and Tamils.

Clothing came to represent even further differentiations of class and social behavior in post-colonial culture, and upper-class clothing in particular was meticulously curated and, once again, imbued with moral significance. However, this was not just in support of conservative moral principles; after the mid-twentieth century, imitating aspects of masculine style became fashionable among a small number of forward-thinking, courageous women in order to assert their right to enjoy traditionally masculine privileges, both in self-expression and behavior.

Local women were inspired by wartime clothing patterns to wear trousers in public, with many adopting elements of menswear as a kind of provocation. This was quickly embraced by many more progressive Sri Lankan women, and gradually, the influence of the emerging feminist movement and other progressive forms of culture could be seen on Sri Lankan women's dress, with short skirts and trousers increasingly common. With the decline of British colonial power in Sri Lanka following the Second World War, and the establishment on an independent Sri Lankan state, it could have been assumed that the influence of Western cultural norms (including fashion) would decline. Interestingly, however, a form of soft cultural influence remained, with Western global capitalist forces asserting a challenge to nationalist religious orthodoxy. The arrival of women's trousers, particularly jeans, from Britain was a watershed moment in Sri Lanka, which changed the face of twentieth-century fashion by making the incorporation of male clothing into women's wardrobes a mainstream style statement. During the 1970s, bell-bottoms became fashionable among young Sri Lankan women, and Western popular culture, from music to television shows, all contributed

---

[37] Martin Wickramasinghe, *Upandasita* (Dehiwela: Tisara Publishers, 1961), p. 44.

to the spread of this style in Sri Lanka. Many Sri Lankan women began to follow the European and American fashions that they saw in Hollywood films,[38] which asserted a style of Western hegemony in a very different fashion to the previous centuries of colonial rule. As Ayesha Wickramasinghe has written:

> Hipster jeans and miniskirts were very popular in the 1960s, and in Sri Lanka this trend continued even to the end of the twentieth century. Shorter-length full-flared skirts, body-hugging miniskirts, shorter length 'A'-lined skirts and 'H'-lined skirts were constructed in hipster style. Most of the short skirts were shorter than the mid-thigh level, with a waistline frequently several inches below the navel, and were frequently worn with very short body-hugging blouses or short blouses. These blouses often had plunging necklines and long sleeves or no sleeves.[39]

Young Sri Lankan women, Wickramasinghe argues, adopted this silhouette, with its overt sexuality, in response the liberalizing moral climate, their exposed legs now being seen as fashionable and attractive. However, in some rural areas conservative attitudes to female dress and sexuality remained, and young women and girls were still sometimes physically assaulted for wearing what was seen as unsuitable clothing. Nevertheless, many continued to wear Western dress and became fluent in the visual language of modern Western styles, adopting mini skirts as wardrobe staples from the 1960s onwards.[40] This time, however, it was not under pressure from a foreign occupation, but the globalized influence of Western capitalism, a power shift which recast a form of soft colonial power as something progressive rather than prescriptive.

As a result of the fashion industry's flourishing in urban areas during the late twentieth century, a backlash occurred among nationalists, with nationalistic rhetoric once more involved in regulating the female body. Due to this new wave of dress politics, Sri Lankan women once again faced pressure from nationalist groups to wear modest, apparently traditional attire. The seeds of this renewed focus upon female modesty had been sewn during the previous few decades, in spite of the liberalizing climate and wide

---

[38] Ayesha Wickramasinghe, "Artistic Review of Sri Lankan Female Fashion and It's Movement," in *Current Trends in Fashion Technology & Textile Engineering*, vol. 3, no. 3 (March 2018), pp. 58-59.
[39] Wickramasinghe, "Artistic Review of Sri Lankan Female Fashion and It's Movement," p. 59.
[40] Wickramasinghe, "Artistic Review of Sri Lankan Female Fashion and It's Movement," p. 59.

embrace of modern fashions. From 1956, as nationalism and Sinhala Buddhist morality started to seem outdated, an increasingly vocal minority of critical voices were raised which condemned women's fashion choices. Some Buddhist monks requested that female devotees refrain from wearing short dresses and skirts, and in 1957, Rev. Hendiyagala Silaratana stated that:

> This is the decline in virtue in our women. Shouldn't we say that it is the women who today more than men desire dancing, tomfoolery like rock and roll, and clothing that does not properly cover the body? Today in the homes of the so-called upper classes, Sinhala customs have completely disappeared. Schools today support rather than discourage these tomfooleries. Would it be wrong to say that it is by imitating the teachers that girls of even very good parents get cultured into bad customs.[41]

Figure 2.8: Women's Health magazine launch a new cover in 2012, showing off a skimpy mini-dress.

Commons.wikimedia.org, public domain.

Since the early days of Sinhalese dress and its fashion for elaborate ornaments, socio-political narratives have wielded significant influence over dress as a

---

[41] Seneviratne, *The New Buddhism in Sri Lanka*, p. 117.

whole. Women were particularly affected by the changing discourses around dress, which had a significant influence over both their clothing choices and social status. Women in different socio-economic strata experienced the politics of dress in various ways, and their understanding of their clothing choices changed with the times, demonstrating a willingness to conform to different sets of norms.

It is evident that dress codes can convey different social aspirations, political ideas and discourses about gender in ways which are particularly evident in Asian societies. Sri Lankan culture gradually transformed in the post-colonial era, including in its attitudes towards dress and style, revealing a highly diverse set of attitudes. Even after the colonial era, Sri Lanka's "repressive conservatism" remained entrenched, and women were encouraged to wear traditional attire such as the saree and *Osari* for official workwear. It took decades for Sri Lanka to adapt its own sense of style, and even professional women did not have much scope to deviate from the national dress code and wear their everyday European-style clothes to work. However, many Sri Lankan women are now confident enough to enjoy their freedom to dress how they choose, with a large number opting to wear more revealing clothes and shorter skirts during their leisure time, and Western-style business attire at work. The influences of the new millennium, with its modernizing forces, can be seen in this more independent style of dress.

In Sri Lanka, then, dress and its socio-political context created several waves of distinct styles and played a role in some of the key social movements of the times. Clothing and the value system that shaped it had ties to both nationalism and colonial moral hegemony, which underpinned ethnic, caste and class identities. Dress was a visual signifier of social capital for certain classes and groups, resulting in a variety of challenges in later Sri Lanka. The changing notion of everyday dress codes in British-colonial Sri Lanka had an influence on the lifestyle of its people, with the nation's dress politics now being seen as a significant part of its cultural legacy in the post-colonial era.

Bibliography

Primary Sources

Government Papers

Ceylon Census at 1901. Ceylon Government Printers, Colombo, 1902.
Ceylon Ordinances. Enacted during the Session of 1866-67, 1870.
Guruge, Ananda. *Anagarika Dharmapala: Return to Righteousness.* Colombo: Department of Cultural Affairs, 1991.
Guruge, Ananda. *Dharmapala Lipi.* Colombo: Government Press, 1991.

Books

Forbes, Jonathan. *Eleven Years in Ceylon.* London: Richard Bently, 1840.
Knox, Robert. *An Historical Relation Of the Island Ceylon.* London: Royal Society, 1681.

Newspapers

Lanka Matha periodical, 1912, Colombo.
Sinhala Bauddaya newspaper, 1910-22.
Sinhala Jatiya newspaper, 1909.

Secondary Sources

Alagiyawanna, K. L. V. "The Social Impact of Missionary Activities in Sri Lanka in The Early 19th Century." In *Journal of the Royal Asiatic Society of Sri Lanka New Series*, vol. 36 (1991), pp. 1-12.

Bahl, Vinay. "Shifting Boundaries of 'Nativity' and 'Modernity' in South Asian Women's Clothes." In *Dialectical Anthropology*, vol. 29, no. 1 (2005), pp. 85-121.

Blumer, Herbert. "Fashion: From Class Differentiation to Collective Selection." *The Sociological Quarterly* vol. 10, no. 3 (1967), pp. 275-291.

Bulten, Luc, Jan Kok, Dries Lina, and Nadeera Rupesinghe. "Contested conjugality? Sinhalese marriage practices in eighteenth-century Dutch colonial Sri Lanka." In *Annales de démographie historique*, vol. 1, no. 135 (2018).

Crill, Rosemary. *The Fabric of India.* London: Victoria and Albert Museum, 2015.

Dissanayake, T.B. and A.B. Colin de Soysa. *Kandyan Law, and Buddhist Ecclesiastical Law.* Colombo: Dharmasamya Press, 1963.

Field, Garrett. *Modernizing Composition: Sinhala Song, Poetry, and Politics in Twentieth century.* California: University of California, 2017.

Jayaneththi, Ramesha. "Women´s attitudes and their social status as discovered from the poems in colonial Sri Lanka." In *Sarathi*. Sri Lanka: Ministry of Cultural affairs, 2003.

Kemper, Steven. *Rescued From The Nation: Anagarika Dharmapala and the Buddhist World.* Chicago: University of Chicago, 2015.

Laver, J. *The Concise History of Costume and Fashion.* New York: Harry N. Abrams, 1969.

Lehmann, Ulrich. *Tigersprung: Fashion in Modernity.* Cambridge, Mass.: MIT Press, 2000.

Maxwell, Alexander. "Analyzing nationalized clothing: nationalism theory meets fashion studies." In *National Identities*, vol. 23, no. 1 (2019).

Meegama, Indrani. *With a Fistful of Rice Buddhist Women and the Making of Mahamaya Girls' College.* Colombo: Mahamaya Old Girls Association, 2003.

Mudiyanse, Nandasena. *Mahayana Monuments in Ceylon.* Maradana: Gunasena, M.D, 1967.

Pathak, Dev Nath and Sasanka Perera. *Culture and Politics in South Asia: Performative Communication.* London: Taylor & Francis, 2017.

Roberts, Michael. *Facets of Modern Ceylon History: Through the Letters of Jeronis Pieris*. Colombo: Hunsa Publishers Ltd, 1975.

Seneviratne, H. L. "The New Buddhism in Sri Lanka." Chicago: The University of Chicago, 1999.

Wickramasinghe, Ayesha. "Artistic Review of Sri Lankan Female Fashion and It's Movement." In *Current Trends in Fashion Technology & Textile Engineering*, vol. 3, no. 3 (March 2018).

Wickramasinghe, Martin. *Upandasita*. Dehiwela: Tisara Publishers, 1961.

Wickramasinghe, Nira. "Some Comments on Dress in Sri Lanka." International Centre for Ethnic Studies, The Thatched Patio. vol 5. no. 1 (1992).

Wickramasinghe, Nira (ed.). *Sri Lanka in the Modern Age: A History*. London: Oxford University Press, 2015.

Wickramasinghe, Nira. *Dressing the Colonised Body: Politics, Clothing, and Identity in Sri Lanka*. Hyderabad: Orient Longman, 2003.

Websites

Boyle, Richard. "Island Dress," 2016: http://serendib.btoptions.lk/article.php?id=1817%EF%BB%BF

Crill, Rosemary. "Indian Textiles: 1,000 Years of Art and Design," 2022: https://oxfordasiantextilegroup.wordpress.com/tag/rosemary-crill

DeLong, Marilyn Revell, "Theories of Fashion," https://fashion-history.lovetoknow.com/fashion-history-eras/theories-fashion

Indian Textiles: 1,000 Years of Art and Design, https://oxfordasiantextilegroup.wordpress.com/tag/rosemary-crill

Hussein, Asiff. "The story of the Rodi: Sri Lanka's 'untouchables,'" http://www.lankalibrary.com/cul/rodi.htm#:~:text=During%20Kandyan%20times%20both%20Rodi,hide%20for%20trapping%20wild%20beasts.

Sarawanan, N. "Lovina Alphonso: A Rodi Waif who 'converted' a British Governor," https://thuppahis.com/2020/04/26/lovina-alphonso-a-rodi-waif-who-converted-a-british-governor/

Sigiriya Frescoes Art, Culture & Heritage. https://www.artra.lk/visual-art/sigiriya-frescoes, 2022

Vilaca, Julia. "Fashion Reflects social changes," 2021: https://fashinnovation.nyc/fashion-reflects-social-changes/

Wettimuny, Shamara. "The Colonial History of Islamophobic Slurs in Sri Lanka." *The History Workshop*, September 20th, 2020. https://www.historyworkshop.org.uk/colonial-history-islamophobia/

Chapter 3

Tilda's New Hat: a case study in Edwardian fashion and working-class identity

Petra Clark
Independent scholar

Figure 3.1: Portrait of a seated young woman in Edwardian dress.

Commons.wikimedia.org, public domain.

Abstract: Chapter Three uses a case study of the fascinating, yet little-remembered, Edwardian drama, *Tilda's New Hat* by George Paston (the pseudonym of Emily Morse Symonds), to examine the themes of dress, gender and class. Taking the form of a critical Introduction to the 1908 one-act play, this chapter explores its intersecting themes of fashion, femininity and working-class identity, presenting it as a significant exploration of female character in Edwardian society, while also looking at its critical reception.

Tilda's New Hat offers a feminist perspective on working-class Edwardian women's dress culture, providing us with a distinctive example through which to explore two very different approaches to fashionable dress in the central female characters of Tilda and Daisy. A neglected work of Edwardian drama, this play foregrounds discussions of dress as a significant mode of self-expression for working-class women of the period, with Tilda herself representing a flamboyant, theatrical type of Edwardian femininity most associated with actresses such as Lily Elsie.

A transcript of the play itself is included at the end of the chapter, as its themes of fashion and class mean that it can itself be seen as a creative and critical essay on Edwardian attitudes to female identity and style.

Keywords: Edwardian drama, *Tilda's New Hat*, George Paston (Emily Morse Symonds), East End, Edwardian fashion, feather club, feminism, hats.

***

George Paston's one-act play, *Tilda's New Hat* (1908), humorously examines the idiom that "clothes make the woman," while offering an intriguing case study to explore the intersections between gender, class, fashion, and identity in Edwardian drama.[1] The play's focus on clothing in both costuming and dialogue is striking for what it reveals about cultural understandings of working-class womanhood, as well as important contemporaneous issues such as women's suffrage and the plumage trade. Far from being the fashion equivalent of a MacGuffin, Tilda's "new hat" is a powerful tool of self-fashioning, both within the character's social and economic class and in the wider cultural context of London at the turn of the twentieth century. This essay serves as a critical introduction to *Tilda's New Hat*, followed by the play text in its entirety with some explanatory notes by the editor of this collection.

---

[1] To my knowledge, Sheila Stowell has provided the most extensive analysis of *Tilda's New Hat* to date: she covers the play in her article "Re[pre]senting Eroticism: The Tyranny of Fashion in Feminist Plays of the Edwardian Age," (1991) and (with Joel H. Kaplan) in the book *Theatre and Fashion: Oscar Wilde to the Suffragettes* (Cambridge: Cambridge University Press, 1994).

far from being deemed vulgar, her style is consistently praised by Mr. Emerson, her would-be admirer, and coveted by Daisy, her would-be rival for his affections. Moreover, *Tilda's New Hat* also seems to encourage playgoers to evaluate and perhaps even emulate Tilda's style.

Historians including Michele Majer, Sheila Stowell, Christopher Breward, Erika Rappaport and Marlis Schweitzer have noted "the reciprocal relationship between fashion and the theater" in the late nineteenth and early twentieth centuries, especially in plays focusing on modern life wherein the actresses' costumes reflected and influenced the latest trends.[13] In *Staging Fashion: 1880-1920*, Majer observes that "For many women, the appeal of observing actresses in performance offered the excitement of seeing new fashions in motion and imagining themselves in the same—or similar—clothes."[14] Upper-class women could order the same couture gown from Worth or Redfern, or commission a close copy, while women of lesser means "might only be able to approximate an actress's particular look."[15] Millinery on stage was also enthusiastically observed and copied: perhaps the most famous example occurred in response to William Edwardes's production of *The Merry Widow* (1907), the first English adaptation of Franz Lehár's operetta *Die lustige Witwe* (1905). *The Merry Widow* caused a sensation when it premiered at Daly's Theatre in London in June 1907, partly due to the lavish costumes that had been designed for the lead actress, Lily Elsie, by the celebrated dressmaker Lucile.[16] Audiences and reviewers were particularly taken with Elsie's "immense black crinoline hat, banded round the crown with silver and two huge pink silk roses nestling under the brim," which she donned in the third act and which set off a craze for "Merry Widow" hats.[17]

---

[13] Michele Majer, "Staging Fashion, 1880-1920" in Staging Fashion, 1880-1920: Jane Hading, Lily Elsie, Billie Burke, Michele Majer (ed), Bard Graduate Center, 2012, p. 28. See also Christopher Breward's Fashioning London: Clothing and the Modern Metropolis (Oxford: Berg, 2004), Erika Diane Rappaport's Shopping for Pleasure: Women in the Making of London's West End (Princeton: Princeton University Press, 2000), and Marlis Schweitzer's When Broadway Was the Runway: Theater, Fashion, and American Culture (Philadelphia: University of Pennsylvania Press, 2009) and "'Darn That Merry Widow Hat': The On- and Offstage Life of a Theatrical Commodity, Circa 1907–1908," Theatre Survey 50:2 (November 2009), pp. 189-221.
[14] Majer, "Staging Fashion, 1880-1920," p. 31.
[15] Majer, "Staging Fashion, 1880-1920," p. 31.
[16] Marlis Schweitzer, "'Darn That Merry Widow Hat': The On- and Offstage Life of a Theatrical Commodity, Circa 1907–1908," *Theatre Survey* 50:2 (November 2009), pp.194-195.
[17] Louise Heilgers, "Delightful Dresses at Daly's," *The Play Pictorial* X, no. 61 (1907), p. 107.

Marlis Schweitzer argues that "the fashion industry led the way in popularizing the Merry Widow hat," but that "commercial industries, most notably publishers of newspapers, magazines, postcards, and sheet music, recognized its potential as an eroticized and easily replicated object."[18] In the months and years that followed *The Merry Widow*'s premiere, popular culture was saturated with references to these hats, and ever larger and more ostentatious versions appeared on the heads of fashion-forward women of all classes. While the plot—and fashion—of *Tilda's New Hat* differs greatly from *The Merry Widow*, one cannot help but wonder if Paston's play capitalized on the popularity of the earlier work and its (in)famous hat. In fact, throughout 1909, the revivals of *Tilda's New Hat* at His Majesty's, Wyndham's, and the Prince of Wales's theatres ran simultaneously and within a few blocks of *The Merry Widow* at Daly's.[19] Even if the two productions were never directly in conversation, they both tapped into the public fascination with "'look at me' styles like the Merry Widow hat."[20] What sets Paston's play apart, however, is its focus on a working-class heroine and her approach to style, which both draws on broader elements of mainstream fashion and is highly specific to her class and locale.

Tilda takes great pride in her own appearance, but much of the comedy—and commentary—of the play comes from the other characters' reactions to it. In her analysis of *Tilda's New Hat*, Sheila Stowell argues that Paston "offers a feminist critique of the conventional linking of women's so-called 'love' of finery to the manipulation of male sexual desire."[21] As the only man in the play and Tilda's suitor, Emerson becomes a target for comedic ridicule owing to his self-important attitude and his facile understanding of almost everything, including fashion. In this, Emerson resembles a more risible version of the type represented by self-taught clerk Leonard Bast in E. M. Forster's roughly contemporaneous novel *Howards End* (1910), "a pathetic victim of bourgeois cultural hegemony" who reads Ruskin simply because that is what he imagines educated people do.[22] Emerson is likewise impressed by texts considered to be "improving" and is easily swayed by appearances, but neglects to deeply examine either. On the other hand, Emerson's erstwhile sweetheart Daisy is well aware of the role played by Tilda's clothes

---

[18] Schweitzer, "'Darn That Merry Widow Hat'," pp. 198-199.
[19] "Theatres," *The Solicitors' Journal and Weekly Reporter* LIII, no.18 (27 February 1909), p. ii.
[20] "Theatres," *The Solicitors' Journal and Weekly Reporter* LIII, p. 200.
[21] Sheila Stowell, "Re[pre]senting Eroticism: The Tyranny of Fashion in Feminist Plays of the Edwardian Age," *Theatre History Studies* 11 (1991), p. 61.
[22] Jonathan Rose, "The History of Education as the History of Reading," *History of Education* 36:4-5 (July-September 2007), p. 601.

in attracting Emerson: "Of course, I know you're more stylish than I am. [...] —if *I* had a hat like that—" to which Tilda archly replies "Hoh, you think Mr. Emerson come after me hat and feathers, do you? [...]"[23] In fact, Emerson is completely enamored of the hat and the overall aesthetic Tilda has created for herself—and later recreates for Daisy—but his "conventional response renders ridiculous man's inability to see women in terms divorced from the erotic appeal of their feminine adornment."[24]

Emerson does not seem to have much interest in either girl's personality or opinions: when he spends time with Tilda, he is either admiring her clothes or droning on about the "Mutual Improvement Debating Society" he belongs to, which he says ladies are allowed to join even if "we don't expect 'em to speak."[25] He does have an interest in "educating" the woman he is involved with, but it seems to be more for the gratification of his own ego than from actual concern for her intellectual cultivation. Tilda, for her part, responds to Emerson's attempts to "form [her] mind" by saying, "I don't want to improve nobody, nor I don't want to be improved meself." [26] This statement is somewhat tongue-in-cheek: Tilda is decidedly not interested in having Emerson's patronizing "improvements" thrust upon her, but she does consistently work to improve her appearance and urges Daisy to do the same. Eventually, Tilda's only use for Emerson seems to be making him "play milliner's dummy" for her, first as she arranges the feathers on her hat and then later as she spruces up Daisy's old one in what Stowell calls "a nice inversion of the conventional caricatures of mannish women."[27] Emerson is concerned that modeling the hats for Tilda will make him look ridiculous, when really his own behavior has done that already—in Tilda's eyes as well as those of the audience.[28]

While Emerson's attraction to both Tilda and Daisy is literally surface-level, Paston does not condemn the women's own interest in fashion—or their strategic use of it. Daisy enters the play "with hair brushed off her forehead" and "very plainly but tidily dressed in a dark skirt, with a cotton or flannelette shirt" and "a flat hat, simply trimmed with ribbon, and perhaps a motor scarf twisted round her neck."[29] After complaining to Tilda about losing Emerson, Tilda chastises, "why don't you get yourself up more stylish? Look at that hat

---

[23] Paston [Emily Morse Symonds], *Tilda's New Hat*, pp. 19-20.
[24] Stowell, "Re[pre]senting Eroticism," p. 61.
[25] Paston [Emily Morse Symonds], *Tilda's New Hat*, p. 11.
[26] Paston [Emily Morse Symonds], *Tilda's New Hat*, p. 11.
[27] Paston [Emily Morse Symonds], *Tilda's New Hat*, p. 12.
[28] Paston [Emily Morse Symonds], *Tilda's New Hat*, p. 12.
[29] Paston [Emily Morse Symonds], *Tilda's New Hat*, p. 17.

now! You can't expect a superior young feller like Mr. Emerson to walk out with a hat like that."[30] Tilda does not necessarily disparage Daisy's fashion on its own merits so much as she (correctly) surmises how it would be perceived by Emerson. To help her friend, Tilda quickly lends Daisy her own prized hat but finds that Daisy's hair and clothes need to be altered to match it, and so gives Daisy a makeover in her own image. Stowell explains, "Tilda's professional reconstruction of Daisy's image stresses process rather than product, making clear by means of its demystification, the artifice of the acceptably dressed female form." [31] Tilda points out Daisy's fashion *faux pas*, all the while dressing and styling Daisy into a version of herself—at least visually. This sartorial sleight of hand has the twofold purpose of deflecting Emerson's (at this point) unwanted attention from Tilda and redirecting it to his former sweetheart. After Daisy's transformation, Emerson tells her "I should hardly have known you [...] You ought always to dress like that," and pays her the same compliment he gave Tilda earlier on her blouse, "Blue's your colour."[32] This not only reveals the fickleness of his affection, but also the shallowness of his discernment. Paston humorously demonstrates how easily clothing can influence someone like Emerson without diminishing Tilda's skilled styling.

Perhaps unsurprisingly, the most interesting discourse about dress in *Tilda's New Hat* occurs between the women characters. Paston uses Tilda's interactions with Daisy and Mrs. Fishwick to explore contrasting fashions for working-class women and the potential implications of each style, both within the play and in the context of turn-of-the-century Britain. For instance, some mid-Victorian social reformers worried that the increasing involvement of girls and women in factory work would give them less time to cultivate what were considered essential domestic skills, such as sewing and mending: instead of virtuously maintaining handmade outfits, working-class women supposedly "wasted their limited resources buying new, fashionable, ready-made clothes."[33] This conflict can be seen between Tilda and her mother, who represents an older generation of working-class woman still aspiring to middle-class Victorian respectability. From the outset, Mrs. Fishwick is described as "a hard-featured woman of the grim and gloomy Puritan type, with drab hair and drab clothes."[34] Even though she disapproves of Tilda's

---

[30] Paston [Emily Morse Symonds], *Tilda's New Hat*, p. 20.
[31] Stowell, "Re[pre]senting Eroticism," p. 61.
[32] Paston [Emily Morse Symonds], *Tilda's New Hat*, pp. 24, 15.
[33] Christine Bayles Kortsch, *Dress Culture in Late Victorian Women's Fiction: Literacy, Textiles, and Activism* (London: Routledge, 2009), p. 40.
[34] Paston [Emily Morse Symonds], *Tilda's New Hat*, p. 7.

style on practical and aesthetic grounds, Mrs. Fishwick is the one who is largely responsible for the creation and maintenance of her daughter's wardrobe. As she sews a striped blouse for Tilda near the beginning of the play, Tilda proudly tells her that she bought the fabric for "Tuppence farthing at the Salvage Sale, and it'll wash and wear forever. Three yards I got. That's six-three the blouse."[35] Mrs. Fishwick points out that Tilda's consumerist calculation doesn't take into account her own labor: "You don't reckon the hooks and the thread and my time."[36] Tilda laughs this off, but her treatment of her mother as a personal seamstress and laundress is a recurring (if humorously handled) argument the women have throughout the play.

In Tilda's mind, the purpose of clothing is first and foremost to please herself, and part of that is distinguishing who she does *not* want to be. For instance, she has little patience for her mother's seemingly outdated ideas of propriety in dress, which is reinforced during conversations about Tilda's prized hat. Mrs. Fishwick exclaims, "I wouldn't have been seen with a thing like that on me head," and would instead opt for "A nice chip bonnet, trimmed with ribbon and tied under me chin, me hair neatly parted, and gathered in a chenille net behind—."[37] This type of bonnet and hairstyle would have been quite outmoded by the time the play premiered, emphasizing Mrs. Fishwick's preference for more conservative working-class feminine styling. Tilda responds contemptuously, "Oh, I dare say. You were in service; you had to say 'Yes' m—no' m.' (*Mimicking*) Catch me demeaning myself! Give me me independence—."[38] Stowell argues that "Tilda views her dress as a marker of social freedom" that "allows her to rise above the stigma of the housemaid's cap" her mother might have experienced.[39] While service and factory work both fell under the umbrella of working-class professions, the distinction Tilda makes here is notable: her flamboyant hat and stylish clothing align her clearly with the typical "factory girl," just as the outfit her mother preferred in her younger days identified her as a domestic worker. Both women are well aware that they exist "within a class system that reads dress as an easy indicator of social standing." [40] While Mrs. Fishwick's ideas about dress seem influenced by winning the approval (or at least avoiding the censure) of her social "betters," Tilda's clothing choices are "a badge of personal independence."[41] Tilda's discretionary income may be small, but

---

[35] Paston [Emily Morse Symonds], *Tilda's New Hat*, p. 8.
[36] Paston [Emily Morse Symonds], *Tilda's New Hat*, p. 8.
[37] Paston [Emily Morse Symonds], *Tilda's New Hat*, p. 9.
[38] Paston [Emily Morse Symonds], *Tilda's New Hat*, p. 9.
[39] Stowell, "Re[pre]senting Eroticism," p. 60.
[40] Stowell, "Re[pre]senting Eroticism," p. 60.
[41] Kaplan and Stowell, *Theatre and Fashion*, p. 168.

every piece of adornment represents money she herself has earned through her labor at the jam factory and is a deliberate statement of her own taste.

Marlis Schweizter argues that "Within the highly competitive world of London fashion in the 1890s and early 1900s, wearing a striking variation of an existing style was an effective strategy for attracting attention and raising one's social status."[42] Tilda certainly takes this approach: the hat in particular is "a symbol of self-indulgence, self-worth and sexuality" for her.[43] When Emerson remarks, "That's a handsome hat—good taste too," Tilda replies "Yes, whatever I has, I must have *good*. Nothing cheap and nasty for *me*."[44] She later asserts that even her "second-best hat with the parakeet trimming" is "better than most girls' best."[45] She encourages Daisy to invest in her looks too, no matter what Daisy's mother thinks is "genteel," demanding "You earn your own money, don't you?"[46] The plumed hat thus transcends its purpose as a mere accessory and becomes a symbol of Tilda's taste and economic independence.

Re-dressing Daisy gives Tilda (and Paston) further opportunities to discuss fashion and its functions. After Daisy expresses concerns about being made to "look fast" and flirtatious, Tilda responds by giving her an "objeck-lesson."[47] Kaplan and Stowell note that "In the process of remaking Daisy, Tilda [...] begins to take on the externals of Daisy herself" with a specific illustrative purpose.[48] Scraping her hair back severely, Tilda tells Daisy, "This is how you walk out with a chap. Fit to scare the motor-busses. Ever see a suffragette after a kick-up with the police-man? The latest fashions for 'Olloway, the new winter health resort. Votes for women!"[49] Tilda links Daisy's austere style with negative stereotypes regarding suffragettes and the women's prison, Holloway, to emphasize how her clothes—and their associations—might be off-putting to someone as small-minded and, frankly, misogynistic as Emerson. As Tessa Boase explains, "Last century's New Woman in her assertive straw boater (slightly masculine, undecorated, hard-edged) had produced the caricature of unmarriageable spinsters in trilbies."[50] However, women involved in suffrage efforts during the Edwardian era were actively

---

[42] Marlis Schweizter, "'Darn That Merry Widow Hat': The On- and Offstage Life of a Theatrical Commodity, Circa 1907–1908," *Theatre Survey* 50:2 (November 2009), p.198.
[43] Boase, *Mrs Pankhurst's Purple Feather*, p. 191.
[44] Paston [Emily Morse Symonds], *Tilda's New Hat*, p. 12.
[45] Paston [Emily Morse Symonds], *Tilda's New Hat*, p. 22.
[46] Paston [Emily Morse Symonds], *Tilda's New Hat*, p. 20.
[47] Paston [Emily Morse Symonds], *Tilda's New Hat*, p. 21.
[48] Kaplan and Stowell, *Theatre and Fashion*, p. 168.
[49] Paston [Emily Morse Symonds], *Tilda's New Hat*, p. 21.
[50] Boase, *Mrs Pankhurst's Purple Feather*, pp. 188-189.

trying to overcome this damaging image by enthusiastically embracing "large, fashionable hats" in order to be seen as "powerful *and* feminine."[51] Paston herself belonged to the Women Writers' Suffrage League and the London Women's Suffrage Society so it seems almost certain she would have known about the double meaning of such millinery.[52] By having Tilda reject a style previously associated with women's activism while promoting the large, flamboyant hat now subtly tied to suffrage, Paston introduces a subversive message regarding women's potential social and political power.

This slyly feminist thread of *Tilda's New Hat* was remarked upon by New Woman writer Ella Hepworth Dixon, who favorably reviewed the play in her column in *The Sketch*: "The ethics of the Modern Woman have permeated, it would seem, even the jam-factories of the East End, for in George Paston's sympathetic little play, 'Tilda's New Hat,' we have the whole theory of the solidarity of women put into dramatic form. [...] What is remarkable about the feminine dramatic work of the day is that in women's plays the female characters display sympathy and kindliness towards each other."[53] Here, Dixon not only praises the refreshing modernity of Paston's play, and particularly its deft portrayal of "the solidarity of women," but also suggests that Tilda's "sympathy and kindliness" are most clearly shown when she puts Daisy's romantic prospects before her own: instead of using her "fearful and wonderful hat" for her own gain, Tilda instead "makes one splendid effect" and "dresses up the forsaken maiden in her own finery."[54] In Paston's play, fashion becomes the medium through which the women reconcile and through which each gets what she wants; it operates as a means of constructing community as well as individual identity. Kaplan and Stowell agree that by the end of the play, Tilda's "triumph resides in her ability to live in a world without 'Rowmeos,' and the kinship she finds with both Daisy and her own mother."[55]

Not all contemporaneous reviews of *Tilda's New Hat* remarked as directly on fashion and feminism, but plenty responded approvingly on the working-class character "types" featured in the play. A review of the first staging in the London-based periodical *The Bystander* praised the "extraordinarily clever portraits of a mother and daughter," adding that "The characterisation and dialogue is instinct with the spirit and humour of the modern tenement

---

[51] Boase, *Mrs Pankhurst's Purple Feather*, p. 189.
[52] "George Paston."
[53] Ella Hepworth Dixon, "Woman's Ways," *The Sketch* LXIV, no. 825 (18th November 1908), p. 191.
[54] Dixon, "Woman's Ways," p. 191.
[55] Kaplan and Stowell, *Theatre and Fashion*, p. 168.

house."[56] Another review in *The Athenaeum* the following January declared it "a play that has flesh and blood in it, a study of low life in which the Cockney woman of the people is shown in her true colours, and a nice balance is kept between shrewishness and good nature. In 'Tilda's New Hat' George Paston gives us three excellent variants of this type—differentiated with the nicest skill by Miss Agnes Thomas, Miss Florence Lloyd, and Miss Sydney Fairbrother—as well as drama that reveals both the depths and shallows of human nature."[57] The perceived accuracy of Tilda as a "Cockney woman of the people" likely owed as much to the numerous journalistic and fictional representations of London's "factory girls" and "coster girls" in the 1880s-1900s, as the "flesh and blood" working-class women of 1908.

In the late nineteenth- and early twentieth-century popular press, working-class Londoners were identified and defined by their clothing in a number of ways. One important contribution to this corpus was Charles Booth's monumental survey of London, *Labour and Life of the People*. In Volume I (1889), social reformer Clara Collet contributed a chapter on "Women's Work," in which she reported her findings about the lives of working women in the East End. While such women were often painted with a broad brush, Collet draws distinctions within this group: "By the 'factory girl' is meant the lower grade of factory workers [...] who are in the majority in the jam factories, and who hold almost undisputed sway in the rope and match factories"—in other words, women like Tilda.[58] Collet then describes the behavior and appearance of "factory girls" in detail.

> She can be recognized on ordinary days by the freedom of her walk, the numbers of her friends, and the shrillness of her laugh. On Saturday evenings and Sunday afternoons she will be found promenading up and down the Bow Road, arm in arm with two or three other girls, sometimes with a young man, but not nearly so frequently as might be imagined. On those occasions she is adorned and decked out, not so much for conquest as for her own personal delight and pleasure, and for the admiration of her fellow women. She wears a gorgeous plush hat with as many large ostrich feathers to match as her funds will run to—bright ruby or scarlet preferred. [...]

---

[56] "The Ninth of November: In Town—And Also in the Country," *The Bystander* XX, no. 259 (18th November 1908), p. 316.
[57] "Drama," *The Athenaeum* no. 4240 (30th January 1909), p. 143.
[58] Clara Collet, "Women's Work," in *Labour and Life of the People, Volume I: East London, Second Edition*, ed. Charles Booth (London: Williams and Norgate, 1889), p. 472.

> She goes to penny gaffs if nothing better is offered her; she revels in the thrilling performances at the Paragon or the music halls.[59]

Several similarities between Collet's description and Tilda's characterization might be drawn here, including Tilda's own love of being "adorned and decked out [...] for her own personal delight and pleasure" and her "gorgeous plush hat" with ostrich feathers.[60] Tilda also expresses enthusiasm for music hall acts such as the duo Tennyson and O'Gorman and George Lashwood's song, "The Twi- Twi- Twilight," which she sings snippets of throughout the play.[61] As for other staged entertainments, she boldly states "I think Shikespeare's overrated," instead preferring the works of Hall Caine, who was an extremely popular novelist and dramatist at the time.[62] In short, Tilda's tastes in fashion, performance and literature align almost perfectly with that of the (stereo)typical factory girl.

Along with the insinuation about a certain level of moral laxity among women of London's lower classes, the description of their distinctive style is remarked on again and again in late-Victorian literature. Montagu Williams's 1893 book *Round London: Down East and Up West* dedicates a chapter to the famous East End matchgirls' strike of 1888 and provides an almost ethnographic study of the factory girls for his (presumably middle-class) readers, including similar details about dress: "Dress is a very important consideration with these young women. They have fashions of their own; they delight in a quantity of colour; and they can no more live without their large hats and huge feathers than 'Arry can live without his bell-bottom trousers."[63] Here, Williams refers to the Cockney character 'Arry, a personification of London's laboring classes created by *Punch* humorist Edwin James Milliken.[64] By alluding to this well-known archetype, Williams seems to suggest that 'Arry's female counterpart was just as distinctive in her clothing choices. Some of Collet's and Williams' observations about working-class style might have been a bit outmoded by 1908, but the fact remained that "huge, gorgeously trimmed hats [...] seem to have been a primary identifying feature

---

[59] Collet, "Women's Work," pp. 472-3.
[60] Collet, "Women's Work," p. 473.
[61] Paston [Emily Morse Symonds], *Tilda's New Hat*, p. 11, 14, 27-28.
[62] Paston [Emily Morse Symonds], *Tilda's New Hat*, p. 12.
[63] Montagu Williams, *Round London: Down East and Up West* (London: Macmillan & Co., 1893), p. 25.
[64] Drew D. Gray, *London's Shadows: The Dark Side of the Victorian City* (London: Bloomsbury, 2010), p. 86.

of London's East End factory workers."[65] Such hats undoubtedly reflected the staying power of the fashion, but also served as visual markers of class that underpinned widely-recognized (stereo)types of working-class women.

These "types" were further established in fictional treatments of London's slums and factory districts, and the female characters who inhabited them. Working-class girls, often generically named "Liza" or "Eliza," were featured in a number of 1890s texts, including the story of "Lizerunt" from Arthur Morrison's *Tales of Mean Streets* (1894), W. Somerset Maugham's novel *Liza of Lambeth* (1897) and William Ernest Henley's poem "'Liza," first published in *London Types* (1898).[66] Such texts drew on and reiterated contemporaneous reportage like Collet's and Williams' about East End women, including their dress and styling. For example, Henley's 'Liza "deems herself *a perfect lady*, / And proves it in her feathers and her fringe," though Henley also notes "Her boots are sacrifices to her hats, / Which knock you speechless—*like a load of bricks!*"[67] Maugham's Liza is likewise "crowned with feathers" and characterized by her bright clothes, "saucy retorts, her laughter, swagger and rowdy country-reel."[68] Jerome Hamilton Buckley points out that Richard Whiteing's 1899 novel *No. 5 John Street* also includes a similar character—this time named Tilda—who, "as far as her limited means will permit, delights in such garish plumage—her huge hat on its hook is the single wall-decoration in her room."[69] In creating her own Tilda, Paston likely owed something to these previous iterations of working-class girls in popular literature, and *Tilda's New Hat* was able to capitalize on the continued recognizability of this type. The feathered hat in particular remained a highly visible indicator of class status as well as suggesting other supposedly intrinsic class-based characteristics.

Like the hats described in earlier factual and fictional accounts, Tilda's is large and trimmed with several ostrich plumes. Feathers had been popular items of adornment for generations, but women's hats decorated with feathers, wings or even entire taxidermy birds, became increasingly popular

---

[65] Catriona M. Parratt, *More Than Mere Amusement: Working-class Women's Leisure in England, 1750-1914* (Boston: Northeastern University Press, 2001), p. 117.

[66] Jerome Hamilton Buckley, "The View from John Street: Richard Whiteing's Social Realism," *Victorian Perspectives: Six Essays*, edited by John Clubbe and Jerome Meckier (Newark: University of Delaware Press, 1989), p. 150-151. Though somewhat later, Eliza Doolittle in George Bernard Shaw's 1913 play *Pygmalion* is arguably also a version of the "Liza" type.

[67] William Ernest Henley, "'Liza," *Hawthorn and Lavender, with Other Verses* (London: David Nutt, 1901), p. 78.

[68] Buckley, "The View from John Street: Richard Whiteing's Social Realism," p. 151.

[69] Buckley, "The View from John Street: Richard Whiteing's Social Realism," p. 150.

in Britain in the late 1800s and continued to be all but ubiquitous through the 1910s. However, this feather boom also engendered fierce debate: feathers "were items of luxury and conspicuous consumption," but such ornaments began to be increasingly seen as cruel and vulgar.[70] This latter opinion was often explicitly tied to concerns about class and the trickle-down effect on fashion: it was assumed that fashionable women of means adopted new styles of plumes and that their example would then be followed by the masses, driving a vicious cycle of demand for more and different kinds of feathers.[71] By the time *Tilda's New Hat* premiered, environmentalists and animal rights campaigners had been working for decades to curtail the killing of wild birds for their feathers—in fact, a bill prohibiting the import of exotic plumage was brought before the House of Lords in May 1908—but the fashion for feathers was far from dead.[72]

Ostrich feathers were perpetual favorites due to their dramatic size, but by the late nineteenth century, most of these feathers were imported from ostrich farms in South Africa rather than being taken from wild birds. These plumes were then processed and prepared for sale by working-class and immigrant labor in the East End of London, "the commercial heart of the global ostrich feather trade."[73] In *Plumes: Ostrich Feathers, Jews, and a Lost World of Global Commerce*, Sarah Abrevaya Stein notes that "the hundreds of small feather manufactories that dotted London's East End were staffed principally by Jewish women and girls" and "as many as 2,000 boys and men and 20,000 girls and women were working in the trade at its peak."[74] Despite their ready availability, ostrich feathers were not necessarily affordable to the women who produced them or to those who worked in other East End manufacturing jobs. Tilda acknowledges to Daisy that she only has her own "long black feathers" because, like many other working-class girls, she belongs to a "feather club."[75] Such clubs were made up of groups of women who collectively contributed to the cost of feathers and then took turns wearing them, or who paid installments towards purchasing the feathers outright.[76] The feather club relied on the social and economic collaboration of

---

[70] Robin W. Doughty, *Feather Fashions and Bird Preservation: A Study in Nature Protection* (Berkeley: University of California Press, 1975), p. 60.
[71] Doughty, *Feather Fashions and Bird Preservation*, p. 14.
[72] Boase, *Mrs Pankhurst's Purple Feather*, pp. 190-191.
[73] Sarah Abrevaya Stein, *Plumes: Ostrich Feathers, Jews, and a Lost World of Global Commerce* (New Haven: Yale University Press, 2008), p. 56.
[74] Stein, *Plumes: Ostrich Feathers, Jews, and a Lost World of Global Commerce*, pp. 57, 63.
[75] Paston [Emily Morse Symonds], *Tilda's New Hat*, p. 20.
[76] G. B. Burgin, "Talks with a Nurse," *The Idler* vol. VIII, no. XLVI (November 1895), p. 333.

women in order to benefit each individual woman—yet another illustration of the play's "theory of the solidarity of women."[77]

These feathers and the hats they adorned were therefore part of a complex tapestry of women's work and identity. Near the end of *Tilda's New Hat*, Paston pulls together many of these threads as Tilda turns her attention from the aesthetic qualities of her own hat to the wider social and economic opportunities presented by millinery. In addition to letting Daisy borrow her prized ostrich feather hat for the weekend, Tilda offers to hold on to Daisy's plain straw hat and "trim it up so's you wouldn't know it" by adding "a couple of yards of ribbon—three-three at the Salvage Sale—and a paradise mount—and a bunch of cherries—and a cut steel buckle."[78] All of these embellishments were commonly used in millinery at the time, so it would not be inconceivable that such a hat actually existed; indeed, many similar hats are depicted or described in contemporaneous trade magazines and in women's periodicals such as *The Lady's Realm* and *Harper's Bazaar*. Tilda jokingly tells Emerson that Daisy's hat is her "first commission in the millingery [sic] line. I shall be setting up in the Bond Street next, and cutting out the Countesses."[79] Bond Street was (and is) renowned for its upscale fashion boutiques, while the competition from "the Countesses" that Tilda says she will be "cutting out" is likely a reference to the extravagant millinery shop run by Countess Fabbricotti on nearby South Molton Street from 1905-1909.[80] So even in jest, Tilda's possible millinery aspirations are quite high.

This scene also gestures at an alternative interpretation for the play's titular headpiece: perhaps Tilda's new hat is not only the plush feathered hat that we see her arranging at the beginning of the play, but also (or instead) the "new" hat Tilda starts creating for Daisy. The former hat reflects prevailing fashions of the day while also representing a quintessential East End style; the latter points to the potential for professional success in millinery and social advancement into the mercantile class. The play's ending does not give any indication of what Tilda will actually do next, except reiterating her reconciliation with both Daisy and her mother—and giving her one last chance to proclaim, "Don't my hat look lovely?"[81]

With its quietly feminist message and unusually detailed portrayals of working-class women, *Tilda's New Hat* is worthy of further examination in scholarship and in the classroom. In particular, Paston's witty commentary on

---

[77] Dixon, "Woman's Ways," p. 191.
[78] Paston [Emily Morse Symonds], *Tilda's New Hat*, p. 22, 23.
[79] Paston [Emily Morse Symonds], *Tilda's New Hat*, p. 23.
[80] Boase, *Mrs Pankhurst's Purple Feather*, p. 142-144.
[81] Paston [Emily Morse Symonds], *Tilda's New Hat*, p. 26.

Edwardian dress and popular culture presents a number of useful inroads for students and scholars of the period as well as those interested in the history of theater, gender, class and fashion in Britain. At its inception, *Tilda's New Hat* not only reflected the past and present of London's working women—and their styles—but was also prescient of what was to come. In August 1911, just a few years after Paston's play premiered, female workers at confectionery, jam, and other factories in the London borough of Bermondsey initiated a massive strike to negotiate higher wages and better working conditions.[82] Writing in 1935, historian George Dangerfield looked back on these strikes and the women strikers: "Many of them, dressed in all their finery, defied the phenomenal temperature with feather boas and fur tippets, as though their strike were some holiday of the soul, long overdue."[83] It isn't hard to imagine Tilda—or someone very like her—among their ranks.

Bibliography

Primary Sources

Plays

Paston, George [Emily Morse Symonds]. *Tilda's New Hat*. London: Samuel French, Ltd., 1909.

Poetry

Henley, William Ernest. "'Liza." *Hawthorn and Lavender, with Other Verses*, p. 78. London: David Nutt, 1901.

Books & Book Chapters

Collet, Clara. "Women's Work." *In Labour and Life of the People, Volume I: East London, Second Edition*, pp. 406-477, edited by Charles Booth. London: Williams and Norgate, 1889.

Williams, Montagu. *Round London: Down East and Up West*. London: Macmillan & Co., 1893.

Periodical Articles

Burgin, G. B. "Talks with a Nurse." *The Idler* Vol. VIII, no. XLVI (November 1895), pp. 329-336.

---

[82] Ursula de la Mare, "Necessity and Rage: The Factory Women's Strikes in Bermondsey, 1911," *History Workshop Journal*, 66.1 (Autumn 2008), p. 62.

[83] George Dangerfield, *The Strange Death of Liberal England* (Stanford: Stanford University Press, 1997), p. 216.

Dixon, Ella Hepworth. "Woman's Ways." *The Sketch* LXIV, no. 825 (18th November 1908), p. 191.

"Drama." *The Athenaeum* No. 4240 (30th January 1909), pp. 143-144.

Heilgers, Louise. "Delightful Dresses at Daly's." *The Play Pictorial* X, no. 61 (1907), pp. 106-107.

"The Ninth of November: In Town—And Also in the Country." *The Bystander* XX, no. 259 (18th November 1908), pp. 316-17.

"Theatres." *The Solicitors' Journal and Weekly Reporter* LIII, no.18 (27 February 1909), p. ii.

Secondary Sources

Books & Book Chapters

Boase, Tessa. *Mrs Pankhurst's Purple Feather: Fashion, Fury and Feminism—Women's Fight for Change*. Minneapolis: Aurum Press, 2018.

Breward, Christopher. *Fashioning London: Clothing and the Modern Metropolis*. Oxford: Berg, 2004.

Buckley, Jerome Hamilton. "The View from John Street: Richard Whiteing's Social Realism." In *Victorian Perspectives: Six Essays*, edited by John Clubbe and Jerome Meckier, pp. 145-156. Newark: University of Delaware Press, 1989.

Dangerfield, George. *The Strange Death of Liberal England*. Stanford: Stanford University Press, 1997.

Doughty, Robin W. *Feather Fashions and Bird Preservation: A Study in Nature Protection*. Berkeley: University of California Press, 1975.

Gray, Drew D. *London's Shadows: The Dark Side of the Victorian City*. London: Bloomsbury, 2010.

Kaplan, Joel H. and Sheila Stowell. *Theatre and Fashion: Oscar Wilde to the Suffragettes*. Cambridge: Cambridge University Press, 1994.

Kortsch, Christine Bayles. *Dress Culture in Late Victorian Women's Fiction: Literacy, Textiles, and Activism*. London: Routledge, 2009.

Majer, Michele. "Staging Fashion, 1880-1920." In *Staging Fashion, 1880-1920: Jane Hading, Lily Elsie, Billie Burke*, edited by Michele Majer, pp. 18-47. New York: Bard Graduate Center, 2012.

Parratt, Catriona M. *More Than Mere Amusement: Working-class Women's Leisure in England, 1750-1914*. Boston: Northeastern University Press, 2001.

Rappaport, Erika Diane. *Shopping for Pleasure: Women in the Making of London's West End*. Princeton: Princeton University Press, 2000.

Schweitzer, Marlis. *When Broadway Was the Runway: Theater, Fashion, and American Culture*. Philadelphia: University of Pennsylvania Press, 2009.

Stein, Sarah Abrevaya. *Plumes: Ostrich Feathers, Jews, and a Lost World of Global Commerce*. New Haven: Yale University Press, 2008.

Journal Articles

de la Mare, Ursula. "Necessity and Rage: The Factory Women's Strikes in Bermondsey, 1911." *History Workshop Journal*, 66.1 (Autumn 2008), pp. 62-80.

Rose, Johnathan. "The History of Education as the History of Reading." *History of Education* 36:4-5 (July-September 2007), pp. 595-605.

Schweitzer, Marlis. "'Darn That Merry Widow Hat': The On- and Offstage Life of a Theatrical Commodity, Circa 1907–1908." *Theatre Survey* 50:2 (November 2009), pp. 189-221.

Stowell, Sheila. "Re[pre]senting Eroticism: The Tyranny of Fashion in Feminist Plays of the Edwardian Age." *Theatre History Studies* 11 (1991), pp. 51-62.

Weig, Heidi. "Amateur Theatricals and the Dramatic Marketplace: Lacy's and French's Acting Editions of Plays," *Nineteenth Century Theatre and Film* 44. 2 (2017), pp. 173–191.

Online Database Articles

Brittenham, Rebecca. "George Paston." In *Late-Victorian and Edwardian British Novelists: Second Series.* Edited by George M. Johnson. Dictionary of Literary Biography Vol. 197. Gale, Detroit, 1999. *Gale Literature Resource Center* (accessed March 1, 2022). https://link.gale.com/apps/doc/H1200008274/LitRC?u=udel_main&sid=bookmark-LitRC&xid=4a0204d8.

"George Paston." *Orlando: Women's Writing in the British Isles from the Beginnings to the Present.* Cambridge: Cambridge University Press, 2020. https://orlando.cambridge.org/profiles/pastge.

Figure 3.2: Edwardian fashion plate, depicting two fashionably dress women in picture hats.

Commons.wikimedia.org, public domain.

Tilda's New Hat

George Paston
Author of "Feed the Brute," etc, etc

—

COPYRIGHT, 1909, BY SAMUEL FRENCH, LTD.

—

CAUTION. — Amateurs and professionals are hereby warned that "Tilda's New Hat," being fully protected under the copyright laws of the United States, Is subject to royalty, and any one presenting the play without consent of the publisher will be liable to the penalties by law provided. Application for the right to produce "Tilda's New Hat" must be made to Samuel French, 28-30 West 38th Street, New York City.

All rights reserved.

NEW YORK	LONDON
SAMUEL FRENCH	SAMUEL FRENCH, LTD.
PUBLISHER	26 SOUTHAMTON ST.
28-30 WEST 38TH STREET	STRAND

Produced at His Majesty's Theatre, 1909.
ORIGINAL CAST.

CHARACTERS.

MRS FISHWICK

TILDA, her daughter
(employed in a Jam Factory)

DAISY MEADOWS

WALTER EMERSON (a Bill Printer)

MISS AGNES THOMAS

MISS FLORENCE LLOYD

MISS SYDNEY FAIRBROTHER

MR. NORMAN PAGE

SCEANE. — Room in a tenement house in Clerkenwell.

TIME. — The present.

TILDA'S NEW HAT

SCENE. – *Living room in a tenement house. The usual cheap furniture but with a certain attempt at smartness in the shape of antimacassars,[84] mats under the lamp and under the vases of artificial flowers. Christmas number pictures on the walls, and picture postcards of the chimneypiece, propped up against the mugs and photograph frames. The is a door opening on the passage, R.C., and a floor leading to the bedroom, L. A window, L.C. Fireplace, L. under the window is a large, old-fashioned bureau or chest of drawers, on which are a looking-glass and some ornaments. There is a couch R. A square table, which should stand in the centre of the room, has been pulled near the fireplace, leaving plenty of floor space, the chairs standing with their backs to the wall, except two armchairs, one on each side of the table. On one of the small chairs a concertina or accordion is lying.*

MRS FISHWICK *sits by the table, L., working on a striped cotton shirt. She is a hard-featured woman of the grim and gloomy Puritan type, with drab hair and drab clothes.*

TILDA *lolls on the couch, R., showing a plentiful display of ankle. She is a dark, showy-looking girl, with black hair puffed out over her ears, and coming low over her forehead in a large fringe or three sausage curls.[85] She wears a fawn skirt and a bright blue satin blouse, very fussily made, with a large cape collar of white crochet lace. Round her collarless neck is a string of big pearl beads, and her dress is fastened by a large gilt brooch. In her ears are large earrings. She wears a number of bangles on her wrists. She is engaged in pinning black ostrich feathers onto a huge black velvet or satin hat.*

MRS. F. (*querulously*). Why ever don't you sew them feathers in, Tilda. The pins'll never hold.

TILDA. Ow, I haven't the patience. When I've pinned 'em, you can tack 'em in...I wish you'd hurry up with that blouse, ma. I want to wear it Monday.

---

[84] A small cloth usually draped over the backs and arms of chairs to prevent soiling of the upholstery. Often made of linen or lace, sometimes with decorative elements such as embroidery. Named after the macassar oil which men used in their hair during the Victorian and Edwardian periods.

[85] A type of ringlet curl very fashionable during the Victorian and Edwardian periods.

MRS. F. (*grumblingly*). This stuff is just like a bit of ticking.[86] Breaks all me needles. Wherever you got it, I don't know –

TILDA. Tuppence farthing at the Salvage Sale, and it'll wash and wear forever. Three yards I got. That's six-three the blouse.

MRS. F. You don't reckon the hooks and the thread and my time.

TILDA. Ow, your time! (*Laughs.*) That's worth a fat lot ain't it?...(*Looks at the clock.*) You'll have to run out in a minute and get some bloater paste[87] for tea.

MRS. F. Why? What for? Who's coming?

TILDA. Mr. Emerson said he might look round on his way to the Institute.

MRS. F. That why you got your best blouse on? You going to walk out with him to-morrow?

TILDA. (*snubbingly.*) Maybe I shall, maybe I shan't.

MRS. F. I thought he was Daisy Meadow's chap. (*Virtuously.*) When *I* was a gal, I didn't take other gals' chaps away.

TILDA. Couldn't get 'em, I suppose.

MRS. F. Get a dozen if I wanted 'em! Ah, things was very different in my young day. *We* didn't stand a soldier drinks, and pay him a bob a kiss.

TILDA. (*firing up.*) And no more don't I. I hope I look higher than a Tommy.

MRS. F. (*disparagingly.*) With your looks you'll have to take what you can get. Why, you ain't got no figure. When I was your age, I had a bust like a band-box.

TILDA. I like to see my own feet.

---

[86] A type of sturdy, tightly woven cloth, traditionally used to cover mattresses.
[87] A kind of fish paste, no longer produced, made from herrings that had been left to 'bloat' and go gamey, then smoked and made into a thick spread.

Tilda's New Hat

MRS. F. And you ain't got a ha'porth o' colour. *My* cheeks were that rosy you could see 'em half a mile away.

TILDA. I should have floured 'em.

MRS. F. Yes, you *would*, and that's why your skin's so coarse. *My* skin was like satin. Ah, dear! I only had to pick and choose.

TILDA. It's a wonder you didn't pick someone better than father.

MRS. F. Your father was all right when I married him.

TILDA. (*pertly.*) Then it was *you* who drove him to the drink?

MRS. F. (*rising.*) I'll drive you somewhere if you give me any more sauce. (*Looking at hat.*) I wouldn't have been seen with a thing like that on me head. A nice chip bonnet, trimmed with ribbon and tied under me chin, me hair neatly parted, and gathered in a chenille net behind –

TILDA (*contemptuously.*) Oh, I dare say. You were in service; you had to say "Yes 'm – no 'm." (*Mimicking.*) Catch me demeaning myself! Give me me independence –

MRS.F. If you like to call it independence, and the boss always after you with the fine-book.

Bell rings.

TILDA. Just run down and see whether that's Mr. Emerson – or the milk.

MRS. F. More like one of them Mulligan kids ringing the bell for a lark. I'll wring his neck if I catch him.

MRS. FISHWICK *exits,* R.C. TILDA *hums a tune, and tries on her hat before the glass.* MRS FISHWICK *returns, followed by* WALTER EMERSON. *He is a tall, pale, dark young man with an austere, earnest expression, and is dressed in a semi-artistic, semi-socialist style. He wears a loose, dark tweed coat, a bright red tie, a rather low collar, and a Trilby hat, which he takes off as he comes into the room. He speaks carefully, and rather mincingly, pronouncing most of his h's. The cockney accent, of the genteeler sort, is still quite perceptible. His manner is serious and soulful, and he gazes yearnfully at* TILDA. *When seated, he twists his legs into knots, and pulls his fingers, as if he were trying to crack the joints.*

MRS. F. It 'taint the milk. It's only Mr. Emerson. (*Sits*, R.)

EMERSON. Good-afternoon, Miss Fishwick. I hope you are very well. I'm sorry Mrs. Fishwick should have had the trouble –

TILDA. Oh, that's all right. (*To* MRS. FISHWICK.) Best put your bonnet on and fetch the paste now.

EMERSON (*perfunctorily*). But cawn't I –

TILDA. No, no, sit down, Mr. Emerson. It does ma good to get a bit of a run.

MRS. F. So *you* think. (*Gets up and puts on an old cricket cap.*) Wait til *you've* got various (*sic*) veins in both legs.

Exit MRS. FISHWICK, L.

EMERSON (*sitting*, R. *Tilda sits on the table*, L.). I took the liberty of bringing you this little volume round, Miss Fishwick. *Five Minutes with the Finest Authors*. There are some beautiful pieces in it. (*Gets up and gives her the book. Sits down on chair*, R. *of the table.*)

TILDA (*carelessly*). Oh, thanks. I like a nice tale meself.

EMERSON (*earnestly*). But don't you think, Miss Fishwick, we ought to read something *instructive*, if it's only for five minutes in the day?

TILDA. Can't say it's a long-felt want –

EMERSON. Now I'm going to try and persuade you to join our Mutual Improvement Debating Society.[88] Ladies are admitted as honorary members. Of course, we don't expect 'em to speak.

TILDA. Oh, don't you? I should speak fast enough if I wanted to.

---

[88] Such educational societies, along with free lectures and courses on diverse topics, formed part of the drive for self-improvement that still characterized British society during the Edwardian period. Here, Symonds is poking fun at Emerson's patronizing earnestness towards his female acquaintances.

EMERSON (*taking out a paper*). I brought the silllibus (*sic*) of our winter session –

TILDA. Silly bus! There is plenty of them about. (*Laughs.*)

EMERSON (*with a pained smile*). I don't think you quite understand. This is a kind of prospectus, gives you the list of lectures, with discussions to follow. Tennyson, Browning, Carlyle, Rusking[89] (*sic*) –

TILDA (*obviously bored*). I've seen Tennyson with O'Gorman at the Met.

EMERSON. *Lord* Tennyson, the powet! (*sic*)

TILDA. Oh, I'm not taking any! I don't want to improve nobody, nor I don't want to be improved meself.

EMERSON (*rising*). Well, now. I think there's nothing like a little *culture*. I've dipped into nearly every volume of the Hundred Best Books, and read some of 'em right through.

TILDA. Chase me!

EMERSON. But I know there's several more books I ought to read before I can call myself a *reely* (*sic*) cultured man. (*With enthusiasm*). Oh, Miss Fishwick, I should so like to form your mind.

TILDA. Form me mind! What's the matter with me mind? Lectures indeed! I got lectures enough when I was a kid.

EMERSON (*with a tolerant smile*). Oh, well, p'raps the dramatic society is more in *your* line. I'll send you tickets for our next show. Part one – Scenes from Hamlet. They've let *me* in for Hamlet.

TILDA. You print the programmes for nothing, don't you? Let's see, it was Rowmeo (*sic*) last time I went. (*Sweetly.*) *You* was Rowmeo.

---

[89] Alfred, Lord Tennyson (1809-1892), Poet Laureate, 1850-1892; Robert Browning (1812-1889), English poet; Thomas Carlyle (1795-1881), Scottish essayist; John Ruskin (1819-1900), English writer and art critic. Together, this group represents a collective of great Victorian thinkers, a concept which would later be satirized by writers such as Lytton Strachey in his ironic biography of nineteenth-century icons, *Eminent Victorians* (1918).

EMERSON *smirks.*

Oh lor, how I did yawn!

EMERSON. Yawn?

TILDA. I think Shikespeare's overrated. Give me 'All Caine.[90]

EMERSON (*distressed*). Oh, Miss Fishwick!

TILDA. Ain't you going to do anything more lively? A c—n song, or a cake walk?

EMERSON. Part two – Recitations by Members of the Society. They've let me in for two.

TILDA. Two!

EMERSON. The Forsaken Veteran and the Little Stowaway. I happen to have the book in my pocket. P'raps you wouldn't mind hearing me me words.

TILDA. Righto. But you've got to play milliner's dummy for me first. I can't get these feathers to me mind.

Puts hat on his head and surveys him thoughtfully. He maintains a dignified attitude.

Yes, those front feathers might be a bit higher. Ah, that's a lot more stylish. Haw, haw, you look got up for 'Amlet now.

EMERSON. Don't make me ridiculous.

TILDA (*pricks her finger*). Oh, damn the pin!

EMERSON (*starts*). I beg your pardon.

TILDA. Oh, it just slipped out. 'Taint s' often I use language before a gentleman. (*Takes hat off.*)

---

[90] Hall Caine (1853-1931) was an extremely popular novelist, dramatist and critic, known for tackling racy subjects such as adultery, divorce and women's rights.

EMERSON (*with solemn admiration*). That's a handsome hat – good taste, too.

TILDA (*complacently*). Yes, whatever I has, I must have *good*. Nothing cheap and nasty for *me*.

EMERSON (*holds out his book and points to the place*). If you don't mind. Top of the page.

TILDA. Oh, all right. Chuck it off your chest.

TILDA *sits on the table, while* EMERSON *stands, centre.*

EMERSON. The Forsaken Veteran.

He strikes an appropriate attitude and bursts into recitation with theatrical expression and exaggerated gesticulation. He should try to "act" the piece with all the vices of the cheap elocutionist.

"Old and feeble, scarred and maimed, a poor old man
    who has fought and bled
In the greatest victories of English arms – I found
    unsheltered and unfed.
The faded ribbons upon his breast, the emblems of
    honour and valiant deed,
Are all the comforts that cheer him now, in his 'oary
    age – *hoary* age and his *hour* of need.
He does not speak with a bitter thought of his treat-
    ment now at his country's hand;
He makes no complaint – complaint – (*Dries up.*)

TILDA (*who has been fidgeting with hat*). Complaint – complaint. (*Hastily looks for place in book and rattles off.*)

"For his heart is loyal to his Emperor King and his

native land."

EMERSON (*starting line afresh*).

> "He makes no complaint, for his heart is loyal to his
> Emperor King and his native land.
> He simply points to his shabby coat, the spot where
> the ribbons adorn his breast,
> 'That's all I'm worth,' he will only say,
> That's all he's worth; we can guess the rest."…

TILDA yawns loudly and openly.

EMERSON (*stopping short*). I'm afraid I'm boring you, Miss Fishwick.

TILDA (*comfortably continuing her yawn*). Ow, no but p'raps you'd better keep the rest till the night. That'll leave me something to look forward to.

Organ strikes up outside

TILDA (*excitedly rushing to the window, and speaking through the last two lines*). Ow, there's an orgin! (*Looking out.*) He's got a monkey. What's that they're playing? Oh, it's "Twi-Twilight" – that's a good song. Ever hear Lashwood[91] sing it? Goes something like this. (*Begins first humming and then singing in provocative style.*)

> "In the twi-twilight,
> Out in the beautiful twilight –
> They all go out for a walk, walk, walk,
> A quiet old spoon and a talk, talk, talk.
> That's the time they long for,

---

[91] George Lashwood (1863-1942) was a popular Edwardian singer, known as the Beau Brummell of the music halls.

>   Just before the night.
>
>   And many a grand little wedding is planned
>
>   In the twi-twilight."

(Dances with high kicks etc.)
The music suddenly gets more rapid.

TILDA. Oh, lor, now we're off!

Whirls round quicker and quicker. EMERSON *has stood leaning forward and gazing at her with devouring eyes. As the music suddenly breaks off,* TILDA *stops whirling, giddy and breathless, and sways towards* EMERSON. *He makes a sudden spring forward, catches her in his arms and kisses her.* TILDA *yields for an instant, then gives him a ringing slap on the face, breaking away as she does so.*

TILDA (*breathlessly*). Call yourself a gentleman – is that the way to treat a lady?

EMERSON (*sobered*). I'm sorry – I forgot myself – just for the moment. I apologize. You'll overlook it, Miss Fishwick?

TILDA (*with a show of resentment*). Don't make too sure of that.

EMERSON. Don't ne hard-hearted, Miss Fishwick. If you *will* look so fetching, how can a poor feller behave himself? (*Insinuatingly.*) You ought always to wear blue, you know. Blue's your colour. (*Touches her sleeve.*)

TILDA. D'ye want a cut lip as well as a thick ear? (*Goes down,* L.)

EMERSON. Do you know what I came for to-day?

TILDA. Came to make a nuisance of yourself.

EMERSON. Came to ask if you'd walk out with me to-morrow? It'ud be lovely in Alexandra Park.

TILDA. Thought you walked out with Miss Meadows.

EMERSON. I suppose a gentleman needn't always walk out with the *same* young lady.

TILDA (*with decision*). He would if he was mine.

EMERSON. Yours would never want a change. Will you – Tilda. (*Tries to take her hand.*) You know I'd do anything in the world for *you*.

TILDA. Would yer? Then p'raps you'll just run round to the cobbler, and fetch my shoes home. (*Crosses,* L.) It's the little man at the corner of East Street – *you* know.

EMERSON. Of course – delighted. (*Following her.*) But first – won't you give me –

TILDA. Oh, the money – I shall forget my own head next; they'll be tenpence to pay – here's a shilling. (*Takes it off mantlepiece.*)

EMERSON (*reproachfully*). You know I didn't mean – (*Takes her outstretched hand with the money, and draws her towards him. She hangs back, coyly.*) Little floweret!

TILDA (*wriggling*). Oh, go on! Get away closer.

EMERSON (*bending towards her*). Just one.

    MRS. FISHWICK's *voice is heard outside in an altercation.*

MRS. F. Better go 'ome and sleep it off, dear.

TILDA (*quickly pushing Emerson away before he can kiss her*). There's ma back again.

EMERSON (*turning away*). Oh, dem!

Enter MRS. FISHWICK

MRS. F. (*speaking into passage*). I may be no lady, but I don't go to bed with me boots on. (*Shuts door.*)

TILDA. Ma, Mr. Emerson's going to run to the cobbler's for my shoes. That'll save you going out again, won't it?

MRS. F. (*sitting down,* R.). You wouldn't get me down them stairs again in a hurry. I wish you could feel my legs.

EMERSON (*at door*). *Au revoir,* as we say in France.

TILDA. So long.

Exit EMERSON.

MRS. F. (*inquisitively*). What you sent him out for? You know your shoes won't be ready afore Monday.

TILDA (L.). Things was getting *warm* – and I wanted a bit of time to think. I don't hardly know me own mind.

MRS. F. If he says "snip" you'd better say "snap." You ain't everybody's money.

TILDA. Glad to be rid of me, wouldn't you?

MRS. F. Yes, and sorry for the man that gets you.

TILDA *takes up striped cotton shirt and examines it critically.*

TILDA. These sleeves ain't set in the same. And there's no draw-tape. And you ain't boned the collar-band. And I told you I wanted white hooks, and you've been and put black ones.

MRS. F. Better make the next yourself. Wonder how long that'll hold together.

Knock at the door.

TILDA. Whoever's that? Come in.

Enter DAISY MEADOWS. *She should be a nice, gentle-looking little girl with hair brushed off her forehead. She is very plainly but tidily dressed in a dark shirk, with a cotton or flannelette shirt. She should wear a flat hat, simply trimmed with ribbon, and perhaps a motor scarf twisted round her neck. She is the sort of girl who looks innocent, yielding and childlike, but has an obstinate will where her own desires are concerned, and generally contrives to get her own way. At this moment she looks pale and agitated, as though she had something on her mind.*

DAISY (*speaking with a nervous tremor in her voice, yet with a certain quiet determination*). Oh, good afternoon.

MRS. F. Oh, it's Miss Meadows. Good afternoon.

DAISY (*in same tone*). I wanted to see you, Tilda.

TILDA (*with assumed carelessness*). Well, here I am, as large as life. Sit down, won't you?

DAISY (*looking at* MRS. FISHWICK). No, I mustn't stop. I'd – I'd got something to say to you, Tilda, but it'll do another time. Or p'raps you could come out for a stroll.

TILDA (*looking at* MRS. FISHWICK, *who settles herself more comfortably in her chair*). Ma – you know you've got to wash out them tan stocking of mine for to-morrow. Why ever don't you go and rub 'em out now. There's plenty of boiling water, and you'll have nice time before tea.

MRS. F. (*with a feeble attempt at rebellion*). But you've got a clean pair in the drawer. There's only a little hold where you always kick your stockings out. I could soon darn that over –

TILDA (*picking up kettle*). I told you I wanted the pair with the clocks for to-morrow. Here, take the kettle. (*Hands it to* MRS. FISHWICK.)

MRS. FISHWICK *takes kettle, and slowly rises.*

TILDA. Get a move on.

MRS. F. (*crossing to the door*, L., *with sarcasm*). Any more little jobs you've got for me?

TILDA (*coolly*). Not just now. Mebbe I shall think of some after tea.

MRS. F. (*going out* L., *grumbling*). I wonder who you'll get to wash and mend for you when I'm gone. Don't suppose I shall be here much longer. Perhaps I shall have an easier time when I'm an angel. (*Exit.*)

TILDA (*turning to* DAISY *with a defiant air*). Well, what is it?

DAISY *comes down, and stands* R.C., *facing* TILDA, *who sits on table swinging her legs.* DAISY *is evidently strung up, and speaks in a quiet tense voice, with a tremor suggestive of the feeling she is holding in. As the scene proceeds, her hold on herself gradually relaxes, and she grows more agitated until the tears come.* TILDA *preserves an air of impudent coolness.*

DAISY. Mr. Emerson's been here.

TILDA. He has.

DAISY. He tea'd with you *last* Saturday.

TILDA. He did.

DAISY. And he saw you home from the Social Monday night.

TILDA. That's so.

DAISY. You're going to walk out with him to-morrow.

TILDA. I am.

DAISY (*bitterly*). I wonder you ain't ashamed.

TILDA (*turning on her*). Well I *ain't*.

DAISY (*with increasing agitation*). We've been walking out for months. Everybody knew he was my chap –

        TILDA *gives an aggravating little laugh.*

But of course, if a girl throws herself at a young feller's head –

TILDA. Oh, shocking! I shouldn't have thought it of you, Daisy.

DAISY (*beginning to melt, and subsiding into chair,* R.). And we wasn't only walking out. We'd settled to get married as soon as he got his rise. (*Sniff.*) We'd begun to get the home together. I'd bought a pair of cut-glass dishes. (*On last word her voice rises to a sob.*)

TILDA (*who has been whistling and swinging her legs, suddenly stops, as if impressed in spite of herself*). Oh – I didn't know that. I did not know you'd begun to get the home together.

DAISY. I'd begun to make my underthings. And now they'll be wasted. I couldn't wear 'em for common. (*Sob.*)

TILDA (*getting off table, and crossing to her*). Oh, for Gawd's sake, don't keep snivelling. Mr. Emerson ain't the only kipper on the barrer. There's plenty of fellers about.

DAISY. But not like Walter. He's so intel-intellectual. They think all the world of him at the Institute; and he said – he said he was going to form my mind. (*Sob.*)

TILDA (*sotto voce*). You've got to get one first.

DAISY. And so gentlemanly! Always takes the outside of the pavement when walking – always lifts his hat at parting and keeps his nails so beautiful –

TILDA (*slowly, with lingering regret*). Yes, no-one can say Mr. Emerson ain't quite the gentleman.

DAISY. Used to call me his little floweret –

    TILDA *turns her head sharply.*

Ain't been near me for a fortnight now. (*Chokes. Then with change of tone.*) Of course, I know you're more stylish than what I am. Mother's kept me that strict. I dare say (*with a curious glance*) – If *I* had a hat like that –

TILDA. Hoh, you think Mr. Emerson comes after me hat and feathers, do you?

DAISY. Yes, and your dressy blowse, and your padded hair.

TILDA. It *ain't* padded…Well, why don't you get yourself up more stylish? Look at that hat now! You can't expect a superior young feller like Mr. Emerson to walk out with a hat like that.

DAISY (*plaintively*). I ain't got no long black feathers.

TILDA. Why ever don't you belong to a feather club, same as me and the other girls?

DAISY. Mother don't think it's nice.

TILDA. Nice be blowed! You earn your own money, don't you? You should have brought your ma up the same as I've brought mine…Give me something with a bit of dash about it. This hat now – (*Putting it on.*)

DAISY. Ow, it's *beau*tiful! I should *love* to wear a hat like that.

TILDA. Would yer? Try it on. Here, take the pin out.

> DAISY *removes her hat, and* TILDA *puts the big hat on* DAISY's *head.*
>
> Lor, don't it look a sight on your little flat head? Why ever don't you fluff your hair out a bit?

DAISY. Mother don't think it's genteel.

TILDA. Genteel be blowed! Come on. Sit right here. Hold still a minute. (*Takes hairpins out of* DAISY's *hair, and brings forward front part.*) Now, *my* hair – I just roll it around me fingers, pop the combs in, and it sticks out like wires. Now then – did I pull you? All done by kindness. Will you have it one curl, or two? This is going to be a little bit of all right.

DAISY. Don't make me look fast, dear.

TILDA (*standing back*). There, that's something like – though I do say it. Run and look at yourself…I'll show you something. (*Quickly takes out her own combs or pins, talking all the time, and flattens her front hair back, leaving her forehead bare.*) This is how you walk out with a chap. Fit to scare the motor-busses. Ever see a suffragette after a kick-up with a policeman? The latest fashions for 'Olloway, the new winter health resort. Votes for women![92]

---

[92] This refers to the increasingly militant tactics of Emmeline Pankhurst's Women's Social and Political Union, known as the Suffragettes, who campaigned for female enfranchisement in the years leading up to the First World War. Many suffragettes were imprisoned for militancy in Holloway Prison and, in 1909, the Scottish artist and author

DAISY. Oh, you are a cure.

> *By this time* TILDA *should have finished business with hair.*

Look at me now. There's an objeck-lesson (*sic*) for you.

DAISY (*giggling*). Oh Tilda, you do look a guy.

TILDA (*putting the big hat on* DAISY *again*). Now the *blowse* is all wrong. Wherever did you get that measly little blowse?

DAISY. Mother chose it.

TILDA (*sniffs*). So I should have guessed. What do you think of mine?

DAISY (*with enthusiasm*). It's perfectly *sweet*. Real dressy, and yet so chaste. I should *love* to wear a blowse like that.

TILDA. Would yer? You can try it on if you like. Here, help me off with this. Hurry up.

DAISY *quickly unhooks* TILDA's *blouse.* TILDA *takes it off, disclosing a pink woven petticoat-body. She helps* DAISY *into it, talking all the time.*

It's too big for you, but it'll go over your own. Lor ain't you slight. Wherever do you put your dinner? Hold still. Blessed if you don't wriggle like a flea on a hot plate. Blow these hooks – wherever ma gets 'em! – and these eyes have got the squint. There – that's the last. Now run and look at yourself in the glass.

DAISY (*running across to glass on wall,* L., *and surveying herself*). Ow, I *do* look nice!

TILDA (*putting on striped cotton shirt her mother has been working at*). Bit of style about you now. That's a dressy blouse, I will say. (*Looking at* DAISY's *hat.*) This hat of yours ain't such a bad *shape*. I could trim it up so you wouldn't know it.

DAISY (*eagerly*). Could you?

Marion Wallace Dunlop went on hunger strike, a tactic which was subsequently adopted by other suffragette campaigners.

TILDA (*hesitates, looking from one hat to the other*). I – er – let's see now – p'raps – (*With a sudden outburst of generosity.*) Tell yer what it is, if you'll leave that old thing behind, I'll lend you my hat to take you over Sunday.

DAISY (*with rapture, yet hardly able to believe in her own good fortune*). Oh, Tilda, you wouldn't really! You can't mean it? *Reely?* (*Crestfallen*). But I ain't got a blowse fit to go with it.

TILDA (*impatiently*). Then set to work and make one, or get your ma to do it.

DAISY (*sadly*). I ain't got a pattern.

TILDA. You don't seem to have got much. Never seen such a little bit of gawd-'elp-us. I – (*Hesitates, eying the smart blouse, and looking down at her own shirt.*) I – um – I'll – no, I wo – (*With another splendid outburst of generosity.*) Tell yer what it is – I'll lend you that blowse to take the pattern off of.

DAISY (*with agonized longing*). Oh, Tilda, but I reely *couldn't* –

TILDA (*mimicking her*). Ow, Daisy, but you reely *could*...It's all right. I can wear my pink velveteen, and my second-best hat with the parrakeet trimming. It's better than most girls' best.

DAISY. Oh, you are an old *dee-ar*! (*Kisses her. With sudden recollection.*) But whatever shall I say to mother?

TILDA. Tell her to go and put her head in a bag – the old blighter. (*Takes concertina from hook on wall.*) Didn't you say you'd been practising for the Choral. What you going to sing?

DAISY. "It's Only a Beautiful Picture – in a Beautiful Golden Frame."

TILDA. Tune the old cow died of. (*Makes noises with the concertina.*) Let's have a verse.

Knock, and enter EMERSON *quickly.*

EMERSON. The man says your shoes won't be ready till – oh – (*Stops short in dismay.*) Oh, beg pardon – I didn't see – (*Jaw drops at finding himself between the two girls, and he looks as though he meant to bolt.*)

TILDA (*easily*). Miss Meadows has just called round to have a practice for the Choral.

EMERSON (*in great confusion and discomfort*). Daisy – Miss Meadows – For the moment I didn't hardly – (*Looking from one to the other.*) Why – you – you've been and changed –

TILDA (*readily and fluently, gong up to back*). I'm going to trim up Daisy's hat, and I've lent her mine to take her over Sunday. It's my first commission in the Millingery (*sic*) line. I shall be setting up in Bond Street next, and cutting out the Countesses. (*Takes length of pink ribbon out of drawer, and comes down to* EMERSON, *who has been standing, R., with his eyes glued on* DAISY, *who sits, L., looking self-conscious and happy.* TILDA *takes him by the shoulders, and pushes him down.*) Sit down, Mr. Emerson, I want my dummy again.

Puts DAISY's *hat on his head, and twists ribbon round it, tying it into big loose bow in front.*

There, with a couple of yards of this ribbon – three-three at the Salvage Sale – and a paradise mount – and a bunch of cherries – and a cut steel buckle, yon wouldn't know this hat again. (*Backs a little to see the effects of her handiwork, and laughs.*) What price Rowmeo now!

EMERSON (*with dignity*). Have you quick done, Miss Fishwick?

TILDA (*removing the hat*). Yes thanks. Mr. Emerson, you make a first-class dummy.

EMERSON (*looking with undisguised admiration at Daisy*). I should hardly have known you, Daisy. You ought always to dress like that. Blue's your colour.

DAISY *bridles.*

TILDA (*draws a wail out of concertina*). You going to the Choral, Mr. Emerson? Daisy is going to sing, "It's Only a Beautiful Picture – In a Beautiful Golden Frame." Come on, Daisy, let's have a verse.

DAISY (*clearing her throat*). Ow, I couldn't, I've got such a shocking cold.

EMERSON (*encouragingly*). Yes, give us a verse, Daisy – that's my favourite song.

TILDA (*boisterously*). Oh, go on! Don't be bashful. Goes something like this, don't it? (*Makes a weird flourish with concertina*).

DAISY (*gently*). I think I could do it best alone, Tilda.

TILDA. Oh, all right – all right.

Stands centre, behind the other two, gently waving concertina in time to the song. EMERSON *sits, with his eyes on* DAISY. *During the last lines, he should mark time with his head or hat, as though moved.* DAISY *sits demurely on her chair, with her feet crossed, and her hands clasped, and sings in a careful, childlike manner, with a little thread of a voice.*

DAISY (*sings*) –

> "If those lips could only speak,
> > If those eyes could only see,
>
> If those beautiful gowlden tresses
> > Were there in realitee.
>
> If I could but take your hand,
> > As I did when I took your name –
> > > (*With sentiment.*)
>
> But it's only a beautiful Pic-ture
> > In a beautiful gowlden frame."

As she stops, there is a faint sigh of pleasurable emotion from the other two.

TILDA (*throwing off the touch of sentiment into which she has been betrayed*). That's something like, ain't it? Knocks spots out of Shakespeare and the improving lecture.

DAISY. Oh, I think Shakespeare's *sweet*. (*With glance at Emerson.*) And I do *love* the lectures.

EMERSON (*jumping up, and crossing to her*). I've got the new syllabus here. I'll show you; Tennyson – Browning –

DAISY. Tennyson's *my* favourite. I can say the Queen o' the May right through.

TILDA. You'll stop to tea, both of you. We've got some bloater paste, and ma'll make us some buttered toast.

DAISY. No, I must be getting home. I told mother I was only running out to the post.

EMERSON (*eagerly*). I'll see you home.

DAISY (*stiffly*). Oh, pray don't trouble, Mr. Emerson. I'm used to walking alone.

EMERSON. It's hardly a step out of my way.

TILDA (*to Daisy*). You'd best *sew* them feathers in, Daisy. They're a bit wobbly, and whatever you do, don't let 'em get a spot of rain.

DAISY (*solemnly*). I'd been drowned myself sooner. Good-bye, old dear. (*Kissing* TILDA *enthusiastically, first on one cheek, then on the other.*) I do think it's so sweet of you. (*Kissing.*)

TILDA (*impatiently*). Oh, all right – that'll do. (*Pushing her aside.*) Good-bye Daisy, good-bye Mr. Emerson. (*Going up.*) I don't think I'll join your Mutual Improvement Society, thank you all the same. I'm afraid of being improved right away.

EMERSON (*coldly*). Good-evening, Miss Fishwick, I think it's a pity when young ladies have no desire for culture. Now Daisy is beginning to form a very correct taste. She can always perceive the clever bits I point out to her, can't you Daisy?

DAISY (*looking up at him*). Yes, Walter. Good-bye, Tilda. (*This should be spoken sweetly over her shoulder.*)

EMERSON *holds open the door for* DAISY, *who peacocks out, followed by* EMERSON. TILDA *stands still for a moment. Then dashes down concertina, and calls.*

TILDA. Ma, you can come up now.

Enter MRS. FISHWICK

MRS. F. (*grumbling*). Time I did. (*Catches sight of* TILDA *and starts.*) Lord a'mighty, whatever you been and done to yourself?

TILDA (*shortly*). Trying out a new style of hairdressing.

MRS. F. (*hanging tan stocking from chimney-piece, and beginning to busy herself with the tea-things*). Better not try that too often, or you'll crack the glass. You couldn't help being born homely, but you needn't go and turn yourself into a reg'lar Aunt Sally.

TILDA (*looking out of the window*). There they go! Don't they look a pair of sillies? Never noticed his leg wasn't straight before. (*Sniffs.*) And ain't his shoulders round? (*Sniffs.*) Don't my hat look lovely? (*Sniffs.*)

MRS. F. (*by table cutting bread*). What you keep sniffing for? I told you you'd catch cold if you left off them warm knickers.

TILDA (*coming down to fireplace*). Is that old kettle boiling? (*Takes up kettle. Then gives a yell, and drops it with a clatter.*) Ow! (*Begins to cry.*)

MRS. F. (*starting*). Sakes alive! What you done now?

TILDA. B-burnt me hand with the beastly old kettle.

Rushes across to MRS. FISHWICK, *flops down on the floor, and hides her face in her mother's lap.*

MRS. F. (*Unexpectedly displaying real maternal tenderness and sympathy*). There, there, it ain't so bad as all that. Let mother see. Why, it ain't even a bit red.

Sob from TILDA

Don't you cry now, my pretty. There's plenty more better than him. You'd get a dozen any day if you held up your finger. The smartest, handsomest girl in Chapel Street, though I say it. There ain't another to hold a candle to you. There – there –

TILDA (*suddenly springing up, and dashing away the tears*). I ain't 'owling for him, so don't you think it. He's a lot too cultured for me. If he ever tries to improve my mind again, I'll improve his face so as his own mother won't know it. With his 'Amlets and his Rowmeos!

MRS. F. (*soothingly, taking up teapot to fill it from the kettle*). No, *you* don't want no Rowmeos; what you want is a cup of mother's tea. (*Begins to hum in cracked voice as she fills teapot.*)

"In the twi-twi-light,

Out in the beautiful twi-light."

TILDA *pricks up her ears at the tune. She is standing up centre. As she looks across at her mother, the hurt, angry look dies away, and her own broad jolly smile begins to dawn.*

"They all go for a walk, walk, walk,

A quiet old spoon and a talk, talk, talk,

TILDA (*begins to laugh and joins in the song*).

"That's the time they long for,

Just before the night,

And many a grand little wedding is planned

In the twi-twi-light."

Dances, while MRS. F. *waves the teapot in one hand, and the lid in the other, and looks on admiringly.*

CURTAIN *descends on* DANCE.

Second CURTAIN *rises on* TILDA *still dancing, and* MRS. FISHWICK *waving the teapot.*

Figure 3.3: Edwardian fashion plate, depicting a fashionable Edwardian hat with feathers.

Commons.wikimedia.org, public domain.

Chapter 4

Refashioning spinsterhood: Edith Sitwell's singular style in British interwar literary culture

Emily Priscott
Independent scholar

Abstract: Chapter Four moves us from the Edwardian era of the previous piece into the 1920s, two distinct eras separated by the First World War. Set against the backdrop of debates about so-called "surplus women" that greeted the 1921 census, this chapter uses a case study of the modernist poet and eccentric Edith Sitwell to examine discourses around both spinsterhood and 1920s dress culture. While female poets, novelists and painters of the period were encouraged to cultivate stylish, photogenic publicity profiles, Sitwell adorned herself in flamboyant costumes, fashioning an image which reinforced her distinctiveness and, like her singleness, subverted the standards of normative femininity.

Using the personal diaries and correspondence of her wide circle of literary friends, such as Virginia Woolf, Siegfried Sassoon and Robert Graves, this chapter examines the ways in which Sitwell's unconventional sense of style, so closely allied to her poetic sensibility, reinforced the perception of her as an eccentric spinster within interwar literary society. Close readings of poems such as "The Sleeping Beauty" and "Elegy on Dead Fashion" offer further insight into what Sassoon termed Sitwell's "poetic plumage" and its relationship to her often outlandish appearance.

Keywords: Edith Sitwell, spinsterhood, singleness, 1920s fashion, interwar literary culture, modernist poetry, Virginia Woolf, Siegfried Sassoon, Cecil Beaton.

***

In 1926, the young photographer Cecil Beaton photographed Edith Sitwell at his family's home in Bayswater, concocting a temporary studio in his sister's bedroom, rigged up with artfully arranged drapery. In the slightly dingy, low-quality light of the finished pictures, Sitwell cuts a doomed, romantic figure, the spray of lilies in her hands emblematic of Victorian aestheticism, her shiny gold shroud giving a twist of Baroque opulence. It was as if someone had dragged Millais' Ophelia from her watery grave and laid her out in a makeshift suburban studio: not the most media-friendly image for the times, perhaps, but as a piece of personal propaganda it perfectly captured Sitwell's style and helped to establish Beaton as the most sought-after photographer of his day.

Figure 4.1: Edith Sitwell, 1926.

Cecil Beaton Archive, (c) Condé Nast.

Edith Sitwell (1887-1964) is known as a series of famous images, from Beaton's photographs to Wyndham Lewis' 1925 vorticist portrait. Her most recent portrayal, by Lia Williams in Terence Davies' Siegfried Sassoon biopic *Benediction* (2022), evokes a queenly, formidable yet shrinkingly sensitive aesthete, dramatic and commanding yet professing herself "deeply wounded"[1] by criticism: in Davies' presentation, she resembles the "electric eel"[2] to which she once compared herself, toweringly tall and willowy, clad in long flowing robes and head-swathing turban. Sitwell's dramatic sense of style brought the fantastical into the everyday, crossing boundaries between formal/informal, and perhaps public/private, without ever adapting much to her surroundings. She had always been a singular figure, resisting the pressure to conform to contemporary trends or beauty standards. During her childhood and adolescence, she had differentiated herself from her overbearing family by developing a distinctive personality, which seemed to resist external social pressures to conform.

By the end of her life, Sitwell's myth would almost eclipse her art; yet her poetry was a part of this self-fashioning which, like her image, sought to challenge orthodox notions of the self. Like the imagist poet Hilda Doolittle (known as H. D.), her particular style of modernism was decorative and, though succinct in composition, ornamental in its colorful imagery,[3] embodying what Sassoon described in his diary as her "fantastic plumage."[4] Despite their very different poetic styles, of all her close friends Sassoon seemed to have the most profound impact on her work, with Sitwell herself writing that he was "the only person to have ever done anything at all for my poetry."[5] As Sassoon would observe in many private scribblings in his diary over the course of their friendship, Sitwell's poetry is as ornamental as she herself was, rich in delicate, decorative imagery which frequently evokes the natural world through artifice and stylized surfaces. Illustrating her allegiance to Symbolist poets such as Baudelaire and Swinburne, both Sitwell's poetry and her highly original sense of style link her to an older, aestheticist tradition, while still supporting her status as an avant-garde modernist.

---

[1] *Benediction*, dir. Terence Davies, 2022.
[2] Richard Green, *Edith Sitwell: Avant Garde Poet, English Genius* (London: Virago, 2011), p. 6.
[3] Sandhya Kimberley Lachmansingh, "'Fashions of the Mind:' Modernism and British Vogue Under the Editorship of Dorothy Todd," (MPhil diss., University of Birmingham, 2010), p. 4.
[4] Siegfried Sassoon, *Journal*, 27 Dec. 1921-13 July 1922 (MS Add.9852/1/18).
[5] Green, *Edith Sitwell*, p. 235.

Yet despite achieving critical acclaim in her own lifetime, by the 1960s, when Movement poets such as Philip Larkin were in ascendance, she was deeply out of fashion. She seemed somehow out of step with the times, the poetic trend for logical positivism making her playful, colorful work seem overly ostentatious and somehow undemocratic. In the words of her biographer, Richard Greene, "She was a flamboyant, combative aristocrat" [...who] achieved a dazzling degree of originality in life and art. [But] there is a mystery about this individuality – how to explain a woman who [...] will not submit to comparison?"[6] Perhaps, over the years, her eccentric character and unique appearance eclipsed her achievements as a poet. Yet as Greene has written, "Her [...] eccentricities [...] were aspects of a struggle to define a meaningful life against the conventional standards of conduct for a woman born under the reign of Queen Victoria," her striking and unconventional style a "direct repost to prevailing standards of feminine beauty."[7]

As Mary Ellen Roach and Joanne Eicher argue in their essay "The Language of Personal Adornment, "dressing oneself can be an aesthetic act."[8] Both dressing and personal display are aesthetically pleasurable, but they are also social, a form of visual communication that contains multiple meanings about gender, class, sexuality and race. For Edith Sitwell, personal adornment was an act of defiance and a means of expressing her individuality. Her appearance, as Victoria Glendinning notes, "was a realization of her dream-self,"[9] part of her quest for creative freedom, the price of which she saw as "permanent resistance."[10] "My face," she wrote in a letter to the dancer Beryl de Zoete in 1956, "awful though it may be, is the only one I've got, and is my copyright, as is [my poetry]."[11] Sitwell's individuality was a fight for her own survival, a creative gasping for air "rooted in the desolation of her family life."[12]

Born into an eccentric, aristocratic family in 1887, the eldest of three siblings, Sitwell was always desperate to break away. While socially and economically privileged, she had spent a strange childhood living between her family's large house in rural Scarborough and their Derbyshire estate,

---

[6] Green, *Edith Sitwell*, pp. 5-6.
[7] *Selected Letters of Edith Sitwell*, ed. Richard Greene (London: Virago Press, 1998), p. xi.
[8] Mary Ellen Roach, and Joanne Bubolz Eicher, "The Language of Personal Adornment," in *The Fabrics of Culture: The Anthropology of Clothing and Adornment*, ed. Justine M. Cordwell and Ronald M. Schwarz (New York: De Gruyter Mouton, 2011), p. 7.
[9] Victoria Glendinning, *Edith Sitwell: A Unicorn Among Lions* (London: Faber and Faber, 2013).
[10] *Selected Letters of Edith Sitwell*, Richard Green (ed), p. xi.
[11] *Selected Letters of Edith Sitwell*, Richard Green (ed), p. 383.
[12] Green, *Edith Sitwell*, p. 4.

Renishaw, with a remote father and cruel alcoholic mother, the latter of whom, Sitwell would later confess "made my childhood and youth a living hell."[13] She was close to her younger brothers, Osbert and Sacherverell, (also poets, with whom she would occasionally collaborate), yet was also understandably jealous of her mother's unconcealed preference for her sons. Imprisoned for fraud in 1915 after accruing huge gambling debts and falling in with a con artist, Lady Ida Sitwell had always adopted a callous, combative attitude towards her daughter which, if she could summon the energy after hours of drinking expensive French brandy in bed, sometimes erupted into physical violence. Her daughter's idiosyncratic appearance did not help matters.

When she was twelve years old, Sitwell later recalled, "it was noticed that my thin body stooped slightly, in a deprecating and rather frightened way," revealing a curvature of the spine and weak ankles which would require correction from a pair of weighted orthopedic boots and a back brace, which she called the "Bastille." At night, her governess locked her legs into a "tightly walled [...] cage," a nose-truss for "cartilaginous deformities" providing additional embarrassment and discomfort during the day.[14] Cultivated at least partly as a steely camouflage for shyness and reticence, Sitwell's flamboyant image could be seen as an act of resistance to this kind of interference, a glittering suit of armor to protect her against further humiliation. In a 1962 interview for the *Daily Mirror*, Sitwell described her first act of sartorial defiance, recalling it as a defining moment of separation from the other girls she knew:

> When I was young I was made to wear tweeds and oval hats and fluffy pale pink and blue in the evening and I hated them, but when I was eighteen I was given £4…I went to a sale and bought a long black velvet dress with long sleeves. Everyone was quite shocked and horrified. For in those days young girls simply didn't wear black velvet. I realised at once [its] shock value and knew I was right to look different from the other girls because I was different and individual.[15]

Later, in the 1920s, and daringly for the time, she painted her nails silver and mother-of-pearl, wore huge rings, bracelets and necklaces, sweeping black, floor-length dresses and large hats and headdresses. As Glendinning writes, "she accentuated her uncontemporary looks, and presented herself in her

---

[13] Green, *Edith Sitwell*, p. 13.
[14] Green, *Edith Sitwell*, p. 40.
[15] *Daily Mirror*, 7th September 1962.

own image."¹⁶ She also claimed to be the inspiration for the "crane-tall Jane" of her poem, "Aubade," taken from her 1923 collection *Bucolic Comedies*, whose lank, toneless "cockscomb-ragged hair" rendered her a "cockscomb flower that none will pluck."¹⁷

This image was prescient, with its undercurrent of thwarted sexuality. Sitwell never married and was, in the parlance of her time, one of the "surplus women" whose matrimonial chances had apparently been dashed by the Great War. As Virginia Nicholson has written, "Thousands of women born between 1885 and 1905, who unquestionably saw marriage as their birthright, [had] it snatched from them by the four bloodiest years in human history."¹⁸ The 1921 census showed that there were roughly 1,750,000 single women living in Britain, and while the war had only deepened an existing population imbalance, it felt like part of its legacy of trauma. As Katherine Holden has argued, women's experiences, their dreams and expectations of life, cannot be explained through statistics alone. The media-led moral panic that characterized much of the newspaper coverage about the census figures showed that pressure to marry only increased in response to women's dwindling chances, contributing to what Holden has called an "aggressively married and heterosexual"¹⁹ climate, in which both living alone and living with a female companion were heavily stigmatized.

There is no evidence, however, that Edith Sitwell ever regarded marriage as her "birthright." When war broke out in 1914, she was already set apart from the expectations that governed the lives of most young, well-bred women. Having spent the previous few years living in Paris with her governess and companion Helen Rootham, it does not appear that either she or her parents put much effort into finding her a suitable husband. She felt more inclined to believe that poetry was her destiny, and with her mother in prison by 1915 and her father wrapped up in his books and landscape gardening, neither was well placed to argue.

While there was a higher proportion of single women in the population as a whole during the 1920s, ideas about single identity itself were starting to change. As Hope Howell Hodgkins has written, singleness among women was more common than it had previously been, yet the concept of spinsterhood

---

[16] Glendinning, *Edith Sitwell*.
[17] Edith Sitwell, "Aubade," *Collected Poems* (London: Duckworth, 1931), p. 177.
[18] Virginia Nicholson, *Singled Out: How Two Million Women Survived without Men After the First World War* (London: Penguin Books Ltd., 2007), Kindle Edition, p. x.
[19] Katherine Holden, *The Shadow of Marriage: Singleness in England, 1914-60* (Manchester: Manchester University Press, 2007), p. 7.

now seemed dated, redolent of a vanished Victorian past.[20] The new type of single woman was a world away from the stereotype of the dreary spinster, who was perceived as drably-dressed and "dowdy."[21] In the years following the First World War, a new, more progressive type of single woman was usurping spinsters in the popular imagination, who was fashionably dressed, independent and slightly transgressive.[22]

All of this served to link women's fashions to modernity itself during the 1920s, a phenomenon which publishing houses were eager to capitalize on with their galleries of stylishly attired women writers. During this period, perceptions of single women were split between flappers and spinsters, two archetypes of single womanhood which were almost diametrically opposed. While the flapper represented progress and modernity, the spinster was a familiar character, deeply rooted in the British psyche. In terms of national archetypes, they could not have been further apart, yet both provided ways of interpreting the "problem" of single women.

As the fashion historian Elizabeth Wilson has observed, it is easy to fall back on clichés and generalizations when discussing the link between fashion and social change.[23] The rise of flapper style following the First World War is a prime example of this, with simplistic assertions of made about post-war fashions symbolizing women's "emancipation." In fact, the years immediately following the First World War witnessed a large-scale attempt to reverse many of the social and economic freedoms that women had experienced during the war (from the implementation of marriage bars across many industries to media-led moral panics about single women); yet, despite this, the huge alterations to women's dress reflected deeper, subtler changes.

While this did not justify a belief in a wholesale transformation in women's status, it did signify that *something* had changed, and while, as the critic D. J. Taylor has written, "full-scale economic autonomy [...] lay some way off [...] the Modern Girl was still capable of provoking outrage in the minds of the people she knocked up against."[24] The new fashions of the 1920s, the bobbed or shingled hair, make-up and shorter, looser skirts, reflected new ideas about women's place in society. Their increased participation in traditionally male areas of employment during the war (with many taking jobs as bus

---

[20] Hope Howell Hodgkins, *Style and the Single Girl: How Modern Women Re-Dressed the Novel, 1922-1977* (Columbus: The Ohio State University Press, 2016), p. 52.
[21] Hodgkins, *Style and the Single Girl*, p. 71.
[22] Hodgkins, *Style and the Single Girl*, p. 52.
[23] Elizabeth Wilson, "Explaining it Away," in *Fashion Theory* (Routledge, 2020), p. 15.
[24] D. J. Taylor, *Bright Young People – The Rise and Fall of a Generation: 1918-1940* (London: Vintage Books, 2008), pp. 44-5.

conductors, shipyard laborers and munitions workers, among other roles), had had a noticeable impact on what they wore, with freedom of movement often taking precedence over a ladylike appearance. For many women, slacks, overalls and knickerbockers became "essential workwear during the war,"[25] and skirts were shorter and more tailored. Loosely belted coats, cardigans and neat blouses replaced tightly-laced bodices, and the scarcity of fabric dyes (the chemicals of which were redirected into the war effort) meant that blacks, browns and whites came to dominate many women's wardrobes. With many families in mourning for husbands, sons and lovers, it chimed with the mood of the times.

While many women lost their jobs to returning soldiers in 1918, a new spirit of independence was perceptible, and the flapper image was part of this. While women were more likely to read about the flapper craze in the popular press than they were to adopt the daringly short tunic dresses and heavy make-up, the flapper personified the spirit of her age. Young, unmarried and frequently to be seen at nightclubs and dancehalls, she symbolized emancipation and modernity.

Within this context, the spinster represented the female "other," a means of embodying problematic female traits which "define[d] the limits of normative feminine behaviour."[26] As Holden has written, characteristics associated with spinsterhood cut across class, yet far from forming a coherent image, they were often contradictory. Prevailing stereotypes could be opportunistic, adapting themselves to different circumstances as if spinsters could be held responsible for whatever female ills society was disposed to pin on them. Because of this they varied ingeniously, casting spinsters simultaneously as "silly, gossipy, affected, sentimental, foolish, fussy and eccentric; or downtrodden, pathetic and spineless [...] Dominating, severe, gaunt or ridged, bitter or frustrated."[27]

While modern single women made "spinsterhood" seem outmoded, as we shall see, many of Edith Sitwell's friends and acquaintances interpreted her personality through the lens of at least some of these perceived character traits. While Sitwell's singleness was itself unexceptional, something about her personality seemed to evoke an outmoded form of spinsterhood. Her extravagant sense of style and her "formidable" personality cast her as an eccentric, singular character, and made her singleness seem as much a part of her identity as her poetry and dress.

---

[25] Daniel Milford-Cottam, *Edwardian Fashion* (Oxford: Shire Publications, 2014), p. 59.
[26] Holden, *The Shadow of Marriage*, p. 101.
[27] Holden, *The Shadow of Marriage*, p. 4.

During the Victorian period, spinsters had been seen as either "pathetic or saintly figure[s],"[28] objects of pity as well as ridicule or disapproval. Yet they had also fulfilled a need in British culture for public-spirited, dedicated women of "good works," Florence Nightingale figures, who would offer themselves up to good causes to compensate for the arid disappointment of their personal lives. As psychological theories gained traction after the First World War, however, these spinsterish traits became more pathologized, an acknowledged symptom of sexual repression.[29] Even spinsters' apparent lack of style was seen as a pathological exhibit, as much a symptom of their singleness as its cause.

To discourage women from accepting spinsterhood too easily, doctors, psychologists and advice columnists frequently made virulent attacks on single women's "emotional abnormality," warning that domestic relationships between women both encouraged lesbianism and posed a threat to the institution of marriage.[30] Even feminist writers such as Vera Brittain, Rebecca West and Stella Brown wrote disparagingly of spinsters, seemingly regarding them as an embarrassment to the cause. While Richard Greene minimizes its significance to her life and art, Sitwell's singleness heavily influenced how she was perceived by many of the people who knew her, whose understanding of her personality and appearance was linked, in their minds, to her marital status.

Both Sitwell's singleness and her personal appearance created an impression of assertive individuality and independence: there was a nexus between them which, though not directly related, worked to create a character. With her highly individualistic sense of style, she certainly could not be characterized as dowdy, yet neither was she conventionally beautiful or feminine. Both her prickly spinsterhood and idiosyncratic sense of taste seemed like legacies of the "bastille," the flowing robes and cowled headdresses — the latter inspired by Henry VII "whom I resemble most strongly"[31] — swathing her fragile body in a sort of decorative shell. Whatever the cause, however, Sitwell's personality conformed to what the social anthropologist Margaret Adams would later refer to as single women's "psychological integrity," by which she meant well-defined personal

---

[28] Holden, *The Shadow of Marriage*, p. 4.
[29] Alison Oram, "Repressed or Thwarted, or Bearer of the New World? The Spinster in Inter-War Feminist Discourse," *Women's History Review*, vol. 1., no. 3 (1992), pp. 413-433, p. 415.
[30] Holden, *The Shadow of Marriage*, p. 4.
[31] *Daily Mirror*, 29th March 1961.

boundaries and a strong streak of independence, traits which were often applauded in men yet stigmatized in women.[32]

Sitwell's own attitude to spinsterhood was ambivalent. While her paternal aunt Florence had been a formative influence on her during her childhood, young Edith had also seen her as an example to be avoided at all costs. Unmarried and intensely religious, Florence had never had much opportunity to forge an independent existence and, as Greene puts it, "seem[ed] always to have lived on the edge of other, more powerful lives."[33] This cannot be said for her niece, however. As a young adult, she was painfully aware that Florence's fate could have been her own, and yet everything about her personality rejected this kind of confinement. In 1905 aged 18, she wrote a short, evocative piece about "two maiden ladies" like Florence, "Standing outside a stuffy bookshop lost in speculation."[34] In rich, fantastical prose, Sitwell conjures up a surreal, mythical world in which these two prosaic spinsters transform into enchanted goddesses, their drab, colorless clothing blossoming into exquisite plumage, which becomes part of the decorative landscape itself:

> The elder of these wore a long dress which burst into a thousand leaves and waterfalls and branches and minor worries. She had hair of the costliest gold thread…and this, when undone, fell in waterfalls until it nearly reached her feet. But at this moment, it was crammed beneath a hat which seemed to have been decorated with all the exports of our colonies – ostrich feathers, fruits, furs and heaven knows what besides.[35]

As a piece of poetic writing it was significant, an early example of the kind of imagery she would use in later poems (which Greene calls "modernist fairy tale[s]"[36] such as "The Sleeping Beauty" (1923) and "Elegy on Dead Fashion" (1926), in which she uses clothing metaphors as symbols of female identity. "The hat," as Greene has noted, "is telling. Edith herself feared the life of the maiden aunt and believed that the spiritual potential of a woman like Florence was wasted in a modern age obsessed with buying and selling."[37] It appears to symbolize a conflict between the "natural" and social selves, in which the unique individual is subsumed into a constricting social role.

---

[32] Emily Priscott, *Singleness in Britain, 1960-1990: Identity, Gender and Social Change* (Delaware: Vernon Press, 2020), p. 6.
[33] Green, *Edith Sitwell*, p. 15.
[34] Green, *Edith Sitwell*.
[35] Green, *Edith Sitwell*, p. 16.
[36] Green, *Edith Sitwell*, p. 178.
[37] Green, *Edith Sitwell*, p. 178.

Written around the same time as Edith bought her black velvet dress, this early prose piece also reveals her dawning awareness of the link between individual identity and personal style, something that she would weaponize seemingly as part of her strategy for avoiding Florence's fate. For Sitwell's frail, willowy frame, clothing would become a form of battle dress, which jarred with the increasingly commercialized relationship between fashion and literary culture.

During the 1920s, an explicit link was formed between contemporary fashions and modernity, which allied chic, modish young women to ideas about social progress; as Hodgkins has written, "dress style became a potent literary weapon to dissociate female identity from marriage."[38] Traditionally, women writers were closely aligned with their marital status in the eyes of the public. While married authors such as Elizabeth Gaskell and Elizabeth Barrett Browning were always professionally referred to as "Mrs," until the early twentieth century unmarried women writers often adopted male pseudonyms. By the 1920s, however, writers such as Jean Rhys and Dorothy L. Sayers (both of whom were actually married) used their own names as part of their literary identities, and were accordingly regarded as honorary single women. While Sayers and Rhys were universally referred to as "miss" in reviews and publicity material, Virginia Woolf had discarded her maiden name of Stephen following her marriage to Leonard Woolf in 1912, her marital status becoming as much a part of her literary identity as Gaskell's and Barrett Browning's had been.[39] Marriage, then, was still considered a cornerstone of women's selfhood, and Rhys and Sayers' decision to keep their maiden names appeared to preserve their status as individuals in their own right rather than extensions of their husbands.

This intricate interplay between literary and marital status reflected deeper concerns about female identity. During the interwar period, literary culture became increasingly commercialized, as publishing houses sought to capitalize on the expansion of celebrity culture following the First World War. In this market-driven context, it became more important than ever for authors to cultivate the right image. For women writers, this meant being fashionably dressed for publicity photographs, in a way that was pleasingly feminine yet also suitably "literary." As Vike Martine Plock has written, "What helped to sell a book was its author's image and reputation,"[40] a cross-over between fashion and literary culture as exemplified by *Vogue* editor Dorothy

---

[38] Hodgkins, *Style and the Single Girl*, p. xx.
[39] Hodgkins, *Style and the Single Girl*, p. 51.
[40] Vike Martina Plock, *Modernism, Fashion and Interwar Women Writers* (Edinburgh: Edinburgh University Press, 2019), p. 3.

Todd, who aimed to elevate fashion by setting it alongside elite art forms. "Seeking to demonstrat[e] the similarities between…fashion and the other art forms of literature, drama, art and architecture," Todd commissioned many well-known, literary authors to write articles for *Vogue*, including Edith Sitwell, Virginia Woolf, Richard Aldington and Aldous Huxley during her brief tenure as editor between 1922 and 1926.[41]

Of course, the concept of celebrity authorship was not new, and nor was the relationship between literature and fashion. Clothing had played an important role in shaping the literary personalities of image-conscious authors such as Lord Byron and Oscar Wilde, whose dandyish attire had personified the link between literature, aesthetics and decorative art.[42] However, the advent of mass media technologies and the birth of a conspicuous commodity culture during the early twentieth century enabled a more strategic dissemination of celebrity culture,[43] and in the years leading up to the First World War literary personalities such as the Decadent poet Olive Custance had taken full advantage of this emerging climate. As would later be the case with Edith Sitwell, "photography and self-fashioning were central to her publicity strategies,"[44] and Custance's carefully choreographed publicity stills regularly appeared in society magazines such as the *Tatler*. Accompanied by captions such as "A pretty poet," Custance contrived to appeal to aristocratic Edwardian standards of beauty through her conspicuously cultivated, "romantic" appearance, a style which Sitwell would willfully flout a decade later. Yet both understood the power of image, and by the 1920s Sitwell would be well placed to exploit the new media potential for self-publicity.

However, while women writers were under increasing pressure to look stylish and distinctive in addition to producing original work, too much individuality was frowned upon in an increasingly competitive commercial industry. Because of this tension, a critical engagement with fashion brings into focus many of the complex debates around authorship and celebrity that characterized the interwar period, highlighting the often "antagonistic relationship between assimilation and differentiation."[45] According to Plock,

---

[41] Lachmansingh, "Fashions of the Mind, p. 1.
[42] Margaret D. Stetz, "Fashioning Modern and Modernist Authorship: Rebecca West in the 1920s and 1930s," in *Fashion and Authorship*, ed. Gerald Egan (Palgrave Macmillan, 2020) pp. 255-272, p. 262.
[43] Vike Martina Plock, *Modernism, Fashion and Interwar Women Writers*, p. 7.
[44] Sarah Parker, "Olive Custance, Nostalgia, and Decadent Conservatism," *Volupté: Interdisciplinary Journal of Decadence Studies*, vol. 2, no. 1 (Spring 2019), pp. 57-81, p. 64.
[45] Plock, *Modernism, Fashion and Interwar Women Writers*, p. 2.

"too much extravagance in writing or authorial posturing could…lead to the same results as extravagance in dress: [...] possible rejection by an intended target audience."[46]

Within this context, fashion, garments themselves, became invested with meanings, sartorial symbols which chimed with contemporary debates about image, art and identity. While modernism was broadly anti-populist and disdainful of the ever-increasing pressure to pander to commercial tastes, by the 1920s it was becoming impossible to entirely shun the publicity-hungry media machine.[47] This was not a problem for Edith Sitwell who, although naturally shy, was also an avid attention-seeker. While she denied ever consciously seeking publicity, she became adept at playing the game, a significant part of which appeared to be maintaining a pretense of ambivalence.

This apparent complicity with celebrity culture seemed starkly at odds with Sitwell's high modernist principles, yet it chimed with the post-war literary climate. Indeed, while Virginia Woolf wrestled with her role in the cultural cross-over between literature, capitalism and fashion, the Sitwell siblings readily splashed themselves across the pages of the popular press, nurtured literary feuds and made inflammatory remarks about fellow writers. When Woolf posed for *Vogue* in 1922 wearing one of her mother's old dresses, however, she was not so much expressing an interest in fashion as making a satirical statement about Victorian culture, in the same spirit that she had hung her great aunt Julia Margaret Cameron's photographic portraits of "great literary men" in the hallway of her Bloomsbury home.[48]

In 1930, Woolf's ambivalence about fashion erupted into open hostility. Despite being hailed in his accompanying notes as "one of the most gravely distinguished women I have ever seen," Woolf was dismayed when Cecil Beaton included a sketch portrait of her in his recently published *Book of Beauty*. While Woolf was not, Beaton conceded, "conventional[ly]" attractive, and "would look like a terrified ghost in an assembly of the accepted raving beauties, she would make each one separately appear vulgar and tawdry."[49] This lyrical eulogy failed to convince the subject herself who, in a letter of complaint to *The Athenaeum*, confessed to feeling exploited and victimized. For Woolf, women's sartorial practices were loaded with social and political significance. In her work, clothing functions symbolically as a means of

---

[46] Plock, *Modernism, Fashion and Interwar Women Writers*, p. 4.
[47] Plock, *Modernism, Fashion and Interwar Women Writers*, p. 5.
[48] Philip Hoare, *RISINGTIDEFALLINGSTAR* (London: Fourth Estate, 2018), p. 90.
[49] Cecil Beaton, *The Book of Beauty* (London: Duckworth, 1930), p. 33.

exploring "frock consciousness," or the ways in which clothing can shape women's self-perception and social awareness.[50]

In her 1933 novel, *The Years*, Woolf explores the influence of women's dress on their social interactions with one another, suggesting that both extreme uniformity and distinctiveness could have negative repercussions. One of the novel's protagonists, Kitty, feels acutely embarrassed by her elaborate eveningwear as she hails a taxi for a matinee opera performance. Her sense of being out of place only evaporates when she arrives at the theatre, her individuality lost in a crowd of similarly dressed women. Her conspicuously elegant frock has essentially become a uniform which now threatens to engulf her and smother her independence.[51] As a marker of social divisions distinctive dress could also, Woolf argued, create rifts between women by encouraging social anxiety and envy; by the same token, however, blanket conformity to seasonal fashions suggested an over-compliance with oppressive socio-economic norms.[52]

This was not a concern for Edith Sitwell, however, who wore her distinctiveness as a mantle of pride. Unlike Woolf, Sitwell was proud of her association with Beaton and the portraits he took of her in 1926. Recalling their first session in his diary, Beaton was struck by her distinctive mix of humor and otherworldliness, finding "her formidable aspect less striking than her sympathetic girlishness."[53] Yet posing outstretched on the floor of his sister's bedroom, clutching a spray of lilies in her "cadaverous" hands, she became a statuesque slab of gothic marble, oddly pure and untouchable; in another picture, Beaton recalled that she had looked "surprisingly Victorian in her crudely Pre-Raphaelite dress, with her matador's jet hat, and necklace…When the hat was discarded she became an Emily Bronte heroine."[54] The results of the session were not so much media-friendly publicity photographs as personal propaganda. Like the portraits Beaton would take of Stephen Tennant the following year in Tennant's silver-foil lined bedroom,[55] these images of Sitwell were archly eloquent of their sitter's mystique. As with Custance before her, this session with Beaton was a

---

[50] Plock, *Modernism, Fashion and Interwar Women Writers*, p. 193.
[51] Plock, *Modernism, Fashion and Interwar Women Writers*, p. 198.
[52] Plock, *Modernism, Fashion and Interwar Women Writers*, p. 198.
[53] Cecil Beaton, *The Wandering Years, 1922-39: Cecil Beaton's Diaries Volume One* (Leeds: Sapere Books, 2018), p. 190.
[54] Beaton, *The Wandering Years, 1922-39*, p. 190.
[55] Philip Hoare, "I Love a Man in Uniform: The Dandy Espirit de Corps," *Fashion Theory*, vol. 9, no. 3 (2005), pp. 263–282, p. 264.

deliberate act of self-fashioning, Sitwell's hard, Plantagenet glamour replacing Custance's slightly wistful romanticism.

While in *The Years,* Kitty's perception of being over-dressed makes her feel acutely self-conscious, Sitwell reveled in her heavily stylized individuality, always turning out to literary engagements in full battle order. At a reading in 1927 where, as the critic from *Truth* magazine noted, "frocks all around and beyond were very good," she turned heads by walking into the hall late, in "a glory of gold tinsel lamé with a huge jewel blazing at her waist."[56] Accompanying Sitwell to the Strand Theatre one night in 1926, Sassoon recorded that, "As might have been expected, [Edith] looked quite out of place among a crowd of dreary vulgar nonentities…(I was proud of being <u>seen</u> with her, I don't mind admitting it)."[57]

It was this type of extreme distinctiveness which, Woolf believed, could potentially drive a wedge between women. Sitwell, however, was not particularly concerned about feminism, or politics more broadly: while she was sympathetic to women's rights, her own uniqueness was far more important to her than a sense of solidarity with other women. While Sitwell explored women's social and aesthetic identities in her poetry, often through dress symbolism, this was less a feminist comment than a reference to her own decorative self at one remove. Sitwell's dramatic style was a projection of her own poetic self, something which Sassoon was particularly attuned to in his appreciation of her work.

For Sassoon, Sitwell's striking image was the key to her poetry, a kind of visual code which elucidated its meaning and significance, and in his diary, he frequently frames Sitwell as a product of her own artistry. Following a performance of her "entertainment" *Façade* in April 1926, he noted that she was "quite beautiful, in a way which corresponds with her poems."[58] In his 1922 review of *Façade* for the *Daily Herald*, entitled "Too fantastic for fat-heads," Sassoon took a broad swipe at the "exasperated gentlemen" critics and anthologists who "busily and brusquely boycott" Sitwell's poetry. "Miss Sitwell's originality has affinities with Aubrey Beardsley," he wrote, "[who], as such, has triumphed over all of the fat-heads of his day. Miss Sitwell will do the same."[59]

Sassoon understood that, for Sitwell, art and image were one, her style itself a poetic pose which, like her Beaton photographs, merged her modernist

---

[56] *Truth*, 30th November 1927.
[57] Siegfried Sassoon, *Journal*, 13 Dec. 1926-11 Mar. 1927 (MS Add.9852/1/24), p. 49.
[58] Siegfried Sassoon, *Journal*, 27 Dec. 1921-13 Jul. 1922 (MS Add.9852/1/18).
[59] Siegfried Sassoon, "Too fantastic for Fat-Heads," *Daily Herald*, 24th May 1922.

aesthetic with a decorative, fin de siècle flair (an allusion underscored by their mutual friendship with Robbie Ross, Oscar Wilde's literary executor and, until his death in 1918, mentor to a coterie of budding young poets).[60] To Sassoon, Sitwell's towering, languid figure, clad in sweeping, floor-length frocks and bright, flashing jewelry, was a Beardsley-esque pen and ink sketch brought to life, a vivid expression of her poetry's "fantastic plumage," draped in her own dress symbolism.

In her poetry, Sitwell often uses dress as a symbol of female identity, through which she also explores wider ideas about history and social progress. In poems such as "Elegy on Dead Fashion" (1926), detailed descriptions of female dress act as metaphors for the layers of suffocating social customs which subsume and crush the individual self. As Greene has observed, the role of social performance and masquerade was one to which Sitwell frequently returned in her poetry, exploring the tension between the authentic self and the projected social self, or "façade." As a devotee of Swinburne, Baudelaire and other late-Romantic and Symbolist poets, Sitwell's poetry is rich in sharp, fragmentary imagery, filled with the same "extravagance, virtuosity and obliqueness"[61] that characterized their verse. For Sitwell, as the critic Ihab Hassan wrote in 1955, "all expression is welded into an image,"[62] her ornamental, almost painterly poems also evocative of the Impressionist art and music she loved.

Along with poets such as H. D., Sitwell's decorative style of writing and use of rich imagery distinguished her from many of her male modernist counterparts, perhaps aligning her more obviously with the experimental, theatrical prose of writers such as Ronald Firbank. As Sassoon suggested, she might have been a character in one of her own poems, an elegant outcast cut adrift from contemporary culture. In "Elegy on Dead Fashion," she expresses a nostalgic yearning for a lost arcadian idyll, whose aesthetic landscape is littered with dead queens and old goddesses. She shares a kinship with these pre-Christian naiads and nymphs, whose lost, decorative world she evokes through rich, repetitive imagery, mourning the march of Time, which has eroded their status and power. Their obsolescence is symbolized through their outmoded, anachronistic dress. We see "Queen Thetis" in "pelisses of tissue/Of marine blue or violet," a wood-nymph "shading her face" with a "deep black velvet bonnet/With blackest ivy for wreaths upon it," and

---

[60] Maureen Borland, *Wilde's Devoted Friend: A Life of Robert Ross* (Oxford: Lennard Publishing, 1990), p. 15.
[61] Ihab H. Hassan, "Edith Sitwell and the Symbolist Tradition," *Comparative Literature*, vol. 7, no. 3 (Summer, 1955), pp. 240- 251, p. 240.
[62] Hassan, "Edith Sitwell and the Symbolist Tradition," p. 245.

Cleopatra in "crinolines of plaided sarsenet." Even the trees are wearing "pelerines," their foliage punningly evoking an out-of-date style magazine ("fashion leaves of eighty years ago").[63]

Figure 4.2: Edith Sitwell, Renishaw estate, 1930.

Cecil Beaton Archive, (c) Condé Nast.

Similarly, "The Sleeping Beauty" (1923) depicts a dream-like world of imaginative languor, in which nature is again portrayed through stylized symbolism. Fairies in "richest trains [and] plumes" inhabit a land of "green and jewelled leaves," "red lacquer buds," "pearled...shores" and "curled and turbaned waves,"[64] the poem's hard beauty evoking the eighteenth-century Japanese lacquer screens that inspired it. Both poems consistently invert the pastoral tradition by depicting nature as ornamental and paradoxically artificial; the natural world is hard and jewel-like, the trees, flowers and fairies

---

[63] Edith Sitwell, "Elegy on Dead Fashion," in *Collected Poems* (London: Duckworth, 1931), pp. 237, 240, 238.
[64] Sitwell, "Elegy on Dead Fashion," p. 2, p. 15.

which populate the landscape depicted through fashion and dress metaphors, evoking the spirit of Wilde's 1891 essay "The Decay of Lying." It is as if the reader is looking at a collage or a series of fashion plates, a sequence of sharply defined pictures placed side by side, linked through repetitive diction and imagery. As Robert Graves wrote in the *Nation and Athenaeum*, this was a "Looking-Glass Land…strewn with memorable images,"[65] as much indebted to Diaghilev's 1921 ballet "The Sleeping Princess" as it was to Tennyson or Shelly.

Like Virginia Woolf posing for *Vogue* in one of her mother's old frocks, both poems are rich in the visual signifiers of Victorian dress; unlike Woolf, however, Sitwell's delicate, painterly evocation of these obsolete fashions is not satirical but, as the title of her 1926 poem suggests, elegiac, even yearning. Her lingering, aesthete's eye takes in a lost world for which, perhaps, she feels a secret longing, delighting in her own detailed descriptions of dress and artifice. In one sense, Victorianism was the antithesis of modernism, its outmoded morality an enemy of modernist conceptions of progress and newness. Yet Sitwell's own sense of style was as anachronistic as that of the protagonists of her poems, her spinsterish personality aligning her, according to the views of many of her contemporaries, to a dead Victorian past. This theme is alluded to in "The Sleeping Beauty," her reworking of the classic fairy tale in which her heroine fails to wake up. In the poem, when Beauty pricks her finger and falls into a trance-like sleep, she is lost to a permanent state of childhood and virginity. Her prince never comes to wake her and, unable to resolve the challenge of adult sexuality, Sitwell keeps her in a perpetual dream state, her stylized, decorative body lost in a land of fairies and evil queens. In this way, as Greene has observed, the princess is saved from the illusion of an imposed, adult identity.[66]

Sitwell's disdain for contemporary style made her an anti-fashion icon. During a period in which capitalism exerted increasing pressure towards salability and uniformity, Sitwell forged a public persona which was both visually extravagant and eccentric. In stark contrast to the clean lines and chic simplicity of 1920s fashions, Sitwell draped herself in "eighteenth-century Venetian costume[s],"[67] "picture-dresses of bright green brocade"[68] and, at a poetry reading in 1927, "trailing skirts and a large black, psychic-looking felt hat."[69]

---

[65] Robert Graves, *Nation and Athenaeum* 19th April 1924.
[66] Green, *Edith Sitwell*, p. 172.
[67] *Daily Mirror*, 8th March 1927.
[68] *Westminster Gazette*, 9th June 1926.
[69] *Westminster Gazette*, 31st October 1927.

Clearly, like Woolf, Sitwell was no slave to fashion. She herself spoke in 1928 of the "deplorable" state of contemporary womenswear, dismissing it as unimaginative and "sterile."[70] There is more than a hint of snobbery in her attitude towards modern fashions. Mass production, textile innovations and the trend for simpler designs had brought stylish, machine-made clothing to a far larger consumer market than had previously been possible. Taking issue with her hostile outlook the *Daily Herald* retorted, "Miss Edith Sitwell may regret that women now dress very much alike. But she cannot deny that…the poor woman is dressed simply and well, and her clothes are no longer a shoddy imitation of the clothes of richer women."[71]

Her aristocratic disdain for fast fashion was a product of her privileged social status, yet also hinted at a deeper sense of idiosyncrasy. She was out of step with the times, her appearance reminiscent of a bygone era. Her "fine instinct for old-time fashion,"[72] as a *Daily Mirror* critic called it, was as anachronistic as her old-fashioned spinsterhood, which seemed to link her to a vanished past. Speaking to John Freeman on *Face to Face* in 1959, she explained her "eccentric, forbidding" style through reference to her "Plantagenet ancestors," to whom she considered herself a "throwback":

> I can't wear fashionable clothes…I really would look *so* extraordinary in coats and skirts. People would doubt the existence of the almighty if they saw me looking like that… [dressing unusually] comes naturally. I'm descended from the most queer, remote sources.[73]

Seated opposite Freeman in the brightly lit television studio, draped in a voluminous fur coat with a huge cameo brooch at her throat, a stiff, black tulle headdress with a sequined rim completely concealing her hair, she has all the poise and dignity of a glamorous Abbess, her curved, plucked eyebrows alight like gothic arches below her high, alabaster forehead.

During the 1920s, however, she was not the only flamboyantly attired spinster in her social circle. Nellie Burton, landlady to a number of "bachelor gentlemen" in Piccadilly's Half Moon Street, was a larger-than-life figure who peeps out from the corners of other people's histories. Always known affectionately as "Burton" to her friends (a legacy of her former position as Lady's Maid to Robbie Ross's mother), she presided over her tenants with

---

[70] *Daily Herald*, 28th October 1928.
[71] *Daily Herald*, 28th October 1928.
[72] *Daily Mirror*, 30th June 1928.
[73] Eckington Parish Television — Dame Edith Sitwell — *Face to Face* Interview 1959. Broadcast 18th November 2014.

motherly devotion, among whom were the eccentric peer Lord Berners, Treasury Secretary Roderick Meicklejohn and a Theosophist named Mr Flemming.

As Ross's landlady, she had been introduced to the Sitwells and his other literary acquaintances, some of whom became close personal friends. Recording an encounter in his diary with "dear N.B," Sassoon related his delight at seeing her "magnificently dressed in green with a dashing black hat and a black feather boa."[74] In early 1918, a time of heightened anxiety and moral panic due to Britain's struggling war effort, Burton had painted Ross's rooms gold in protest against the prevailing climate of moral persecution.[75] One visitor, Squire Sprigg, described the scene in a letter to his son, with Burton resplendent in a mauve dressing-gown, "smoking a cigarette…like a bad character in a Hogarth print…the background of gilt paper, bits of bronze…and workmen's tools recalled some such moral picture as *The Debutante's Downfall*."[76]

Of course, being a spinster was not a prerequisite for dressing extravagantly. Another of Sitwell's contemporaries was the upper-class bohemian salonnière Lady Ottoline Morrell, wife of the pacifist Liberal MP Philip Morrell and also famous for her flamboyant style. However, while Sitwell and Morrell were two of Sassoon's closest friends during the 1920s and 1930s, their personalities could not have been more dissimilar, which his contrasting responses to them clearly illustrate. If Sitwell was, for Sassoon, a hard, strikingly bejeweled Aubrey Beardsley illustration, then Morrell was as willowy and romantic as a Rossetti heroine.[77] A far less imposing figure than Sitwell, she, like Kitty in *The Years*, was vulnerable to bouts of insecurity about her choices of clothing. On a trip to Mells in Somerset to stay with the Horner family, she had packed her favorite dresses but decided that "when shaken out and worn they seemed absurdly fantastic and unfitting for the company and the surroundings."[78]

Perhaps Margaret Adams would diagnose a lack of psychological integrity in Morrell's insecurity, which seemed to communicate itself to others. When Ross had introduced them in 1916, Sassoon later recalled being "embarrassed" by Morrell's appearance which, he wrote, "seemed to have been artificially imposed on the rest of her personality […] at that period the paint and powder

---

[74] Siegfried Sassoon, *Journal*, 12 Mar. 1927-28 Sep. 1927 (MS Add.9852/1/25), p. 94.
[75] Hoare, "I Love a Man in Uniform, p. 265.
[76] Borland, *Wilde's Devoted Friend*, p. 272.
[77] Siegfried Sassoon, *Siegfried's Journey* (London: Faber & Faber, 1945), p. 9.
[78] Juliet Nicholson, *The Perfect Summer: Dancing into Shadow in 1911* (London: John Murray, 2006), p. 212.

and purple hair were a definite impediment to my [...] appreciation of her splendid qualities."[79] He never expressed such reservations over Burton's or Sitwell's appearance, or that of his extremely flamboyant lover, Stephen Tennant. Perhaps this sense of vulnerability explains why Morrell was so much more susceptible than Sitwell to being satirized by her (usually male) writer friends such as Aldous Huxley, D. H. Lawrence and W. J. Turner.

Sassoon was not alone in his fascination with Edith Sitwell, though he was among the most sympathetic of her friends during the 1920s and 1930s. Attempting to decode her was a popular pastime among her friends and acquaintances, who often focused on the two aspects of Sitwell's character that, as a woman, made her distinctive: her appearance and her singleness. Their comments reveal intricate theories of gender, illustrating the ways in which assumptions about appearance, class and marital status could merge, with stereotypes about "old maids" often providing a means of understanding her character. The traits associated with spinsterhood in the popular imagination seemed to stick to Sitwell; we see them at work in letters and diary entries about her, which often fall back on stereotypes to explain her to the writer, descriptions which dwell on both her appearance and her status as a "traditional spinster," as if one could explain the other. Both were taken as mutually reinforcing aspects of her eccentricity, different strands of a personality type which could be called upon to account for her.

Recalling their first meeting in her diary in 1918, Virginia Woolf had described Sitwell as "a tall young woman...curiously finished off with a high green silk head-dress, concealing her hair, so that it is not known whether she has any."[80] She had puzzled Woolf, who thought her "severe, implacable and tremendous,"[81] yet somehow inexplicable. It was only after having dinner with the three Sitwells in 1925 that she had an epiphany, realizing that Edith was "a well-born Victorian spinster...Edith is an old maid [...] She is, I guess, a little fussy, very kind and beautifully mannered [...] & timid & admiring & easy & poor."[82]

In 1926, Woolf described an encounter with Sitwell in the street, noting that she was "dressed, on a windy, March day, in a three decker skirt of red spotted cotton [...] She is a curious product [...] sensitive, affectionate, lonely, having to thread her way home [...] to Bayswater to help cook dinner [...] In other

---

[79] Sassoon, *Siegfried's Journey*, p. 9.
[80] Virginia Woolf, *A Moment's Liberty: A Shorter Diary*, ed. Anne Oliver Bell (London: Chatto & Windus, 1990), p. 57.
[81] Virginia Woolf, *The Diary of Virginia Woolf: 1925-30, Volume 3*, ed. Anne Oliver Bell (London: Penguin Classic, 1982), p. 24.
[82] Woolf, *The Diary of Virginia Woolf*, p. 24.

ages she would have been a cloistered nun."[83] This reference to what Sassoon referred to in his diary as Sitwell's "dreary" Bayswater flat was where she lived with her old governess and now close friend Helen Rootham, a musician and Theosophist, whom the writer and aesthete Harold Acton referred to as "the essential hysterical intellectual spinster," but who was also "something of a rebel."[84] Describing a party there for Gertrude Stein in 1926, Woolf recalled that Stein had been "throned on a broken settee (all Edith's furniture is derelict, to make up for which she is stuck about with jewels like a drowned mer-maiden)."[85]

While, in the post-war climate, a general sense of disapproval hung over women taking flats together, it still provided a route to freedom and independence for middle- and upper-class women, and as Greene has noted, "Without Helen, Edith's existence might have mirrored that of her Aunt Florence."[86] The Bayswater flat was shabby, genteelly down-at-heel, the living room a "bare room with a lamp, many books, a bedroom divan and a piano."[87] It was not without originality and style, however, with Osbert providing red and gold hangings for her bedroom and green and gold ones for Helen's. Here, from 1916 onwards, Edith and Helen began their literary "at homes," with regular visitors including Siegfried Sassoon, W. B. Yeats, T. S. Eliot, Virginia Woolf and E. M. Forster.[88]

As Woolf's comments suggest, however, Sitwell's domestic life sat uneasily with her extravagant, poetic appearance, and many found it difficult to imagine her performing ordinary domestic chores. In fact, as some of her closer friends discovered, Sitwell's rather formidable literary image disguised an essential shyness and domesticity that was starkly at odds with her public persona. Robert Graves, describing one of her visits to the home he shared with his wife, Nancy, in 1918, recalled his shock at discovering that she was "a very good knitter [...] It was a surprise, after reading her poems, to find her gentle, domesticated, and even devout."[89] On another visit, following the birth of their third child Caroline, "she spent her time sitting on the sofa and hemming handkerchiefs."[90] The contents of Sitwell's suitcase was, however,

---

[83] Woolf, *The Diary of Virginia Woolf*, p. 132.
[84] Green, *Edith Sitwell*, p. 141.
[85] Virginia Woolf, *A Change Of Perspective — The Letters Of Virginia Woolf Volume 3: 1923 – 1928*, ed. Nigel Nicholson, and J. Trautmann (London: The Hogarth Press, 1977), pp. 269-70.
[86] Green, *Edith Sitwell*, p. 42.
[87] Green, *Edith Sitwell*, p. 42.
[88] Green, *Edith Sitwell*, p. 113.
[89] Robert Graves, *Goodbye to All That* (London: Penguin, 1999), p. 158.
[90] Graves, *Goodbye to All That*, p. 294.

Refashioning spinsterhood   131

more characteristic; according to Graves, she had brought "books, manuscripts and an eighteenth-century brocade coat," which she had had to lug from the train station herself due to her host's rugby injury. Graves had remained unrepentant: "She was a fine strapping woman who could carry her own case."[91] This anecdote seems to epitomize the conflicting sides of Sitwell's personality; at heart, as Graves suggests, she was a spinster of the meeker and milder kind than many people assumed. Yet she carried her other self with her in the extravagant brocade coat, stuffed into an old suitcase like a security blanket.

While Beaton had glimpsed Sitwell's milder, "girlish" side during their 1926 photography session, Harold Acton remained unconvinced. Describing her as a "sex-starved spinster" to her first biographer John Pearson shortly after her death, he concluded, "dear Edith wasn't exactly what you'd call cuddly."[92] For Acton, Sitwell's unconventional appearance seemed somehow incompatible with the traditions of romance and courtship. She was too spiky, too remote and unwomanly to fall in love, an impression evoked again by her portrayal in Terence Davies' *Benediction*, in which Ivor Novello waspishly remarks of her that, "she isn't a woman, she's an animated meringue."[93] Sitwell herself, however, had never been opposed to marriage, and seems to have regretted the lack of romance in her life. At 70, she tearfully confided to her secretary, Elisabeth Salter, that she had "never had a passionate relationship and felt that she was built for it."[94]

There had been near romances; her greatest love was the homosexual Russian artist Pavel Tchelitchew, with whom she sustained a close yet tempestuous friendship for 30 years. In 1914, she reportedly fell in love with the Chilean artist, boxer and drug addict Alvaro de Guevara, who threw her over for Nancy Cunard. She even claimed to have been briefly engaged to Guevara until, so she told the socialite Allanah Harper in 1924, someone had warned her that he had VD.[95] Her attachment to Sassoon also seems to have been partly romantic, and while Sassoon himself went on to marry Hester Gatty in 1933, it would take a torturously protracted break-up with Stephen Tennant to scar him sufficiently first. In 1926, he was surprised when his friend, the writer and critic Edmund Gosse, had asked him if he "would like to marry Edith?" Confiding to his diary later that night that while "this remarkable question did not embarrass me at all," he had told Gosse that he

---

[91] Graves, *Goodbye to All That*, p. 158.
[92] Green, *Edith Sitwell*, p. 117.
[93] *Benediction*, dir. Terence Davies, 2022.
[94] Green, *Edith Sitwell*, p. 118.
[95] Green, *Edith Sitwell*, p. 117.

"didn't think poets should marry one another."[96] A few weeks later, however, he was musing that "Edith thinks about me more than is good for her," something which Gosse had evidently also noticed.

However, for Sitwell, marriage and romance were not to be, and with her singular character and arresting appearance, it was not surprising that she nurtured a deep affinity for Elizabeth I. In 1946 she published a popular biography of the childhood of the Virgin Queen, *Fanfare for Elizabeth*, following it with a sequel, *Queens of the Hive*, in 1962. While writing the second book she had hired an astrologer to make a detailed comparison of their birth charts, who had found that, while Sitwell's horoscope was "a great deal more inventive and artistic than was [Elizabeth's]...I should say that both mentally and emotionally you are akin to the great Queen."[97]

Such a conclusion might flatter anyone, but for Sitwell it was an affirmation of the way she had chosen to live her life – her eccentric yet undeniably regal appearance, her dedication to her work, her singleness. While she had written of Mademoiselle Richarde, an elderly governess character from her *Troy Park* sequence of poems (1925), "She lived and rattled in the emptiness/Of other people's splendours; her rich dress/Had muffled her loneliness of heart,"[98] she herself was not lonely. While Mademoiselle Richarde, like her aunt Florence, lived on the edges of other people's lives, Edith Sitwell's version of spinsterhood was far less austere and sad. While at odds with the liberalizing ideals of the times, Sitwell nurtured a spirit of emotional and artistic independence which, for her, felt like a victory.

In 1962, two years before her death, she was interviewed for the *Daily Mirror* by Marjorie Proops. Visiting Sitwell in her small flat in Hampstead (where she had moved from Bayswater several years before), a clearly captivated Proops found her "in bed...Her white velvet jacket fastened with a huge pinkish brooch, big as a king-size cigarette packet."[99] Reflecting on their shared, "very female" love of clothes, Proops nevertheless perceived a stark difference in their inspiration: "I wear the sort of clothes I think men will like," she wrote. "She wears the sort of clothes SHE likes and never mind WHO disapproves"[100] (capitals in original). Harold Acton may have dismissed Sitwell as a "sex-starved spinster," but her appearance still reflected an aura of defiant self-containment:

---

[96] Siegfried Sassoon, *Journal*, 13 Dec. 1926-11 Mar. 1927 (MS Add.9852/1/24), p. 145.
[97] Green, *Edith Sitwell*, p. 434.
[98] Sitwell, Edith, *Collected Poems*, p. 143.
[99] *Daily Mirror*, 7th September 1962.
[100] *Daily Mirror*, 7th September 1962.

> For years she's been known as an eccentric, weirdly dressed in medieval clothes, her hooded eyelids and impressive high forehead making her seem like a figure out of a fantastic past...The twentieth-century candlewick bedspread seemed like an oddly out-of-place covering for this beautifully bizarre woman.[101]

The more time passed, the more anachronistic Sitwell appeared. By the 1960s, her virginal spinsterhood seemed like even more of a relic than it had in the 1920s, with the sexual revolution but a whisper away. Yet, as Proops' clear enjoyment of her subject shows, she had won the right to be taken seriously. While her poetry may have fallen off the cultural radar, she was now regarded as a "living legend."[102] Despite the shifting context of her times, Sitwell still stood out. In an age of "surplus women," Sitwell's spinsterhood had still seemed distinctive; her singularity of character had always made her appear somehow *more* single than other single women, her appearance a marker of her individuality and self-sufficiency. While women writers were under increasing pressure to use their appearance to sell books by the 1920s, Sitwell had smashed the boundaries of feminine beauty norms with her outlandish costumes. Both her singleness and her style became symbols of her extreme distinction, rather than ways in which she could fade into the background of social custom.

Bibliography

Primary Sources

Books

Beaton, *The Book of Beauty*. London: Duckworth, 1930.

Manuscript Diaries

Sassoon Journals, Cambridge Digital Library, DOI: Sassoon Journals (cam.ac.uk)
Journal, 27 Dec. 1921-13 July 1922 (MS Add.9852/1/18).
Journal, 10 June 1926-12 Dec. 1926 (MS Add.9852/1/23).
Journal, 13 Dec. 1926-11 Mar. 1927 (MS Add.9852/1/24).
Journal, 12 Mar. 1927-28 Sep. 1927 (MS Add.9852/1/25).

Published Diaries

Beaton, Cecil. *The Wandering Years, 1922-39: Cecil Beaton's Diaries Volume One*. Leeds: Sapere Books, 2018.

---

[101] *Daily Mirror*, 7th September 1962.
[102] *Daily Mirror*, 7th September 1962.

Woolf, Virginia. *The Diary of Virginia Woolf: 1925-30*, Vol. 3, edited by Anne Oliver Bell. London: Penguin Classic, 1982.

Woolf, Virginia. *A Moment's Liberty: A Shorter Diary*, edited by Anne Oliver Bell. London: Chatto & Windus, 1990.

Poetry

Sitwell, Edith. *Collected Poems*. London: Duckworth, 1931.

Autobiography

Graves, Robert. *Goodbye to All That*. London: Penguin, 1999.

Sassoon, Siegfried. *Siegfried's Journey*. London: Faber & Faber, 1945.

Letters

Selected Letters of Edith Sitwell. Edited by Richard Greene. London: Virago Press, 1998.

Woolf, Virginia. *A Change of Perspective - The Letters of Virginia Woolf Volume 3: 1923 – 1928*. Edited by Nigel Nicholson, and J. Trautmann. London: The Hogarth Press, 1977.

Digitized Newspapers

Daily Herald, 28th October 1928.
Daily Mirror, 8th March, 1927.
Daily Mirror, 30th June 1928.
Daily Mirror, 7th September 1962.
Nation and Athenaeum, 19th April 1924.
Truth, 30th November 1927.
Westminster Gazette, 9th June 1926.
Westminster Gazette, 31st October 1927.

Film

Benediction, dir. Terence Davis, 2022.

Secondary Sources

Books

Borland, Maureen. *Wilde's Devoted Friend: A Life of Robert Ross*. Oxford: Lennard Publishing, 1990.

Glendinning, Victoria. *Edith Sitwell: A Unicorn Among Lions*. London: Faber and Faber, 2013.

Green, Richard. Edith Sitwell: Avant Garde Poet, English Genius. London: Virago, 2011.

Hoare, Philip. *RISINGTIDEFALLINGSTAR*. London: Fourth Estate, 2018.

Hodgkins, Hope Howell. *Style and the Single Girl: How Modern Women Re-Dressed the Novel, 1922-1977*. Columbus: The Ohio State University Press, 2016.

Holden, Katherine. *The Shadow of Marriage: Singleness in England, 1914-60*. Manchester: Manchester University Press, 2007.

Milford-Cottam, Daniel. *Edwardian Fashion*. Oxford: Shire Publications, 2014.

Nicholson, Juliet. *The Perfect Summer: Dancing into Shadow in 1911*. London: John Murray, 2006.

Nicholson, Virginia. *Singled Out: How Two Million Women Survived without Men After the First World War*. London: Penguin Books Ltd, 2007, Kindle Edition.

Plock, Vike Martina. *Modernism, Fashion and Interwar Women Writers*. Edinburgh: Edinburgh University Press, 2019.

Priscott, Emily. *Singleness in Britain, 1960-1990: Identity, Gender and Social Change*. Delaware: Vernon Press, 2020.

Roach, Mary Ellen and Eicher, Joanne Bubolz. "The Language of Personal Adornment." In *The Fabrics of Culture: The Anthropology of Clothing and Adornment*, edited by Justine M. Cordwell, and Ronald M. Schwarz. New York: De Gruyter Mouton, 2011.

Stetz, Margaret D. "Fashioning Modern and Modernist Authorship: Rebecca West in the 1920s and 1930s," In *Fashion and Authorship*, edited by Gerald Egan, 255-272. Palgrave Macmillan, 2020.

Wilson, Elizabeth. "Explaining it Away." In *Fashion Theory*. Routledge, 2020.

Taylor, D. J. *Bright Young People – The Rise and Fall of a Generation: 1918-1940*. London: Vintage Books, 2008.

Journal Articles

Hassan, Ihab, H. "Edith Sitwell and the Symbolist Tradition." *Comparative Literature*, vol. 7, no. 3 (Summer, 1955), pp. 240- 251.

Hoare, Philip. "I Love a Man in Uniform: The Dandy Espirit de Corps." *Fashion Theory*, vol. 9, no. 3 (2005), pp. 263–282.

Oram, Alison. "Repressed or Thwarted, or Bearer of the New World? The Spinster in Inter-War Feminist Discourse." *Women's History Review*, vol. 1., no. 3, (1992), pp. 413-433.

Parker, Sarah. "Olive Custance, Nostalgia, and Decadent Conservatism." *Volupté: Interdisciplinary Journal of Decadence Studies*, vol. 2, no. 1, (Spring 2019), pp. 57-81.

Unpublished Thesis

Lachmansingh, Sandhya Kimberley. "'Fashions of the Mind:' Modernism and British Vogue Under the Editorship of Dorothy Todd," (MPhil diss.), University of Birmingham, 2010.

Chapter 5

British Jewish identity: Linda Grant as a flâneuse and 'thoughtful dresser'

Margaret D. Stetz
University of Delaware

Abstract: Chapter Five considers the notion of the British Jewish flâneuse following the Second World War, challenging the notion of the *flâneur* as essentially male. This chapter builds upon Lauren Elkin's 2016 work *Flâneuse* with a feminist perspective, using Linda Grant's collection of essays *The Thoughtful Dresser* (2009) to explore the relationship between female Jewish identity, shopping and urban culture, and suggests that shopping, a means through which women can legitimately occupy public space by walking through streets, can itself be an act of *flânerie*.

Exploring the role of fashion in British Jewish flâneuse culture, this chapter also looks at the significance of dress in the personal memories of Holocaust survivors such as Katerina Deutsch, whose memories of ripping the hem of her prison dress at Auschwitz and tying it in her hair remind Grant of the powerful and humanizing significance of personal style choices. The chapter concludes with an analysis of the novelist Anita Brookner's use of clothing in fashioning a distinctive sense of self as a British Jewish woman in post-war culture.

Keywords: Linda Grant, *flâneuse*, British Jewish identity, Second World War, Holocaust, Anita Brookner, New Look, Dior, Chanel, shopping methodology.

***

The history of British Jewish identity, from the late-nineteenth century to the present, has often been a story involving dress, as well as one frequently seen in relation to urban culture. As Rachel Kolsky reports in *Vintage Glamour in London's East End* (2014), in places such as Whitechapel and Spitalfields with large Jewish communities, it was "the 'schmatte' [meaning "rag" or clothing] trade that predominated" throughout the first half of the twentieth century.[1] Much of the life and labor of the local population focused on "millinery, buttonhole making, designing, cutting, selling fabrics, dressmaking or managing a factory."[2]

This association with the manufacture and marketing of clothing proved both a blessing and a curse in terms of integrating Jews, many of whom had arrived as non-English-speaking immigrants from Eastern Europe, into the literal and metaphorical fabric of the nation. On the one hand, it positioned Jews as essential to everyday life; they were the backbone of institutions that were eventually embraced as iconic, as well as utilitarian. Such was the case, for instance, with the Marks & Spencer chain of shops, which began in 1884 as a "penny bazaar" market stall in Leeds run by Michael Marks, who had arrived from Russian-controlled Poland to escape persecution, and which went on to become a major clothing retailer.[3] On the other hand, the image of Jews was tied to the world of dress and fashion, a sphere that has long been connected to women and has thus been both feminized and demeaned. At the same time, this focus on clothes-making and clothes-selling confined working-class Jews in particular to specific locations in the popular imagination—i.e., to spaces where various aspects of the garment industry were carried out—as opposed to being seen as full participants in the life of the city as a whole, or as consumers rather than producers.

Even without this traditional link between British Jews and what was often perceived as the lower-status occupation of fabricating and selling clothing, Jewish identity has long been a fraught subject in Britain. In historical terms, there has never been a period when anti-Semitism was not a widespread problem, or when Jews were accepted as being completely and unquestionably British. This has led theorists such as Eitan Bar-Yosef and Nadia Valman, in their Introduction to *"The Jew" in Late-Victorian and Edwardian Culture* (2009), to refer to the ongoing condition of "the Jews' liminality" and of the "political, social, and cultural construction of Jewish otherness" in Britain.[4] Writing in 2021 for an American readership in the U. S. magazine *The Nation* about the pervasiveness of anti-Jewish feeling in British political circles, even among those on the Labourite left, Rachel Shabi

---

[1] Rachel Kolsky, "Boris's East End," in *Vintage Glamour in London's East End*, ed. Michael Greisman (London: Hoxton Mini Press, 2014), pp. 6–7.
[2] Kolsky, "Boris's East End," p. 7.
[3] [Anon], "Marks in Time," https://marksintime.marksandspencer.com/ms-'history/timeline/art968.
[4] Eitan Bar-Yosef, and Nadia Valman, "Introduction," in *"The Jew" in Late-Victorian and Edwardian Culture* (Houndmills, UK: Palgrave Macmillan, 2009), pp. 4–5.

reminds readers that it is "a misunderstanding of anti-Semitism to focus on individual acts of bigotry rather than a permeating culture. Racial prejudice is better understood as an ever-present, easily animated force in society."[5] Although there have been times when anti-Semitism has risen to the level of acts of violence, it has more often appeared as a steady and consistent bias operating at a lower register, making British Jews feel as though they do not deserve the rights of full citizenship and that, if they are targeted, they should not expect to be defended. As David Baddiel puts it in *Jews Don't Count* (2021), "When people talk about anti-Semitism, what they tend to mean is an active process."[6] Baddiel finds greater evidence instead of "absences. Of something—a concern, a protectiveness, a championing, a cry for increased visibility, whatever it might be—*not* being applied to Jews"[7] (italics in original). Related observations have led Todd M. Endelman to conclude that "the history of the Jews in Britain[,]" while not "a sorry or unenviable tale of failure," has also not been a true "success story" either.[8] Complicating the picture is the fact that "toleration" of Jews by non-Jewish Britons has always been "qualified by a lack of respect for Jewish concerns and Jewish difference. In addition, Jewishness remained a stigmatized quality at all times."[9]

Not even literature and other high-art forms in Britain have been exempt from this pattern. What Carolyn Betensky has called the "casual racism" or "throwaway reference" to Jews in negative terms that so frequently disfigured nineteenth-century British texts turns up with distressing frequency in twentieth and sometimes even twenty-first century examples, as well.[10] This has led Jo Glanville, writing for the blog of the *London Review of Books* in 2020, to declare, "A proper purge of the antisemites [sic] who are currently honored in British culture would empty the bookshelves, the galleries and the concert halls."[11]

---

[5] Rachel Shabi, "British Labour's Jewish Problem," *The Nation*, vol. 311, no. 13 (Dec. 28, 2020–Jan. 4, 2021), p. 30.
[6] David Baddiel, *Jews Don't Count* (London: TLS Books, 2021), p. 14.
[7] Baddiel, p. 14.
[8] Todd M. Endelman, *The Jews of Britain, 1656 to 2000* (Berkeley: University of California Press, 2002), p. 268.
[9] Endelman, *The Jews of Britain, 1656 to 2000*, p. 262.
[10] Carolyn Betensky, "Casual Racism in Victorian Literature," *Victorian Literature and Culture*, vol. 47, no. 4 (2019), p. 724.
[11] Jo Glanville, "What Difference Would It Make?" *London Review of Books Blog*, 5th December 2020, https://www.lrb.co.uk/blog/2020/december/what-difference-would-it-make

Figure 5.1: Linda Grant, *The Thoughtful Dresser*.

Courtesy of Little Brown Book Group Limited.

It is against this backdrop of disrespect for dress, for items and interests associated with women, and also for Jews in Britain, that the career of Linda Grant (b. 1951) must be placed. In her work as a novelist, journalist and especially as a critic, she has insisted publicly and defiantly upon her attraction to fashion, her feminist defense of women and their concerns, and her proud heritage as a British Jew. She has, moreover, laid claim to a further identity that remains much in dispute when it comes to women who wish to assert it: that of *flâneuse*. For Grant, all of these issues are inextricably connected, and all come together both clearly and successfully in her 2009 collection of essays, *The Thoughtful Dresser*. It was no accident that the subtitle appended to the U.S. edition—"The Art of Adornment, The Pleasures of Shopping, and Why Clothes Matter"— concluded with a phrase that highlighted her argument throughout about the importance of dress, binding together all of the elements of the text as a whole, along with those associated explicitly with her discussion of both communal and individual identity in the book's central chapter, "Making a Self: The Creation of I."[12] Walking through cities, and also shopping in them, as a woman and as a Jew, inspires Grant to be a "thoughtful dresser." She is always aware of how she presents herself and also of how others see her. This is true whether in the streets of London or in her writing, as she remains perpetually conscious of the historical backdrop of racialized, gendered and class-based forms of oppression and, in contrast, of her own familial Jewish counter-tradition of self-assertion, self-creation and aspiration expressed through clothing.

The first chapter of Grant's *The Thoughtful Dresser* is titled, "In Which a Woman Buys a Pair of Shoes." That "Woman," as readers learn immediately, is a version of Grant herself, who begins by telling them, "One day last summer, at the moment of waking, I knew that I had to go out and buy new shoes. Shoes which fulfilled another function, apart from walking. I wanted high-heeled shoes."[13] Although this narrative starts by explicitly downplaying the ordinary functionality of shoes by removing them from the practical business of walking, it quickly turns into an account of walking, nonetheless. These shoes will not be purchased online, nor will they be found in a single location; instead, the hunt for them will become a quest that takes, so to speak, a great deal of shoe leather to accomplish—the task of "working my way down all the shoe shops of the street" and eventually winding up in a department store.[14] Grant links the difficulty of finding the right shoes to her Jewish heritage: "I

---

[12] Linda Grant, "Making a Self: The Creation of I," in *The Thoughtful Dresser* (London: Virago, 2009), p. 153-80.
[13] Grant, *The Thoughtful Dresser*, p. 1.
[14] Grant, *The Thoughtful Dresser*, p. 2.

have inherited from my Eastern European immigrant ancestors wide feet, thick ankles and heavy calves [. . .] and no amount of exercise will ever fix the problem."[15] Here, she comes close to echoing what Shelly Zer-Zion reports in her 2008 essay, "The Wanderer's Shoe," regarding traditional beliefs in Jewish Otherness as written on the body and, specifically, on the feet of Jews, who were reputed by anti-Semitic physicians to suffer more often from a "deformation" such as flat-footedness.[16] The pursuit of what Grant desires, therefore, will entail her concertedly seeking it through shopping, which means walking through the urban landscape, conscious always of feeling her body's unwelcome difference from the normative beauty standard of "good legs" and, simultaneously, of her wish to be visible in a positive way in public spaces.[17] With the purchase of the "high-heeled, difficult, indeed impossible shoes" that she covets, she knows that "above all I'm making a statement, and that statement says: look at me [. . .] That the message was *be seen*. Be a presence in the world"[18] (italics in original).

Throughout *The Thoughtful Dresser*, Grant will describe numerous such expeditions, especially those undertaken in London. Sometimes, she will be in search of a particular item of clothing, but on other occasions, in search instead of an experience, an emotion, that may not involve any actual purchase of goods. As she writes in a later chapter, "To the Shops," for her and perhaps for every other woman who haunts them in a similar frame of mind, "Shops, like cinemas, are dream factories. They sell glamour and illusions and unfulfillable desires. We see the goods, but most of them we can't have; yet it is usually enough to be amongst them, for a few hours."[19] Grant understands the visiting of shops to be an aesthetic enterprise and an opportunity for self-cultivation, "akin to spending an hour or so in the National Gallery, wandering from room to room and educating one's eye"; it is not necessarily a form of "shopping at all, but an exercise in pleasure and self-education, just to see what is in the shops."[20]

Grant's practice is, in other words, a kind of surveying of the cultural landscape in the heart of the urban environment, performed at leisure and on foot—a deliberate act of *flânerie*. Its historical antecedent was the nineteenth-century pastime associated primarily, if not exclusively, with a male figure.

---

[15] Grant, *The Thoughtful Dresser*, p. 2.
[16] Shelly Zer-Zion, "The Wanderer's Shoe. The Cobbler's Penalty: The Wandering Jew in Search of Salvation," in *Jews and Shoes*, ed. Edna Nashon (Oxford: Berg, 2008), p. 137.
[17] Grant, *The Thoughtful Dresser*, p. 2.
[18] Grant, *The Thoughtful Dresser*, p. 4.
[19] Grant, *The Thoughtful Dresser*, pp. 76–77.
[20] Grant, *The Thoughtful Dresser*, pp. 78–79.

The *flâneur*, as he came to be known, was a new type of character whom Helen Richards describes as "a man who enjoyed wandering anonymously, interested yet detached, through the city streets. He was the possessor of the gaze, objectifying the inhabitants of the city, noting their activities and appearance for his own enjoyment."[21]

Whether there is or ever can be such a thing as a woman engaged in true *flânerie*, which assumes that the watcher can pass unhindered at her own chosen pace through urban locations, has long been a topic of controversy. Indeed, this gendered dispute is so well known and so longstanding that one of Linda Grant's contemporaries, the American author Sigrid Nunez (b. 1951), incorporated it into her 2018 novel, *The Friend*. There, the first-person dramatized narrator remembers the actions of a former lover, who was both a writer and a teacher of creative writing, and his assertions on social media:

> You posted an essay, "How to Be a Flâneur," on the custom of urban strolling and loitering and its place in literary culture. You caught some flak for questioning whether there could really be such a thing as a flâneuse. You didn't think it was possible for a woman to wander the streets in the same spirit and manner as a man. A female pedestrian was subject to constant disruptions, stares, comments, catcalls, gropes [. . .]
>
> You concluded that, for women, the equivalent was probably shopping—specifically, the kind of browsing people do when they're not looking to buy something.
>
> I didn't think you were wrong about any of this.[22]

That is certainly how Grant presents shopping in *The Thoughtful Dresser*—i.e., as a self-conscious act of *flânerie*. She is aware, moreover, of the history of this contested subject. In "To the Shops," she discusses Émile Zola's 1883 novel, *Au Bonheur des Dames* (translated here as *The Ladies Paradise*), which introduced to literature the idea of the department store, a nineteenth-century invention, as the prime site of *flânerie* for women in particular:

> Plate-glass windows and electric light enabled the window display, and turned window-shopping along the grand boulevards into the activity

---

[21] Helen Richards, "*Sex and the City*: A Visible *Flâneuse* for the Postmodern Era?" *Continuum: Journal of Media & Cultural Studies*, vol. 17, no. 2 (2003), p. 150.
[22] Sigrid Nunez, *The Friend* (New York: Riverhead Books, 2018), p. 4.

of the *flaneur*. To be out on the streets, to be walking along and seeing objects of beauty and desire displayed along its pavements! [. . .] was this not better than being at home with a Victorian paterfamilias, a Victorian-sized family and a crew of maidservants to manage?[23]

Here, Grant echoes the conclusions of critics such as Anne Friedberg who, as Helen Richards notes, asserted that women in the nineteenth century and afterwards had turned to "shopping and the department store" for access to "a public space where women were free to wander aimlessly, to look at people and the latest fashions, without the prospect of being labelled loose women. In the department store a woman could become a *flaneuse*."[24]

This would seem to settle the question as to whether a woman writer today, such as Linda Grant, can assume this identity too, particularly as she traverses shopping districts and exercises her right there to gaze unimpeded at the urban spectacle. Such a long record of others having done precisely what Grant has done might be expected to allay all doubts as to women's ability to reproduce what Matthew Beaumont, in his 2020 volume *The Walker*, refers to as "the *flâneur*'s alertness and attentiveness to his environment" and his "state of concentration-in-distraction on the streets."[25] Surprisingly, however, it appears that little about this issue has been resolved; even after the publication of *The Thoughtful Dresser*, the possibility of female *flânerie* has remained something to be argued about and defended.

In 2016, the journalist and critic Lauren Elkin felt the need to devote an entire book-length study—parts of which also circulated in Britain as a BBC Radio 4 program— to championing the cause that Grant had taken up more briefly in 2009. Elkin's *Flâneuse: Women Walk the City in Paris, New York, Tokyo, Venice and London* aggressively protests the fact that *flânerie* continues to be, just as much as in the nineteenth-century, a gendered privilege, and that literary expressions of it are still dominated by men: "The great writers of the city, the great psychogeographers, the ones that you read about in the *Observer* on weekends: they are all men, and at any given moment you'll also find them writing about each other's work, creating a reified canon of masculine writer-walkers. As if a penis were a requisite walking appendage, like a cane."[26] Anger over this disparity leads her to insist, somewhat defiantly,

---

[23] Grant, *The Thoughtful Dresser*, p. 75.
[24] Richards, "*Sex and the City*: A Visible *Flâneuse* for the Postmodern Era?", p. 151.
[25] Matthew Beaumont, *The Walker: On Finding and Losing Yourself in the Modern City* (London: Verso, 2020), p. 19.
[26] Lauren Elkin, *Flâneuse: Women Walk the City in Paris, New York, Tokyo, Venice and London* (London: Chatto & Windus, 2016), p. 19.

that "The *flâneuse* does exist," even when that figure goes unrecognized as such, and that she has been part of the urban scene all along, "whenever we have deviated from the paths laid out for us, lighting out for our own territories" whether in life or in literature.[27] To do so is still, according to Elkin, a "transgressive act."[28] In Linda Grant's view, however, it becomes doubly transgressive when it involves a woman writer seeking out and then describing urban experiences that have been devalued by men, such as walking to and through shops and department stores that are dedicated to displaying items of dress—precisely, in other words, what Grant herself is committed to doing. Elizabeth Wilson refers to the *flâneur* "as a man of pleasure, as a man who takes visual possession of the city" as his form of pleasure.[29] Grant insists upon her own right to revel in the pleasures of diverse forms of window-shopping, which might on some occasions involve acts of purchasing the goods she spies, but more often relies on a fleeting sense of possession by the eyes alone.

Where Grant differs most from a number of other commentators on the topic of the *flâneuse*, however, is on its relationship to the issue of visibility/invisibility in terms of a public identity. Among the most prominent critics to take this up has been Janet Wolff, who in *Feminine Sentences* (1990) stated unequivocally that "The experience of anonymity in the city, the fleeting, impersonal contacts [. . .] the possibility of unmolested strolling and observation [. . .] were entirely the experiences of men[,]" beginning in the nineteenth century and going forward in time.[30] Seeing invisibility as both a desirable and a necessary condition, she would deny the existence of such *flânerie* as Grant would later claim for herself. Wolff would, however, later rethink this formulation in an essay titled "Keynote: Unmapped Spaces— Gender, Generation and the City" for the *Feminist Review* in 2010. There, she would advance the proposition that women do achieve the requisite state of being unnoticed as they age, for "in our culture older women *are*, in a certain sense, 'invisible'"[31] (italics in original). She would suggest, moreover, that "despite the damage invisibility inflicts on older women[,]" there are also "possible advantages" that "not being seen bestows on them[,]" including the option of passing with true "freedom" through urban spaces, as they no

---

[27] Elkin, *Flâneuse*, p. 23.
[28] Elkin, *Flâneuse*, p. 20.
[29] Elizabeth Wilson, "The Invisible *Flâneur*," *New Left Review*, no. 191 (January–February 1992), p. 98.
[30] Janet Wolff, *Feminine Sentences: Essays on Women and Culture* (Cambridge, UK: Polity Press, 1990), p. 58.
[31] Janet Wolff, "Keynote: Unmapped Spaces—Gender, Generation and the City," *Feminist Review*, no. 96 (2010), p. 6.

longer "draw attention."³² It is, of course, worth noting what Wolff herself does not mention: that her theories may apply only to white women—indeed, only to white men, as well—as numerous people of color in Britain and other parts of the Global North have recorded their unwelcome experience of being watched with suspicion and of having their access to both public and commercial spaces challenged, regardless of their gender or age.

But what Wolff welcomes—i.e., the prospect of becoming invisible as an older (white) woman—is precisely what Linda Grant is determined to counter through the medium of dress, "Because at my age, born in the 1950s, there is nothing that people would like better than to pretend you are invisible."³³ Dress functions here as a means of resistance, of pushing back against those who would erase her, as she negotiates the urban terrain in her *flânerie*. As she explains in the essay "In Which a Woman Buys a Pair of Shoes," the impulse to go in search of high heels grew directly from her wish to make "a statement, and that statement says: look at me."³⁴ The almost-unwearable, but attention-getting and extremely expensive designer shoes that she would eventually purchase were intended to be the bearers of a message, and "the message was *be seen*. Be a presence in the world."³⁵ (italics in original). While other women might "crave anonymity" Grant announces unreservedly that hers is "another point of view" regarding how to move across the urban landscape.³⁶

Throughout *The Thoughtful Dresser*, Grant makes plain that she attributes this perspective to her heritage as a Jew, specifically as one who was raised in Britain as the descendant of "immigrant grandparents who fled conscription in the Russian army at the turn of the last century to arrive, safely, on the shores of England" to settle in Liverpool.³⁷ Arriving without money and confined to occupations in the textile trade that limited their incomes, Grant's forebearers nonetheless learned quickly to use "clothes as a weapon, as armor, as a means of gaining respect in the eyes of a frequently hostile world[,]" meaning a class-based and also anti-Semitic one:³⁸ "My grandparents had an innate understanding of the importance of clothes [. . . and] instinctively knew that they would be judged on how they dressed, and the better impression they made as they moved upwards in society, the better things would go for

---

³² Wolff, "Keynote: Unmapped Spaces—Gender, Generation and the City," p. 6.
³³ Grant, *The Thoughtful Dresser*, p. 4.
³⁴ Grant, *The Thoughtful Dresser*, p. 4.
³⁵ Grant, *The Thoughtful Dresser*, p. 4.
³⁶ Grant, *The Thoughtful Dresser*, p. 4.
³⁷ Grant, *The Thoughtful Dresser*, p. 159.
³⁸ Grant, *The Thoughtful Dresser*, p. 160.

them."[39] This was also a philosophy passed down to the generation of Grant's parents: "The six children of these two old people knew that clothes maketh the new immigrant. They spent a fortune on clothes."[40]

Grant's family was hardly alone in such beliefs. Even in the economic depths of the Depression, as Edwina Ehrman recounts in "Cinema, Fashion and Hope in London's East End," many British Jews who "worked in the clothing trade as tailors, couturiers, dress designers, cutters, seamstresses, milliners, sales assistants and mannequins[,]" used their access to fashionable items to present themselves in public as exemplars of taste and style.[41] They did so, moreover, at a moment when worldwide anti-Semitism (including British anti-Semitism) was at its most virulent, and when visibility came both with heightened risks and with an increased need to make a positive visual statement about themselves that boosted their own self-respect. As Ehrman says, "Wearing smart, fashionable clothes was important to them professionally and personally, even in the troubled times of the 1930s."[42]

The connection between Jewish identity and the pressure to distinguish oneself proudly as a stylish spectacle, regardless of the dangers that such visibility might entail, is an idea that Grant pursues in a number of ways. Indeed, it informs one of the main organizing motifs that run throughout *The Thoughtful Dresser*, as Grant follows the story of a Holocaust survivor known as "Catherine Hill," who appears as the biographical focus of three separate essays: "Catherine Hill: Never Wear Black"; "Catherine Hill: Dinner with Armani"; and "Catherine Hill: I Am Fashion." But the life of this Hungarian-born Jew, who eventually settled in Canada after the Second World War and opened a fashionable boutique in Toronto, also provides the narrative frame that begins and ends the final essay of the volume, "The Red Shoe," Linda Grant's meditation on the museum at Auschwitz, with its display of footwear left behind by those murdered in the death camp. *The Thoughtful Dresser*, therefore, which opens with Linda Grant expressing her own desire to be seen as she wishes to be seen by selecting a pair of impractical, attention-getting designer shoes, concludes with her coming upon, in the glass case filled with discarded shoes at Auschwitz, a single red high-heeled woman's pump, presumably owned once by a Jewish woman like herself. The reflections that follow lead her back to the memory of Catherine Hill's suffering and survival,

---

[39] Grant, *The Thoughtful Dresser*, p. 159.
[40] Grant, *The Thoughtful Dresser*, p. 159.
[41] Edwina Ehrman, "Cinema, Fashion and Hope in London's East End," in *Vintage Glamour in London's East End*, ed. Michael Greisman (London: Hoxton Mini Press, 2014), p. 14.
[42] Ehrman, "Cinema, Fashion and Hope in London's East End," p. 14.

while reaffirming her own resolution to assert her identity through what she wears, no matter what, and to champion the importance of a self-created image.

As Grant writes in an essay titled "Depths and Surfaces: Fashion and Catastrophe," dress offers the comfort of beautiful surfaces, and "when you have stared into the black depths, you don't long for more depths, but scramble to get back to the surface."[43] *The Thoughtful Dresser* celebrates its author's own right, along with the right of all women, to gaze and to comment on those surfaces, while indulging in a fantasy life of desires that expand her self-definition. In "To the Shops," she proclaims, "I'm entitled. Entitled to be walking along Bond Street and entitled to go inside Hermès and inquire the length of the waiting list for a Birkin handbag . . . And why not put yourself on the waiting list for something you can't afford, because the fact you are on the waiting list implies that you are the sort of person who might one day own a Birkin . . . even though you know perfectly well that you won't?"[44]

These almost defiant statements of what Grant feels "entitled" to, as a woman traveling along the streets of London in the early twenty-first century, recur throughout the volume, as though in direct response to the counternarrative that she offers regarding the victimization of Catherine Hill. They set up, in fact, a rhythmic fluctuation between surfaces and depths, embodied in the very different experiences of the two Jewish women who grew up in different places and eras. Yet even when taking readers into the depths, Grant's focus remains on how women such as Catherine Hill and other women Holocaust survivors have maintained a sense of self and clung to an individual identity, against all odds, through the medium of dress.

The full horror of the story of Katerina Deutsch, who later became "Catherine Hill," the successful merchandiser of high-end women's clothing in Canada and self-conscious wearer of *haute couture*, is not revealed until Grant reaches the last of the essays devoted to her, "Catherine Hill: I Am Fashion." As Grant tells it, Deutsch's pre-war life as an adolescent from a middle-class, cosmopolitan family in Hungary was a model of personal liberty, expressed through the ability to walk alone, observe and speculate—in other words, to act as an autonomous *flâneuse*: "Wandering the streets of her town, she would look up at people's windows and wonder who lived there and what kinds of lives they had."[45] She quotes Deutsch as saying, "'I had such freedom. I could go out at night. I could walk the streets, aged fourteen

---

[43] Grant, *The Thoughtful Dresser*, p. 262.
[44] Grant, *The Thoughtful Dresser*, p. 69–70.
[45] Grant, *The Thoughtful Dresser*, p. 269.

or fifteen, and nobody cared.'"[46] At the same time, her life was structured by expectations and opportunities involving dress: "Clothes were of paramount significance to the Jewish family, almost as important as food"; she was given "new outfits" for the religious holidays, including "the patent-leather shoes, the white socks, the new dress."[47] All of these marks of class-based privilege— the ability to engage in *flânerie* and the access to new and attractive clothing—vanished instantly when, in "1944 the genocide of the Hungarian Jews began" and the entire Deutsch family was sent to Auschwitz-Birkenau.[48]

The defining moment in Deutsch's experience and, in many ways, the philosophical climax of Grant's argument regarding, as the final phrase in the subtitle of the U.S. edition of *The Thoughtful Dresser* volume suggests, "Why Clothes Matter," comes in the extermination camp. Living in a state of despair and terror, the adolescent Deutsch, both of whose parents had already been murdered, stood amid a crowd of women one morning during roll call. In the camp, her head had been shaved of its "beautiful black hair. Her mother had braided her hair and put ribbons in it. Now she was bald."[49] Shivering in the cold, she wore nothing but a prisoner's "burlap uniform, a striped dress."[50] Grant quotes Deutsch's own description of what happened next:

> So this striped thing, it was so long, and all I could think about was, my God, I'm so cold and I'm missing my hair [. . .] I took the bottom of the dress and I tore a whole strip around and I rolled it and I put it on [my head], I made a ribbon and I tied it, and I said, *that's beautiful*. And I felt that my mother was tying my ribbons and it gave me a moment of content.[51] (italics in original)

With this act of resistance through the making of "a kind of hat, a form of millinery"[52]—thus, through a *material* protest against what Linda Grant details as the Nazis' deliberate "dehumanising" of their Jewish "victims, by turning them into what they called *Stücke*, pieces,"[53] before eventually dematerializing them entirely, as smoke from the chimneys of Auschwitz— Deutsch reclaims a self. As she put it years later, her Nazi persecutors "'could

---

[46] Grant, *The Thoughtful Dresser*, p. 268.
[47] Grant, *The Thoughtful Dresser*, p. 267.
[48] Grant, *The Thoughtful Dresser*, p. 270.
[49] Grant, *The Thoughtful Dresser*, p. 275.
[50] Grant, *The Thoughtful Dresser*, p. 276.
[51] Grant, *The Thoughtful Dresser*, p. 276.
[52] Grant, *The Thoughtful Dresser*, p. 276.
[53] Grant, *The Thoughtful Dresser*, p. 274.

not take away my desire to be feminine, and a woman.'"⁵⁴ In *The Thoughtful Dresser*, gender is defined explicitly through a particular relationship to clothing and to aesthetics, through the desire for contact with the beautiful and with a self-created bodily display, whether that happens in a department store, on a city street or even on the site of a concentration camp.

After the liberation of Auschwitz, Deutsch would, according to Grant, return fully to the world of the living only when, in 1947, she traveled to Rome. There, in what Deutsch herself called "a city of joy, vibrant and alive[,]'" she "walked along the Via Veneto" where the "opulence of the emotions brought her back to life."⁵⁵ This was the *flânerie* of a Jewish woman survivor—not a demonstration of detachment, as one finds with the traditional masculine figure of the *flâneur*, but a method of reattachment. The freedom to stroll the streets and to be an autonomous spectator led to a recovery of her past and a renewal of engagement with the present, once again through the medium of physical beauty. Linda Grant quotes Deutsch as saying, "'And in the beauty of Rome, the beauty I had had with my parents was also there, in Rome.'"⁵⁶

From the story of Katerina Deutsch, who literally re-fashioned herself into the retailer of clothes and style expert named Catherine Hill, Grant takes much of her own inspiration as a modern British Jewish woman and writer. But the example of Deutsch/Hill is not, of course, the sole model of significance to her. Equally important, if uncited throughout *The Thoughtful Dresser*, is the influence of the critic and novelist Anita Brookner (1928–2016) who, like Grant, was born in England but grew up in a family of Jewish immigrants. In interviews, Grant has often spoken reverently of Brooker's *oeuvre*, telling a reporter for the British newspaper the *Guardian*, for instance, that *Hotel du Lac* (1984) is the one book to which she always returns, because it is "the perfect novel about romantic love and how the idea of it can shape or deform your whole identity."⁵⁷ Elsewhere, in a longer 2015 conversation conducted by Silvia Pellicer-Ortín, Grant has elaborated on her feelings, saying, "I am a huge admirer of Anita Brookner, of the massive work of hers[,]" and that "I would like to breathe the same air as her. I think she has wonderful style and I really admire what she does."⁵⁸

---

⁵⁴ Grant, *The Thoughtful Dresser*, p. 278.
⁵⁵ Grant, *The Thoughtful Dresser*, p. 281.
⁵⁶ Grant, *The Thoughtful Dresser*, p. 282.
⁵⁷ Lisa Allardyce, "Linda Grant: 'I Was Brought Up with Paranoia," The Guardian, 20ᵗʰ April 2019, https://www.theguardian.com/books/2019/apr/20/linda-grant-a-stranger-city-interview-london.
⁵⁸ Silvia Pellicer-Ortín, "Linda Grant: An Interview," *Atlantis: Journal of the Spanish Association of Anglo-American Studies*, vol. 37, no. 2 (December 2015), p. 213.

The phrase "wonderful style" is a wide-ranging and multi-sided one, suggesting a reference both to Brookner's prose and to her self-presentation in general, including her appearance. Brookner was famously attentive to the latter. Carefully staged publicity photographs across the decades, even those issued when she was well into her eighties, often showed her in crisply ironed shirts, sometimes worn under tailored jackets. These outfits were accompanied by her flawlessly arranged and dyed red hair and by dark pink lipstick, exemplifying an image of professional dignity and polish befitting someone who, before her career as a novelist, was an academic—a professor of art history, trained to be sensitive to visual matters.

Brookner was an astute commentator, too, on the subject of clothing, as seen especially in a 1982 article, titled "Dressing and Undressing," that has enjoyed a second life in Rosemary Hill's anthology *Frock Consciousness: Writing about Clothes from the London Review of Books* (2019). There Anita Brookner extolled the aesthetic of Gabrielle "Coco" Chanel (1883–1971), on which she had clearly based her own: "She was also a work of art in her own right, always dressed to kill, always impeccable, always unapproachable. At an age when women decline into comfortable shoes and a vagueness of outline[,]" Chanel remained "upright, impassive, confiding nothing" and obviously conceding nothing to the advancing years.[59] This was defiant style, created by someone who began as a social outsider, the child of "a feckless pedlar and a peasant woman in a tiny village[,]" but who fought her way up to enjoy life at the center of Paris, in an apartment filled with "priceless" antiques.[60] The other exemplar of "style" whom Brookner described approvingly in that same essay was the British writer and performer Quentin Crisp (1908–1999), the out gay man and "dandy" who used dress as a means "of self-creation, of self-validation[,]" and who understood style to be "an affair of the spirit, a moral undertaking" as well as an expression of identity, particularly in the face of a hostile, homophobic world.[61]

It was, however, through her own fictional protagonists—some of whom were, like the author herself, British Jews, and by definition social outsiders in an anti-Semitic environment—that Anita Brookner interrogated most rigorously the implications of dress and its relationship not only to who one is, but to how one lives and to how one is treated. This was never truer than in her 1983 novel, *Look at Me*. Certainly, it is no coincidence that a key phrase used by Linda Grant in the opening essay of *The Thoughtful Dresser* serves as

---

[59] Anita Brookner, "Dressing and Undressing," in *Frock Consciousness: Writing about Clothes from the London Review of Books*, ed. Rosemary Hill (London: LRB, 2019), p. 14.
[60] Brookner, "Dressing and Undressing," p. 12.
[61] Brookner, "Dressing and Undressing," pp. 16–17.

a direct invocation of that work. Grant writes about her purchase of a pair of shoes that she hopes they will command the attention of passersby: "But above all I'm making a statement, and that statement says: look at me."[62] These are quite literally spectator pumps, designed to speak up on her behalf to spectators, making her physical presence known and saving her from the fate of Brookner's Frances Hinton, a librarian and writer living in London who, in *Look at Me*, finds herself increasingly reduced to social obscurity and sexual invisibility.

Frances Hinton's antithesis and later nemesis is her erstwhile (non-Jewish) friend, Alix Fraser. Unlike Frances, Alix has "such an aura of power that she claimed one's entire attention."[63] This is something achieved not merely through how she deploys her voice and body, but through her clothing, such as the "fur coat" that she slips out of and tosses casually, to announce her arrival and to mark her territory, along with the "very tight black jersey dress, cut low at the front" that, in a crucial scene, assists her in holding the desirous gaze of two men simultaneously, one of whom Frances loves hopelessly.[64] In contrast, Frances remains "neat" and unnoticed in her "grey dress"—"rather plain: not a hair out of place" and seemingly desexualized, "like some beady Victorian child."[65] By the end of Brookner's novel, Frances feels that she has been condemned, due to the moral scruples engrained in her and underpinning her choice of modest clothing, to "dwindle," trapped in "various prospective prisons—old age, silence, solitude."[66] This realization is "the ultimate sadness," which is figured in terms of shopping and dress; Frances thinks of her ruined and now discarded dreams of being seen, appreciated, and loved as "dropping away from me as if they had been fashionable clothes which I had perhaps tried on in a shop and then regretfully laid aside, as being . . . not suitable"[67] (ellipses in original). In contrast, Linda Grant declares throughout the opening essay of *The Thoughtful Dresser*, "In Which a Woman Buys a Pair of Shoes," her determination to use unmistakably attention-demanding designer high heels as a means to avoid just such a prospect of fading and vanishing from view, counting on them to speak the very words that Frances cannot bring herself to enunciate, even through the medium of her clothes: "look at me."[68]

---

[62] Grant, *The Thoughtful Dresser*, p. 4.
[63] Anita Brookner, *Look at Me* (New York: Pantheon, 1983), p. 47.
[64] Brookner, *Look at Me*, p. 48; p. 157.
[65] Brookner, *Look at Me*, p. 155.
[66] Brookner, *Look at Me*, p. 179; p. 181.
[67] Brookner, *Look at Me*, p. 181.
[68] Grant, *The Thoughtful Dresser*, p. 4.

But there is an additional reason why Grant's text is haunted by the shade of Brookner's Frances Hinton, the woman writer from a British Jewish background who seems fated by the ethical standards imparted by her upbringing to disappear from the London landscape. *Look at Me* demonstrates that the creation of an identity does not happen in a vacuum, nor is it a response to the larger social world alone; for a woman, it is also a process that occurs in relation to the influence of a mother, and it is expressed in outward terms through the acceptance or rejection of the mother's style. At the novel's conclusion, Frances Hinton signals the abandonment of all thoughts of pursuing the hedonistic path laid out by Alix Fraser, in her furs and body-revealing dress, by retreating to her late mother's bedroom, where "her clothes were still hanging in the wardrobe, and her narrow shoes marshalled in their usual impeccable rows."[69] She puts on, moreover, a long white garment that she recognizes as "one of the nightgowns I had bought for my mother[,]" which has lain unworn in a drawer, thus merging her own identity entirely with that of her dead parent through this intimate, yet also shroud-like item.[70]

In both "To the Shops" and in the central chapter of *The Thoughtful Dresser*, titled "Making a Self: The Creation of I," Linda Grant, too, wrestles with the issue of how a woman establishes a personal identity, and she acknowledges that the process begins in the setting of the home, using her own family history as an illustration. As she writes, "Clothes are a lifelong journey into acquiring an identity," and the journey involves exercising a series of decisions that sometimes lead to a reproduction of the maternal example but are sometimes a deliberate reaction against it.[71] In the case of Grant's mother, growing up with Russian immigrant parents, the identity she wished to forge was that of an English lady. Part of that sense of achieving Englishness would come from her own rejection of the maternal example, involving the eschewal of Orthodox Jewish traditions: "The chief separation between my maternal grandmother and her daughter was that the older woman, in ritual religious observance, shaved her head and wore a wig, and my mother didn't"; it was a choice symbolic of what she desired to be: "Not wearing a wig made her feel English on the inside, even though English was not, in fact, her first language."[72] At the same time, during the post-Second World War period, the class-based image of the lady prevailing in Britain required a close approximation of the Parisian mode, known as the "New Look," that had been

---

[69] Brookner, *Look at Me*, p. 176.
[70] Brookner, *Look at Me*, p. 175.
[71] Grant, *The Thoughtful Dresser*, p. 162.
[72] Grant, *The Thoughtful Dresser*, p. 161.

created and popularized by Christian Dior. This was the ideal to which Grant's mother aspired:

> The corsetry, the lipstick, the conical brassieres, the jewels, the alligator handbags, the seamed stockings carefully straightened before you left the house: all this hard work of being a woman—its preparation, its painful underpinnings, its cleverly maintained illusions—was precisely what she craved. She wanted to be standing next to my father in her evening clothes, a little sequined clutch in her hand.[73]

Figure 5.2: 1954 Dior cocktail dress

Public domain.

---

[73] Grant, *The Thoughtful Dresser*, p. 163.

As charted in *The Thoughtful Dresser*, Linda Grant's own identity would also be forged through the medium of dress; indeed, this experience of self-discovery would form the basis of her pronouncement that "The defining moment in the life of a young girl is the moment when she is able to choose her own clothes."[74] In "Making a Self: The Creation of I," she is clear about this "moment" as being equivalent in importance to the religious coming-of-age rites in Judaism, for "When you start to dress yourself, you are beginning your own future, the subtle, everyday construction of who you are through what you wear."[75] Grant's transition into a specifically English womanhood coincides with a revolution in British fashion: "I reached my teens at a seminal point, when couture was dying and being replaced by boutique," due in large part to the influence of Mary Quant, who had rebelled against being "trussed up, choked, caged, by clothing" of the sort that Grant's mother had coveted and eventually possessed.[76] In the late 1960s and early 1970s, Grant's would be a casual, Bohemian, yet also class-specific style—accessorized with "coloured tights" and "hennaed hair"—achieved through the purchase of cheap, secondhand clothes that would align her appearance with that of other young British women and against that of the previous generation: "It was the style of university-educated girls with an interest in fashion, [and] not much money." [77] Such a style also had the effect of dividing her identity from that of her mother, whose lasting antipathy to Grant's taste would survive even into the grim final years when she seemed otherwise lost in the fog of advanced dementia. Grant reveals, in "To the Shops," that at a time when "the part of her brain which controlled language began to malfunction" and she could speak only a mashup of syllables from Yiddish and English, she could still express her disapproval, so that "Her last words to me as mother to daughter, the person she knew to be her daughter and not merely someone she knew, had been stated a few months earlier [before her death]: 'I don't like your hair.'"[78]

Dress, as the sociologist Joanne Entwistle observes, "lies on the boundary between self and other"; it "does not only belong to our bodies but to the social world as well."[79] In "Making a Self: The Creation of I," Grant attributes her mother's preferences in dress to specific matters of personal history, interpreting her enduring attachment to the highly ornamented aesthetic of

---

[74] Grant, *The Thoughtful Dresser*, p. 164.
[75] Grant, *The Thoughtful Dresser*, p. 164
[76] Grant, *The Thoughtful Dresser*, p. 163.
[77] Grant, *The Thoughtful Dresser*, p. 167.
[78] Grant, *The Thoughtful Dresser*, pp. 59–60.
[79] Joanne Entwistle, "The Dressed Body," in *The Fashion Reader*, second edition, ed. Linda Welters and Abby Lillethun (Oxford and New York: Berg, 2011), p. 138.

Christian Dior's post-1947 "New Look" to a desire to erase memories of the loss of loved ones and the fear of death from the Blitz during the Second World War: "short skirts, the hair in a roll, the clumsy platform shoes" were associated with wartime and thus with the pain of having "first a brother, then a fiancé" killed in battle, as well as with "the night terrors of the air raids" in Liverpool, which "she really wanted to forget about."[80] Grant fails to consider, however, whether additional reasons underlay her mother's determination to forge an entirely new image as quickly as possible and to adopt an identity based not merely on dressing, but on "dressing up," through the wearing of what Grant describes as elaborate, hyper-feminine "costumes" that signaled a privileged and secure social position.[81] Some of those motives, although perhaps not at the level of consciousness, may have been political in origin. For Jews of Eastern European heritage, as Phyllis Lassner's work on Jewish war refugees reminds us, the early 1940s brought constant, distressing reminders of their precarious existence even in Britain, where the "government was ambivalent about rescuing" those who shared their identities: "When war broke out, tribunals were set up to interview and classify resident aliens. Initially very few were interned, but after the fall of France in May 1940, large numbers of well-intentioned foreigners were locked up as a result of growing panic about 'enemy aliens.'"[82] Given her foreign parentage, it would have been difficult for Grant's mother not to feel uneasy and often unwelcome during that time of national "panic."

The "New Look" offered a mode of self-presentation that could distance the wearer from everything associated with those anxious years. What the adolescent Linda Grant viewed with distaste as clothes designed not to be "comfortable," but to represent "how you built your femininity,"[83] starting with tight and constricting underwear, clearly had a different and a literally *supportive* meaning for her mother. The corsets of the 1950s were indeed *foundation* garments for her— welcome signifiers of having entered a period when a more solid sense of social belonging seemed at last within reach for a first-generation British Jewish woman. This certainly was not what the French couturier Christian Dior had in mind, in creating his signature mode, and, as Einav Rabinovitch Fox rightly states, "when fashion is used to convey cultural values and attitudes, the wearer is not the only one formulating the message.

---

[80] Grant, *The Thoughtful Dresser*, p. 162.
[81] Grant, *The Thoughtful Dresser*, p. 163.
[82] Phyllis Lassner, "The Art of Lamentation: Josef Herman's Humanist Expressionism," *Shofar: An Interdisciplinary Journal of Jewish Studies*, vol. 37, no. 3 (Winter 2019), p. 179.
[83] Grant, *The Thoughtful Dresser*, p. 163.

The designer, the manufacturer of the garment, as well as the audience who decipher it, all take part in the process."[84] Nevertheless, the wearer's own desire to speak through dress is hardly a negligible matter, and clothes present a potent visual vocabulary, whether for long or short-term use. The well-known labor, lengthy preparations, and attention to details required for the proper wearing of Dior's "Bar" suit—which depended, as Grant describes in the chapter titled "Seeing 'Bar': The Art of Pleasure," on an array of "underpinnings in the form of underwired bustiers, girdles, tulle and horsehair petticoats, and a strap-on device called a peplum."[85] —might well have felt to Grant's mother as an assertion of self-worth and a tacit demand for acknowledgment by others of her worth in a social, not merely an economic, sense. Such a style proudly, if subtly, affirmed the dignity of her supposedly "alien" body as a work of artifice and art, deserving of its right to be accepted as part of the British nation's corpus.

When considering from the vantage point of maturity her own relationship to dress, Linda Grant writes, "Grappling with this construction of the self through clothes, and the desire to express myself, I gradually realised, or returned to, what I'd known in my teens: that identities can be fixed, or they can be ephemeral, an identity for a day or an identity which you keep in the wardrobe and bring out for various occasions."[86] Identity is, therefore, a process both shaped by and shaping the daily rituals of dressing. But only so much of this identity-making, of course, will lie within the control of the dresser, regardless of how (to quote the title of Grant's volume) "thoughtful" she may be. Grant ends the volume's pivotal chapter, "Making a Self: The Creation of I," by noting that "the world judges us on our external dimensions."[87]; it does not, of course, make its judgments on externals alone, nor are various facets of identity always capable of being either advertised or erased by external means, such as sartorial ones, according to the wishes of the individual. Although, as the journalist and fashion scholar Shahidha Bari suggests, "This idea that 'being' and 'appearing' might be entangled, rather than opposed, is an alluring and persuasive one,"[88] such a notion is, of course, a simplification. When it comes to race, ethnicity, and religion, identities can also be imposed by others—and along with those identities, forms of oppression, political exclusion, or even sentences of death—regardless of the

---

[84] Einav Rabinovitch Fox, *Dressed for Freedom: The Fashionable Politics of American Feminism* (Urbana, IL: University of Illinois Press, 2021), p. 9.
[85] Grant, *The Thoughtful Dresser*, p. 26.
[86] Grant, *The Thoughtful Dresser*, p. 168.
[87] Grant, *The Thoughtful Dresser*, p. 180.
[88] Shahidha Bari, *Dressed: The Secret Life of Clothes*, Jonathan Cape, London, 2019, p. 17.

subject's own sense of being or choice of appearance. This is one of the lessons that emerges repeatedly throughout the three chapters devoted to Katerina Deutsch/Catherine Hill in *The Thoughtful Dresser*: however strong or weak her identification with Judaism may have been, she was forced to attach to whatever she wore a yellow Star of David and, later, to have a number tattooed onto her flesh at Auschwitz-Birkenau. Grant remains haunted by the story of Deutsch/Hill's utter lack of agency under Nazi persecution, yet inspired, too, by her later efforts to restore some degree of agency by means of fashion, especially through the "therapeutic" function of "shopping for clothes."[89]

In *The Thoughtful Dresser*, Linda Grant self-consciously performs the role of a *flâneuse* who takes a walk and invites readers to accompany her on her rambles, hearing her observations along the way. Her literary excursions involve not only surveying the shopfronts of London's Oxford Street, but staring into the windows of British and European history from the Second World War onwards, while paying particular attention to the impact that history has had on Jewish women like herself.

Figure 5.3: A *flâneuse's* paradise, Oxford Street, 2006.

Public domain.

---

[89] Grant, *The Thoughtful Dresser*, p. 285.

It is unfortunate that Grant's arguments as to "Why Clothes Matter" seem not to have exerted greater, more widespread influence and that, ten years after the publication of *The Thoughtful Dresser*, Shahidha Bari still found it necessary to insist defensively in *Dressed: The Secret Life of Clothes*, her own 2019 volume for the British publisher, Jonathan Cape, "When we disregard dress, relegating it to a superficial concern, we obstruct a mode of understanding ourselves and others."[90] This was, of course, the very point Grant already had made both vehemently and eloquently throughout her work. A cynic might conclude that the absence of any major shift in public opinion, following the circulation of *The Thoughtful Dresser*, bore some relation to Grant's focus throughout on Jewishness, as though this were a further illustration of David Baddiel's conclusion, reflected in the title of his 2021 book that, at least in Britain, *Jews Don't Count*. Even though Grant succeeded in issuing her bold command to "look at me," it is not clear that audiences were actually listening and absorbing the importance of what she had to tell them about identity and dress. Despite this, her 2009 volume, *The Thoughtful Dresser*, still serves as a salutary example of a woman writer bravely professing that she deserves attention and attempting openly to attract it, whether through the crafting of memorable prose or the purchase of a pair of high-heeled shoes.

Bibliography

Primary Sources

Essays

Grant, Linda. *The Thoughtful Dresser*. London: Virago, 2009.

Interviews

Allardyce, Lisa. "Linda Grant: 'I Was Brought Up with Paranoia," *The Guardian*, 20th April 2019, https://www.theguardian.com/books/2019/apr/20/linda-grant-a-stranger-city-interview-london. Accessed October 28, 2021.

Pellicer-Ortín, Silvia. "Linda Grant: An Interview," *Atlantis: Journal of the Spanish Association of Anglo-American Studies*, vol. 37, no. 2 (December 2015), pp. 201–215.

Secondary Sources

Books

Baddiel, David. *Jews Don't Count*. London: TLS Books, 2021.

---

[90] Bari, *Dressed: The Secret Life of Clothes*, p. 17.

Bari, Shahidha. *Dressed: The Secret Life of Clothes*. London: Jonathan Cape, 2019.

Bar-Yosef, Eitan and Nadia Valman. "Introduction." *"The Jew" in Late-Victorian and Edwardian Culture*. Houndmills, UK: Palgrave Macmillan, 2009, pp. 1–27.

Beaumont, Matthew. *The Walker: On Finding and Losing Yourself in the Modern City*. London: Verso, 2020.

Brookner, Anita. "Dressing and Undressing." In *Frock Consciousness: Writing about Clothes from the London Review of Books*, edited by Rosemary Hill. London: LRB, 2019, pp. 6–17.

Brookner, Anita. *Look at Me*. New York: Pantheon, 1983.

Ehrman, Edwina. "Cinema, Fashion and Hope in London's East End." In *Vintage Glamour in London's East End*, edited by Michael Greisman. London: Hoxton Mini Press, 2014, pp. 14–15.

Elkin, Lauren. *Flâneuse: Women Walk the City in Paris, New York, Tokyo, Venice and London*. London: Chatto & Windus, 2016.

Endelman, Todd M. *The Jews of Britain, 1656 to 2000*. Berkeley: University of California Press, 2002.

Entwistle, Joanne. "The Dressed Body." In *The Fashion Reader*, second edition, edited by Linda Welters and Abby Lillethun, pp. 138–149. Oxford and New York: Berg, 2011.

Fox, Einav Rabinovitch. *Dressed for Freedom: The Fashionable Politics of American Feminism*. Urbana, IL: University of Illinois Press, 2021.

Kolsky, Rachel. "Boris's East End." In *Vintage Glamour in London's East End*, edited by Michael Greisman. London: Hoxton Mini Press, 2014, pp. 6–7.

Nunez, Sigrid. *The Friend*. New York: Riverhead Books, 2018.

Wolff, Janet. *Feminine Sentences: Essays on Women and Culture*. Cambridge UK: Polity Press, 1990.

Zer-Zion, Shelly. "The Wanderer's Shoe. The Cobbler's Penalty: The Wandering Jew in Search of Salvation." In *Jews and Shoes*, edited by Edna Nashon, pp. 133–48. Oxford: Berg, Oxford, 2008.

Journal Articles

Betensky, Carolyn. "Casual Racism in Victorian Literature." *Victorian Literature and* Culture, vol. 47, no. 4 (2019), pp. 723–51.

Lassner, Phyllis. "The Art of Lamentation: Josef Herman's Humanist Expressionism." *Shofar: An Interdisciplinary Journal of Jewish Studies*, vol. 37, no. 3 (Winter 2019), pp. 171–202.

Richards, Helen. "*Sex and the City*: A Visible *Flâneuse* for the Postmodern Era?" *Continuum: Journal of Media & Cultural Studies*, vol. 17, no. 2 (2003), pp. 147–57.

Shabi, Rachel. "British Labour's Jewish Problem." *The Nation*, vol. 311, no. 13 (Dec. 28, 2020–Jan. 4, 2021), pp. 28–31.

Wilson, Elizabeth. "The Invisible *Flâneur*." *New Left Review*, 191 (January–February 1992), pp. 90–110.

Wolff, Janet. "Keynote: Unmapped Spaces—Gender, Generation and the City." *Feminist Review*, 96 (2010), pp. 6–19.

Websites

[Anon]. "Marks in Time," https://marksintime.marksandspencer.com/ms-'history/timeline/art968, accessed September 12, 2021.

Glanville, Jo. "What Difference Would It Make?" *London Review of Books Blog*, December 5, 2020, https://www.lrb.co.uk/blog/2020/december/what-difference-would-it-make , accessed September 12, 2021.

List of contributors

Chloe Northrop is a Professor of History at Tarrant County College, Texas. She received her Ph.D. in History with a minor in Art History from the University of North Texas. Her dissertation was on the exchanges of fashionable goods throughout the British Atlantic World in the eighteenth century. In 2022 Vernon Press published her edited collection *The Hamilton Phenomenon*, a diverse selection of essays exploring the cultural significance of the Broadway musical *Hamilton*.

Ramesha Jayaneththi serves as a senior lecturer in the Department of History at the University of Peradeniya, Sri Lanka. As part of her research-based MA programme, she studied for a few semesters at the Centre for Historical Studies, Jawaharlal Nehru, University of India. Her MA thesis was written on Census and Identity politics in British colonial Sri Lanka. Ramesha has been able to obtain an MPhil degree in Buddhist History from the University of Peradeniya. She is now reading her PhD at the Institute for Social Movements, Ruhr University of Bochum, Germany under the supervision of Prof. Stefan Berger. Her research interests are identity politics, nationalism, historiography, and Buddhist studies.

Dr. Petra Clark earned her PhD in English in 2019 from the University of Delaware, where she also received her MA in 2012. Her research interests include late nineteenth-century periodicals, British and American women's writing, Aestheticism and Decadence, visual and material culture, and gender and sexuality studies; her scholarship on these and other topics has been published in *Victorian Periodicals Review*, *Adaptation*, the *Journal of Victorian Culture*, and *English Literature in Transition, 1880-1920*. Dr. Clark taught undergraduate courses in literature and writing for nine years and she now works in Special Collections at the University of Delaware Library.

Emily Priscott is a social historian and writer. She completed her doctorate in Contemporary History at the University of Sussex in 2019, where she specialized in late-20th-century gender history. Her thesis formed the basis for her first book, *Singleness in Britain, 1960-1990: Identity, Gender and Social Change*, which was published in 2020 by Vernon Press. Her most recent work focuses on the relationship between fashion, singleness and interwar literary culture, which she built on as the inspiration for this collection.

Margaret D. Stetz is the Mae and Robert Carter Professor of Women's Studies and Professor of Humanities at the University of Delaware, USA. She has published more than 120 essays in journals and edited volumes, while also curating or co-curating numerous exhibitions on late-nineteenth-century art and print culture. Her most recent book was the exhibition catalogue *Aubrey Beardsley, 150 Years Young* (Grolier/University of Chicago Press, 2022). She is also a widely published poet. In 2015, she was named by the magazine *Diverse: Issues in Higher Education* to its list of the 25 top women in U. S. higher education.

Index

A

Acton, Harold, 130, 131, 132
Anti-Semitism, 138, 139, 147
Auschwitz, xxii, 147, 149, 150, 158

B

Baddiel, David, 139
Beardsley, Aubrey, 123, 124, 128
Beaton, Cecil, 109, 110, 111, 121, 122, 123, 131, 133
Beckford, William of Somerly, 4, 5, 6, 11, 12, 14, 26, 27, 29
Benediction, 111, 131
Body politics, xvii, xxii, 23, 36, 38, 42, 43, 53, 56, 58, 59, 117, 142, 157
British colonialism, xix, xx, 35, 42, 43
Brodbelt, Francis Rigby, 10
Brookner, Anita, xxii, 150–53
Brunias, Agostino, 18, 30

C

Caste, 35, 36, 37, 38, 41, 42, 43, 46, 47, 48, 60
Collet, Clara, 74
Conversation pieces, xx, xxiii, 1, 2, 3, 5, 13, 14, 15, 17, 18, 20, 21, 23, 25, 26, 28, 29
Costume, xv, 67, 68, 126, 133
Cosway, Richard, 10
Crisp, Quentin, 151
Custance, Olive, 120, 122, 123

D

Daily Herald, 123, 127
Deutsch, Katerina (Catherine Hill), 148, 149, 150, 158
Devises Act, 23
Dixon, Ella Hepworth, 73

E

East End, 66, 73, 74, 75, 76, 77, 78, 137, 138, 147, 160
East India Company, 42
Edward East and Family. See Edward Pusey and His Family
Edwardian drama, xvii, xix, xxi, 64, 66, 67
Elkin, Lauren, xxii, 144, 145

F

Factory girls, 74, 75
Factory strikes, 79
Feather club, 77, 99
Feminism, 73, 123
  women's suffrage, 64, 73, 99
First World War, xxi, 66, 99, 114, 115, 117, 119, 120, 135
Flânerie, xxiii, 142, 143, 144, 145, 146, 149, 150
Flâneur, xxii, 143, 144, 145, 150
Flâneuse, xxii, 137, 143, 144, 160

G

Gardner, Daniel, 7, 8, 29
Genre pieces, 2

George Robertson, 29
Grant, Linda, xv, xxii, 141
Graves, Robert, 126, 130

H

H. D (Hilda Doolittle), 111, 124
Hats, 69, 75, 113
    chip bonnet, 71, 87
    feather hat, xxii, 66, 76, 78
    flat hat, 69, 95
    Merry Widow, 67
Henley, William Ernest, 76
Henry, James, 24, 25, 29
Holocaust, xxiii, 147, 148

J

Jamaica, xvii, xx, 1, 2, 3, 4, 6, 7, 9, 11, 13, 14, 15, 18, 20, 21, 22, 23, 24, 26, 27, 28, 29, 30, 31
Jewish identity, xix, xxii, 137, 138, 139, 141, 142, 147

K

Kandyan kingdom, 41, 43, 46
Knox, Robert, 42

L

Long, Edward, 13, 18, 28

M

Millinery, 67, 78, 149
Modernism, xv, xvii, xix, xxiii, 111, 118, 121, 123, 124, 126
Morrell, Lady Ottoline, 128
Moulton, Sara Barrett, 9

N

Nationalism, xx, 35, 51, 53, 55, 59, 60, 61
New Look, xxii, 153, 156
New Woman, 72, 73

O

Osariya, 38, 41, 42, 54, 55
Ostrich feather trade, 77

P

Paston, George (Emily Morse Symonds), xxi, 64, 65, 68, 69, 70, 72, 73, 74, 78
Photography, xii, 45, 47, 54, 109, 119, 120, 131
Pinkie, 9
Pusey, Benjamin and Mary, 16, 29
Pusey, Richard and Jane, see also Pusey, William, 18, 29

R

Robertson, George, 11
Ross, Robert, 124, 127

S

Saree, 37, 38, 41, 54, 55, 60
Sassoon, Siegfried, 111, 123, 124, 128, 129, 130, 131, 132, 133, 134
Schaw, Janet, 22, 29
Second World War, xxii, 57, 147, 153, 156, 158
Sexuality, xii, xvi, 40, 58, 72, 112, 114
Sigiriya frescos, 38
Single identity, xiii, xix, xxi, 72, 114, 115, 116, 117, 118, 119, 126, 127, 129, 130, 131, 132, 133

Sitwell, Edith, xiv, xix, xxi, xxii, 109
Sitwell, Osbert, 113, 130
Sitwell, Sacherverell, 113

T

Tamil culture, 36, 41, 43, 54, 55
Taylor, Simon, 6, 7, 8, 29
Tennant, Stephen, 122, 129, 131
The Athenaeum, 74, 121
The Merry Widow, 67, 68
Thistlewood, Thomas, 26
Tilda's New Hat, xix, xxi, 64, 65, 66, 68, 70, 73, 74, 77, 78, 83

V

van Dyckian style, 5
Vogue, 111, 119, 121, 126, 135

W

Wickstead, William, xx, xxi, xxiii, 2, 3, 4, 5, 9, 11, 13, 14, 15, 16, 17, 20, 25, 26, 27, 28, 29, 30
Wilde, Oscar, 120, 124, 126
Williams, Montagu, 75
Woolf, Virginia, xiv, xv, 119, 120, 121, 122, 123, 126, 127, 129, 130
Working-class identity, xix, xxi, 66, 68, 70, 71, 73, 74, 75, 76, 79
Working-class stereotypes, 73, 74, 76

Z

Zoffany, Johann, 2, 4, 5, 7, 14, 17, 26, 28, 31

www.ingramcontent.com/pod-product-compliance
Lightning Source LLC
Chambersburg PA
CBHW061448300426
44114CB00014B/1884